WATER FROM STONE

Florida Museum of Natural History: Ripley P. Bullen Series

WATER FROM STONE

ARCHAEOLOGY AND CONSERVATION AT FLORIDA'S SPRINGS

JASON O'DONOUGHUE

University of Florida Press
Gainesville

22 21 20 19 18 17   6 5 4 3 2 1

Library of Congress Cataloging-in-Publication Data
Names: O'Donoughue, Jason M., 1979– author.
Title: Water from stone : archaeology and conservation at Florida's springs /
Jason O'Donoughue.
Other titles: Ripley P. Bullen series.
Description: Gainesville : University of Florida Press, 2017. | Series:
Florida Museum of Natural History: Ripley P. Bullen series | Includes
bibliographical references and index.
Identifiers: LCCN 2017005512 | ISBN 9781683400097 (cloth : acid-free paper)
Subjects: LCSH: Indians of North America—Florida—Saint Johns River
Valley—Antiquities. | Excavations (Archaeology)—Florida—Saint Johns
River Valley. | Springs—Florida—Saint Johns River Valley. | Saint Johns
River Valley (Fla.)—History. | Saint Johns River Valley
(Fla.)—Antiquities.
Classification: LCC E78.F6 O36 2017 | DDC 975.9/18—dc23
LC record available at https://lccn.loc.gov/2017005512

UF PRESS

**UNIVERSITY
OF FLORIDA**

University of Florida Press
15 Northwest 15th Street
Gainesville, FL 32611-2079
http://upress.ufl.edu

To Amanda

CONTENTS

FIGURES

TABLES

ACKNOWLEDGMENTS

This book owes its existence to many individuals and institutions that supported and contributed to its fruition. The fieldwork for this project was carried out by the University of Florida Laboratory of Southeastern Archaeology and St. Johns Archaeological Field School, both directed by Ken Sassaman. My thanks to the Juniper Hunt Club of Louisville, Kentucky, for granting access to their property adjacent to Silver Glen Springs and for supporting our research there. Triel Lindstrom, Archaeologist with the Florida Department of Environmental Protection, Division of Recreation and Parks, facilitated the fieldwork at Silver and Weeki Wachee springs, while Dave Dickens, Chief of the Bureau of Administrative and Operations at the Suwannee River Water Management District enabled the research at Otter Springs. We are also thankful to U.S. Forest Service Archaeologist Ray Willis and Heritage Program Manager Rhonda Kimbrough for lending their support and expertise to the projects at Salt and Silver Glen springs. Funding for this research was provided by the Hyatt and Cici Brown Endowment for Florida Archaeology and a John W. Griffin Grant from the Florida Archaeological Council.

I was assisted in the field by many individuals and am grateful for the hard work and companionship of Meggan Blessing, Randy Crones, Julie Duggins, Zack Gilmore, Kristen Hall, Erik Johanson, Brad Lanning, Ginessa Mahar, Micah Mones, Asa Randall, Johanna Talcott, Shaun West, and Mark Winburn. Numerous field school students and lab volunteers contributed to this research by sorting, cataloguing, and analyzing materials, but Anthony Boucher and Catherine Aust went well beyond what was required of them. I also extend my thanks to Jon Endonino of Eastern Kentucky University, who performed the lithic provenance determinations presented in chapter 5 and graciously shared data from other sites. Likewise, I thank John Jaeger of the Department of Geological Sciences at the University of Florida for loaning the vibracoring unit used at Silver Glen Springs, and Paulette McFadden for assisting in the lab and field.

Portions of chapter 3 were originally published in *The Archaeology of Events* and are reprinted here with permission from the University of Alabama Press. My thanks to Claire Lewis Evans and Wendi Schnaufer for facilitating this. I also owe a debt of gratitude to photographers Jennifer Adler, John Moran, and Amanda O'Donoughue for allowing me to use their stunning work, although not all of it appears here. Historical photographs of springs were provided by the State Archives of Florida. The editorial team at the University of Florida Press, especially Judith Knight and Nichole Manosh, was exceedingly patient while providing just the right amount of prodding to keep me moving through the process. They have my sincere thanks, as do reviewers David Anderson and Christopher Rodning for input that vastly improved the final product.

I would be remiss if I did not acknowledge the countless professional colleagues who helped me develop ideas and provided data and insights of their own. Ken Sassaman inspired my initial interest in Florida archaeology, and he continues to be a source of encouragement and support. Ken challenged me to address the relevance of archaeology to modern problems and policy issues, particularly Florida springs conservation. More than anyone else, he facilitated this research. I draw heavily on the work of Asa Randall and Zack Gilmore in these pages. I appreciate their willingness to share data and am thankful for the foundation they provided for this research. Susan Gillespie has had a profound influence on my intellectual development. I am truly grateful for her steadfast support and for advice and critique that is always insightful. Many of the ideas presented here were spawned by conversations with mentors, colleagues, and friends, including David Anderson, Meggan Blessing, Mark Brenner, Josh Goodwin, Willie Harris, Ginessa Mahar, and Shane Miller. Despite the influence of these individuals, I alone am responsible for any deficiencies or errors of interpretation.

I am deeply indebted to my family, especially my parents, Michael and Catherine O'Donoughue, for support that never faltered. More recently, my two sons have brought immeasurable joy to my life and help me to keep things in perspective. Finally, my wife, Amanda, has been a true partner in life. I am in awe of the creative capacity of her love as an artist, mother, and wife. She has endured the best and worst of me with equal measures of patience and grace. I am forever grateful to her.

1

SMOKE ON THE WATER

I SAT ON THE DOCK and watched a steady parade of boats putter past—motorboats, houseboats, pontoons, the occasional party barge. All were converging on a spot just upstream. Silver Glen Springs, or "the Glen" as it's called locally, is a large artesian spring that spills some 65 million gallons of water per day out of the Floridan Aquifer, one of the most productive aquifers in the world. The spring water spouts up from two caverns in the limestone bedrock to form a circular pool of azure water that is 73 degrees year-round. The spring is a bracing respite from searing summer heat, and a warm-water refuge for manatees and other aquatic life in the winter.

Silver Glen is a popular spot for visitors arriving by car and boat alike. Located on the eastern edge of the Ocala National Forest, it is a short jaunt by water from Lake George and the St. Johns River. A U.S. Forest Service recreation area surrounds the spring pool, where for a modest fee visitors can access a swimming area and manicured lawn replete with picnic tables, charcoal grills, canoe rentals, and cold Coca-Cola. On a summer holiday weekend, the flotilla of boats stretches from the edge of the spring pool, down the half-mile-long spring run, and into Lake George (Figure 1.1). According to a local land manager, non-holiday weekends are often even busier, because there are fewer law enforcement officers patrolling the water.

This particular Thursday afternoon was July 2, and Independence Day revelers were already pouring in. All, or virtually all, would claim to love the place and, perhaps more so, the party. But they would also likely be oblivious to, or dismissive of, the impact that such a large gathering of people has on the spring—clouds of exhaust, cooking grease spilt overboard, beer cans on the shore, eelgrass and other aquatic plants trampled,

Figure 1.1. Aerial view of Silver Glen Springs on a typical holiday weekend. Photograph by Overexposed Aerial Photography.

and so on. Perhaps more than any other spring on the river, Silver Glen suffers for its popularity.

Silver Glen has drawn a crowd for far longer than most people realize. The land surrounding Silver Glen Springs and its run into Lake George once housed some of the most imposing pre-Columbian mounds in the entire state, and it remains one of Florida's premier archaeological sites. Artifacts dating to the Paleiondian period have been recovered beneath the water of both the spring and lake, indicating human visitation to the area in excess of 10,000 years ago. By 4,000 years ago Silver Glen Springs was a virtual metropolis, bustling with people. Some made their lives here, visiting the springs frequently. Others came from afar, making the pilgrimage across swamp and sandhill, river and ridge. At that time, Silver Glen was a regional aggregation site that hosted large social gatherings, much as it does today. These people came from an area spanning hundreds of kilometers and brought with them distinctive goods used in mortuary rites, ritualized feasting, and mound building (Gilmore 2016).

But this is a hidden history, a history of events erased or forgotten with the passage of time and only now being resuscitated. To wit, a Forest Service sign marking a 5,000-year-old burial mound remarks, simply, that digging or removal of artifacts is prohibited. Although the site has been well known to artifact collectors, few people, local or tourist, appreciate the scale and significance of Silver Glen Springs in Florida's history.

THE PLIGHT OF FLORIDA'S SPRINGS

Of the many iconic places on the Florida landscape, springs are perhaps the most beguiling. In 1938 Marjorie Kinnan Rawlings published *The Yearling*, in which she wrote of Jody's spring, a small collection of "sand boils" a few hundred feet from the main pool of Silver Glen:

> A spring as clear as well water bubbled up from nowhere in the sand. It was as though the banks cupped green leafy hands to hold it. There was a whirlpool where the water rose from the earth. Grains of sand boiled in it. Beyond the bank, the parent spring bubbled up at a higher level, cut itself a channel through white limestone and began to run rapidly down-hill to make a creek. The creek joined Lake George, Lake George was a part of the St. John's River, the great river flowed northward and into the sea. It excited Jody to watch the beginning of the ocean. There were other beginnings, true, but this one was his own. He liked to think that no one came here but himself and the wild animals and the thirsty birds. (Rawlings 1938:4)

She was not the first to be so enamored of Florida's springs. In 1776 William Bartram remarked on springs "emerging from the blue ether of another world" (1996:150). The poet Sidney Lanier, on visiting Silver Springs a century later (Figure 1.2), wrote: "the whole spring, in a great blaze of

Figure 1.2. Silver Springs ca. 1876, as it would have appeared to Sidney Lanier and others visiting in the late nineteenth century. Courtesy of the State Archives of Florida.

sunlight, shone like an enormous fluid jewel that without decreasing forever lapsed away upward in successive exhalations of dissolving sheens and glittering colors" (Lanier 1876:38).

Florida is home to over 1,000 artesian springs, the largest concentration of such features in the world (Figure 1.3). The best known, like Silver and Silver Glen, are enormous pools that dive into caverns of seemingly limitless depth, drawing throngs of visitors. Others are little more than gurgling puddles, nestled inconspicuously under verdant canopies of sweetgum, magnolia, and tupelo. The water they bring forth from deep in the earth—cool, clear, dancing in the dappled sunlight—stands in sharp contrast to the tannic rivers, lakes, swamps, and wetlands prevalent in Florida. Springs are places of light and life. These "watering holes for the spirit" (Burt 2003:E5) are laced with a mystique that elicits awe and wonder. Pioneering environmentalist Marjory Stoneman Douglas (1967:24) referred to springs as "bowls of liquid light," while Archie Carr (1996:63) considered them to be "the singular blessing of the Florida landscape." For many, springs are reflective of something authentically Floridian that, unlike beaches and amusement parks, is largely untrammeled by droves of interlopers from the north. In short, springs are significant places in the culture, identity, and heritage of Floridians.

Florida's springs have great economic value as well. Annually more than two million people visit the Florida State Parks that feature springs,

generating several million dollars in revenue for the state (Florida Department of Environmental Protection [FDEP] 2014). In addition to the revenue generated by park admission fees, springs provide jobs and financial
stimulus to surrounding areas. Estimates of the economic benefit to the
communities around just four springs—Homosassa, Ichetucknee, Volusia
Blue, and Wakulla—range from $10 million to $23 million each (Bonn
and Bell 2003), and Silver Springs alone contributes in excess of $60 mil-
lion annually to the local economy (Bonn 2004).

Ecologically, springs are seen as unique habitats in need of protection
from the impacts of development and overuse (Florida Springs Initiative
2007; Pittman 2012a). Springs are distinctive hydrological systems, with
exceptional water clarity and near-constant temperature and chemistry.
Many are critical habitats for endemic and endangered species of flora
and fauna (Shelton 2005; Walsh 2001). Springs were central to the development of systems ecology, through the work of Howard Odum beginning in the 1950s (Knight 2015; Odum 1957a, 1957b). As steady-state
systems, springs continue to be "important sites for studying ecosystem
energetics and trophic dynamics" (Liebowitz et al. 2014:2010).

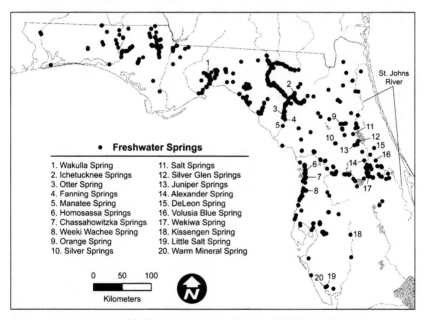

Figure 1.3. Distribution of freshwater springs in Florida, highlighting locations
discussed in the text. Springs data from the Florida Department of Environmental
Protection (2012).

The economic, cultural, and scientific value of springs hinges on their physical properties—water clarity, temperature, and purity—and the health of spring ecosystems. But Florida's springs are imperiled. Reports of dense algal mats covering spring bottoms and floating on the surface began in the mid-1980s and have become increasingly common (Florida Springs Task Force 2000; Stevenson et al. 2007). These algal mats choke out springs' flora and fauna and detract from their aesthetic appeal. Reporting on the state of Wakulla Springs in northwest Florida (Figure 1.4), Doug Struck lamented: "the algae is a black fuzz that coats the bottom and sucks up all the light. The luxurious waving eelgrass is pretty patchy, the schools of fish are mostly missing. The Wakulla Springs of my childhood swimming hole, the Wakulla Springs of jeweled luminescence, now exists only in memories" (quoted in Shockman 2015).

Algal proliferation is largely attributed to increases in nitrate concentration in spring waters. Nitrate, a form of nitrogen, is the most commonly elevated pollutant in the Floridan Aquifer and is primarily introduced from fertilizers used in agricultural and residential applications (Brown et al. 2008; Jones et al. 1996; Katz 2004; Knight 2015; Phelps 2004). In 1950 nitrate concentration in Florida springs generally ranged from 0.05–0.1 mg/L. By 2004 the average nitrate concentration in Florida springs had increased by an order of magnitude, and values as high as 7.5 mg/L were recorded (Heffernan et al. 2010; Strong 2004). The Florida DEP considers many large springs to be legally impaired because of elevated nitrate (Knight 2015:77). Whether elevated nitrate is the sole and direct cause of algal proliferation is debated, but nitrate has other detrimental impacts, including adverse health effects for humans and springs fauna and eutrophication of downstream aquatic environments (Heffernan et al. 2010; Knight 2015).

In addition to water-quality impairment, many springs have witnessed reduced flow since the mid-twentieth century (Weber et al. 2006; Williams 2006). Groundwater extracted from the Floridan Aquifer supplies potable water to most of Florida's residents and is the primary source of freshwater for agricultural irrigation, mining, and other commercial uses (Marella 2014). Knight (2015:57) calculated the average reduction of spring flow in each of four state water management districts (WMDs) from 1930 to 2009. These range from a 16 percent average reduction in the Northwest Florida WMD to 48 percent in the Suwannee River WMD. Declining spring flow adversely impacts wildlife habitat and reduces food

Figure 1.4. Aerial view overlooking Wakulla Springs in 1967. Photograph by Richard Parks, courtesy of the State Archives of Florida.

availability as spring flow is correlated with primary production (Knight 2015:319–333). A portion of spring-flow reduction may be caused by climatic fluctuations (i.e., long-term changes in precipitation [Munch et al. 2006]), but groundwater pumping is the prime factor.

The plight of Florida's springs has not gone unnoticed. Advocacy and outreach groups have grown in prominence over the past decade, as has the voice of concerned citizens and the attention paid by media outlets (e.g., *Gainesville Sun* and *Ocala Star-Banner* 2013; Pittman 2012a; Knight 2008, 2012, 2015; Moran 2013; *Tampa Bay Times* 2012; Tolbert 2010).The threats facing springs, coupled with their cultural, economic, and ecological importance, led the state legislature to allocate over $24 million to springs protection from 2001 to 2011 through the auspices of the Florida Springs Initiative. Although this program was terminated in 2011, more recent financial allocations have been made to springs restoration projects by the Florida DEP and state WMDs (FDEP 2015, 2016).

However, this concern with the uncertain future of springs, of the unknown changes that will come, belies a view of springs as primordial.

Take, for example, the Springs Eternal Project (springseternalproject.org), a collaborative effort to promote springs conservation that has featured art exhibitions in museums and on public transportation vehicles. Projects such as these are commendable and have been quite successful in educating the public and motivating conservation by foregrounding the aesthetic appeal and fragility of springs. However, in so doing, a narrative is unintentionally constructed that paints springs as unchanging—relics of an ancient, pristine Florida landscape that have endured for millennia, only to buckle under the onslaught of modernity. This has the unfortunate side effect of downplaying the significance of springs in the lives of pre-Columbian Floridians, beyond claims that springs were sacred, for example, as "the home or shrine of their 'water gods'" (Knight 2015:211).

Springs, perhaps more than any other target of conservation, embody a contradiction. Many have been heavily modified, in both ancient and modern times, by humans. This includes the apparent terraforming and landscape modification of mound building, channel widening, dredging, and the installation of recreational infrastructure, and the more pernicious alterations of water quality and flow through chemical pollution and groundwater pumping. Is there a more "cultural" place? But what people value, what they seek to conserve, are not the cultural features, but the natural—the cool, clear water, the fragile ecosystems. Conservation efforts focus on the modern alteration of these places, often eliding the thousands of years of transformation that preceded it. They seek to restore springs to a pristine condition.

Anthropologists and others have long recognized that the notion of a pristine American landscape prior to European intervention is a myth (e.g., Delcourt and Delcourt 2004; Denevan 1992; Mann 2006). Anthropologists further recognize that "nature" and "natural places" (as opposed to "culture" or "cultural places") are concepts peculiar to Western thought that artificially separate the civilized human realm from the realm of the exterior, the wild, the other (e.g., Dwyer 1996; Olwig 1993). However, these insights have not penetrated conservation policy. Indeed, the notion of pristine nature is codified in federal law. The Wilderness Act[1] defines "wilderness" as "an area where the earth and its community of life are untrammeled by man" and as "land retaining its primeval character and influence, without permanent improvements or human habitation, which is protected and managed so as to preserve its natural conditions." But there are few, if any, places in North America that have not been impacted by humans, and anthropogenic climate change affects the entire globe. Nor can we simply strip away the cultural veneer—the buildings, pollutants, and scoured landscapes—to arrive at something natural or pristine.

Springs have a deep history of entanglement with humanity that has been overlooked in these treatments. If we are to anticipate the future of Florida's springs, and intervene to alter it, then it behooves us to explore that history. This book is a study of Florida springs archaeology. With over 1,000 springs in the state, obviously I cannot address them all. Rather, I focus on the springs of the St. Johns River valley. I do so for two reasons: first, because these are the springs I know best and of which I have first-hand experience and, second, because in this region springs have been explicitly used to explain past cultural practices. But by focusing on these springs I hope not only to add to our understanding of specific locales, but also to unearth patterns and processes relevant to springs elsewhere.

Springs and the Archaeology of Florida

In contrast to the eternal sameness of springs, the narrative of pre-Columbian Florida and the St. Johns River valley has largely been one of gradual change (e.g., Milanich 1994; Miller 1998). In brief, it is generally thought that as the environment of Florida shifted from cold, arid conditions of the last glaciation to an amenable "near-modern" state, the people of Florida took advantage of newly available resources, populations grew, and culture slowly became more complex. Eventually, these ancient Floridians shed the simple, nomadic life of hunting and gathering to settle down in villages with hierarchy, domestication, religion, monumental architecture, and other trappings of civilization. Archaeological interpretations thus tend to emphasize the environment, ecology, subsistence, population growth, and adaptation as driving factors during early antiquity. Considerations of politics, power, symbolic life, and the like are reserved for the complex societies of more recent times.

In keeping with this perspective, springs feature prominently in reconstructions of the Paleoindian (ca. 13,500–11,500 cal BP) and Archaic (ca. 11,500–3500 cal BP) periods but fall by the wayside when the emphasis shifts to social, cultural, or ideological explanations for the later Woodland (3500–1200 cal BP) and Mississippian periods (1200–500 cal BP). Further, when springs are considered it is only for their ecological potential—as sources of freshwater, contributors to productive aquatic ecosystems, or attractors of large game (e.g., Dunbar 1991; Miller 1992). Any social or cultural significance of springs is generally discounted. An illustrative example is provided by Little Salt Spring, one of the most prominent archaeological sites in Florida (Clausen et al. 1979; Purdy 1991:139–158). The spring itself contains a bounty of ancient materials, including bone, wood, and antler tools, and the remains of an extinct species of giant land tortoise that are in excess of 13,000 years old. These materials were recovered from subaqueous deposits nearly 26 m below the current surface of the spring. In addition, the land surrounding the spring features a large Middle Archaic village and pond mortuary, in use from approximately 7,000 to 5,000 years ago. The cemetery is estimated to contain over 1,000 individuals, some of whom were buried with funerary offerings, such as a wooden tablet engraved with a bird effigy (Purdy 1991:148). The bodies were wrapped with grass and placed on biers of wax myrtle before being interred in peat adjacent to the spring. This was clearly an important place in the past, but in a discussion of the site, Milanich (1994:80) glosses over these aspects, musing "the spring first was occupied during Paleoindian times. Middle Archaic peoples apparently also found the spring a convenient source of water."

However, springs and other karst features have been implicated as key resources driving settlement patterns during the Paleoindian period of Florida (Dunbar 1991; Dunbar and Waller 1983; Neill 1964). While Florida is today characterized by abundant surface water, it was considerably drier during the late Pleistocene and early Holocene. Paleoenvironmental studies indicate that prior to approximately 9000 cal BP, Florida was arid and prairie-like with limited surface water (e.g., Watts et al. 1996; Watts and Hansen 1988; see chapter 2 for further discussion). Likewise, sea-level reconstructions suggest that seas were more than 80 m lower than present when humans first occupied Florida around 13,500 cal BP (Balsillie and Donoghue 2011; Otvos 2004). Given these conditions, it has been argued that deep sinkholes and springs were some of the few locales where freshwater would have been reliably available (Dunbar 1991; Neill 1964). Although nomadic, Paleoindian populations may have been tethered to springs, frequently revisiting them in the course of their subsistence pursuits. These watering holes would also have attracted large game, thus affording people ample hunting opportunities. Thulman (2009:271) concluded that "reliable water sources were the strongest environmental constraint on the occupation patterns [of Paleoindians]." It has generally been thought that this settlement pattern persisted for several millennia, although the subsequent Early Archaic period remains understudied (Milanich 1994:62–63).

In the St. Johns River valley, it was not until the Middle Archaic and the inception of the Mount Taylor era (7400–4600 cal BP) that this pattern changed to one of riverine adaptation and sedentary settlement. Mounds and middens composed of freshwater shell were first constructed at that time, and Mount Taylor era archaeological sites in the St. Johns River valley are much more numerous than earlier sites, suggesting population growth or influx as people took advantage of newly abundant resources and adopted a lifestyle focused on the river.

Miller (1992, 1998) has hypothesized that spring flow was the key variable in the initiation of riverine adaptation and the consequent appearance of shell sites on the St. Johns River. He argues that under the arid conditions of the late Pleistocene and early Holocene there was insufficient water in the Floridan Aquifer to support springs. Lacking this input of fresh groundwater—estimated to provide nearly one-third of the total water flowing in the river—the hydrologic regime of the St. Johns was likely far different from that of today (Miller 1998:67). It may have been a small, rapidly flowing stream, or channeled water may have been discontinuous, seasonally variable, or nonexistent. Regardless, Miller argued that the productive hydric habitats that today characterize the St. Johns River valley would not exist absent the input of groundwater from springs.

Under this scenario, "it seems probable that the appearance of people on the St. Johns River in such great numbers . . . coincided with the appearance of habitats for freshwater snails" (Miller 1998:68). Again, spring flow is the linchpin. As sea level and climate approached modern conditions, water tables rose and pressure within the Floridan Aquifer reached a tipping point, resulting in the onset of artesian spring flow. This new input of freshwater, coupled with rising seas, inundated the St. Johns River valley and led directly to the development of ecologically productive aquatic biomes. Importantly, as humans were drawn in greater numbers to the valley, they "mapped on" to these habitats, making particular use of booming populations of shellfish (Milanich 1994:87). Thus, the onset of artesian spring flow provided the ecological conditions that underwrote the riverine adaptation characteristic of the Mount Taylor way of life.

Although this model is parsimonious, it reduces the changing cultural practices evinced by the deposition of shellfish to a process of passive adaptation to a climate change event. Further, the notion that springs exist only in a binary state—either flowing or not flowing—invokes a simplistic model of springs hydrology and the impacts of sea level and precipitation on aquifer pressure and spring discharge. Given that the springs of the region vary in elevation, depth, and underlying geology, initial artesian flow may have been heterogeneous, time transgressive, and punctuated. In addition, more recent studies of the Floridan Aquifer indicate that recharge rates, aquifer permeability, groundwater flow, and other parameters are highly variable across the state, underscoring that generalized models must be tested with local, empirical evidence (Hughes et al. 2009; Miller 1997; Moore et al. 2009; Reese and Richardson 2008).

THE PAST AND FUTURE OF FLORIDA'S SPRINGS

A principal argument of this book is that springs were key to cultural evolution in Florida, but not solely because of the subsistence opportunities they afforded. This is particularly true for developments that took place during the Archaic period in the St. Johns River valley. In what follows, I draw on the archaeological record of springs in the region to construct an alternative explanation for their significance. Springs were variously used as habitation sites, repositories for the dead, and loci for mound-building activities. Throughout this varied history of use, springs have been the site of social gatherings that connected people near and far. People were drawn to not only the physical and aesthetic qualities of springs, but also the material legacies left by past visitors.

As a study of springs archaeology, this book is about the past. But it is also about the future, or rather, what we imagine the future of Florida's springs could be. Springs have long been important places on the Florida landscape. But today they face an abundance of threats, to the extent that their survival seems tenuous. Contemporary conservation narratives are rarely informed by archaeological data, instead relying on a trope of eternal, pristine springs that inadvertently downplays their past significance. However, if conservationists have glossed over the historical significance of springs, this is in no small measure due to the narratives produced by archaeologists and our lack of engagement with interested parties outside the discipline. But archaeology *can* provide an important tonic, a perspective that emphasizes both the dynamic nature of springs and their deep history of entanglement with humans. Thus, a second principal argument of this book is that archaeology can contribute in meaningful, substantive ways to springs conservation efforts and that the historical value of springs is key to their future preservation.

My approach in this book is informed by phenomenology and historical ecology. I adopt the perspective that springs were not simply storehouses of ecological potential. Rather, they were socially significant places on the landscape with important experiential qualities, much as they are today. However, I do not seek to deny the importance of the material conditions and biological necessities confronted by people. Rather, I take issue with the uncritical use of models that emphasize optimization and passive adaptation. Everywhere that people interact with each other and the surrounding world, they do so in a distinctive cultural and historical milieu. Thus, in order to explore the significance of springs, it is necessary to examine the ecological, cultural, and historical threads through which people engaged these places.

In particular, I draw on entanglement theory, as developed by Hodder (2011a, 2011b, 2012) as a tool for exploring these innumerable threads weaving through time and space. Entanglement theory derives from thing theory in the social sciences, itself derived from the work of phenomenologist Martin Heidegger (Brown 2001; Heidegger 1971). This position takes as a starting point the etymology of the word *thing* as a gathering or assembly in Old English and Old High German (Hodder 2011a:157, 2011b:177; Olsen 2003). It emphasizes the dual capacity of things to appear to humans as discrete, bounded entities, while surreptitiously depending on other things "along chains of interdependence in which many other actors are involved—human, institutional, legalistic, bureaucratic, and so on" (Hodder 2011a:157).

Entanglement theory highlights the relationships between humans and things in terms of *dependence* and *dependency*. Relationships of dependence are relatively straightforward. We humans rely, or depend, on many things to get by in our daily lives. These are enabling relationships. But this is equally true of the things we rely on. They too depend on other things, and on people, for their continued operation and existence. However, our enabling reliance on things inevitably becomes constraining. We become beholden to them and slide into relationships of *dependency*. My mobile phone, for example, enables numerous forms of connection and makes many tasks much simpler to perform. But because the phone itself depends on so many things to function—the parts and labor of its manufacture, a battery, cellular connection, and the like—I am inadvertently drawn into the phone's relationships with these other things. And these relationships expand across time and space to include global commodities markets, labor strikes in manufacturing plants, and the ethics of extracting conflict minerals from distant countries. These relationships, coupled with the tendency of things to malfunction or decay, constrain my actions. My relationship with the phone requires that I recharge it periodically, update apps and firmware, pay the bill, and otherwise act to maintain it. Entanglement, then, is the dialectical tension between the enabling and constraining aspects of human–thing interaction.

There is more to be said about entanglement theory in chapter 6. The intervening chapters draw on this perspective to illuminate various aspects of the springs' relationship to humans and to other things. In chapter 2 I review the geological context of Florida's springs and the St. Johns River valley. This provides a basis for understanding the abundance of springs in Florida and the forces that drive their geographic distribution and hydrology. The chapter begins with a sketch of the geologic history of the Florida Platform and the formation of the Floridan Aquifer System, with emphasis on those events and processes relevant to springs. This is followed by a discussion of the environmental factors affecting spring flow and how these may have been impacted by global and regional climatic changes since the peak of the last glaciation. Finally, I set the stage for what follows by discussing the geomorphology of the St. Johns River valley and the springs that feed into it.

Chapter 3 tackles head-on the question of spring origins, and particularly the intertwined genesis of spring flow and shell mounding in the St. Johns River valley. I argue that the onset of spring flow has been treated as an ecological founding event by archaeologists. After discussing the concepts of event and non-event as they are used here, I develop a critique of this interpretation from three directions. Focusing on the middle portion of the St. Johns River valley, where shell mounds and springs are most densely concentrated, I present a geographic information systems (GIS)–based model of pressure within the Floridan Aquifer that approximates conditions of the early to middle Holocene. This is done neither to predict precisely which springs are most vulnerable to aquifer reductions nor to quantify the magnitude of reduction required to negatively impact springs. Rather, this model is used to critique the notion that the onset of spring flow would have been uniform and rapid across the valley. Following this, I discuss the early archaeological and hydrological records of two springs—Salt and Silver Glen—and the implications of these for nascent shell mounding in the region. To anticipate the results, available evidence indicates that these springs, at least, began flowing far earlier than previously thought and were visited often by Mount Taylor people who were not piling shell along their shores. The onset of spring flow was thus not, in itself, a significant event that precipitated rapid changes in human lifeways in the St. Johns River valley.

If in chapter 3 I present a critique of the ecological explanation for springs' significance, in chapters 4 and 5 I sketch an alternative interpretation of the use and significance of springs in Florida. Chapter 4 deals with Silver Glen Springs directly. This was the site of the largest freshwater shell mounds in the St. Johns River valley and greater American Southeast. I consider whether Silver Glen Springs was considered sacred in the past and whether all springs might have an inherent sanctity. Silver Glen went through several transformations over its history—from habitation space to mortuary and back again—but throughout was the focal point of regional gatherings that persisted for several millennia and reached impressive scale. Since the earliest inhabitation of the region, springs have drawn people in and have been the focus of gatherings big and small. Foregrounding the sociality of springs draws our attention away from their physical parameters, but the two are recursively linked. If springs have been considered sacred, it is a consequence of both their physicality and the history of sociality they manifest.

Chapter 5 expands the scope of inquiry to other springs, both within and outside the St. Johns River valley. I consider the ways that springs link people across the peninsula of Florida, and I present the results of archaeological reconnaissance at Silver Springs—the largest spring in Florida and the westernmost feeding into the St. Johns River. The artifacts recovered during this survey include a massive assemblage of lithic debitage and tools, far outstripping the known assemblages from other springs in the region. Raw material suitable for the production of flaked stone tools is absent in the St. Johns River valley. I use least-cost modeling to examine the optimal pathways for the movement of toolstone from source areas in western peninsular Florida to four sites in the St. Johns River valley with ample lithic assemblages. I do this specifically to evaluate the hypothesis that Silver Springs and places like it were gateways or conduits for the movement of people and objects into the valley. I evaluate the proposed least-cost paths with lithic provenance and debitage data. Grappling with these results requires a widened perspective on springs archaeology and underscores the divergent nature of the material assemblage at individual springs.

As discussed above, conservation narratives largely gloss over the historical significance of Florida's springs, couching them as timeless parts of an Edenic, unspoiled Florida. Rather, the ecological, economic, and aesthetic significance of springs are emphasized. Chapter 6 begins with discussion of some of the contemporary tensions and debates surrounding springs, including barriers to their conservation. Following this, I explore the ways that the past is presented in media coverage and springs conservation efforts. I then return explicitly to entanglement theory, examining the myriad ways that springs are caught up with geological, hydrological, social, economic, and political forces. Summarizing the preceding chapters, I stake the claim that conservation can be fruitfully enhanced by an archaeological sensibility that draws attention to springs' historical significance and to the remnants of the past still visible in the present. Indeed, the archaeological and historical significance of springs should be intrinsic to their value today. I further argue that there is continuity between past and present practice, with springs functioning as gathering places that draw people for ritual purposes. Today these rituals are recreational—family gatherings, weekend retreats, holiday festivities—that bring people from diverse geographies and backgrounds (Figure 1.5). This continuity of practice provides a bridge spanning the chasm of time and demonstrating the relevance of past experience to modern conundrums.

All of this points to a way forward. The goal of conservation cannot be time reversal or a return to pristine conditions. This would entail the erasure of all the sedimented activities at springs, both ancient and recent. Nor can conservation be an attempt to maintain the status quo, as is implied by "sustainability" efforts. Rather, conservation should be forward looking, aimed toward future states yet to come that are consonant with our desired use of springs. The lessons of the past show that springs have long been significant, perhaps sacred, places. Sanctification was enabled

Figure 1.5. Madison Blue Spring. Photograph by Amanda O'Donoughue, used with permission.

through personal experience of these unique places in the context of social gatherings that themselves were motivated by the presence of accumulated historical significance. This should inform our conservation efforts and encourage continued use of springs for recreation (i.e., for social gatherings), while placing greater emphasis on their historical significance to foster a sense of reverence that, in turn, will help mobilize public sentiment and political will.

2

SPRINGS GEOLOGY

The sinkhole was not unexpected. The warning signs had been there for years. Too much water sucked out from beneath the earth, and too many buildings built atop it, especially in the area surrounding Winter Park, an affluent suburb of Orlando (Huber 2012; McLeod 1986; Robison 1987). The spring of 1981 was a particularly dry one, with near-record drought conditions. One stifling May evening, Mae Rose Williams stepped outside to the beckoning call of her dog, Muffin, who was tearing around the yard in a frenzy. Unable to calm the canine, or to grasp what had upset her, she watched, aghast, as a 40-year-old sycamore tree disappeared from the corner of her yard with a "queer, swishing" sound (Robison 1987). The next day her home followed the tree into the abyss (Figure 2.1).

This was the beginning of the famous Winter Park Sinkhole of 1981. The crater eventually expanded to over 100 m wide and 30 m deep, causing an estimated $4 million in damage (Huber 2012). Along with Mae Rose Williams's house, the sink claimed the municipal swimming pool, a portion of two city streets, an auto shop, and as many as a half dozen Porsches. The drama with which this unfolded captured global attention, drawing tourists and gripping viewers on network news broadcasts. Eventually the sinkhole would stabilize, fill with water, and be dubbed "Lake Rose" in Williams's honor. The chaos wrought by the birth of Lake Rose is barely perceptible in the tranquil, tree-lined scene today.

The same factors that conspired to cleave the earth that day in Winter Park—prolonged drought, groundwater withdrawals, development—are today sapping the water from Florida's springs. Both springs and sinkholes are features typical of karst terrains, ultimately formed by the movement of water across and through the limestone bedrock of Florida. In what follows I discuss the geologic context and history of Florida's springs and the

Figure 2.1. The home of Mae Rose Williams descends into the Winter Park sinkhole, May 9, 1981. Courtesy of the U.S. Geological Survey.

factors that affect their formation, distribution, and operation. I do so to illuminate the physical parameters of Florida's artesian abundance while providing a basis for evaluating how varying environmental conditions can impact spring flow. The ways that these factors intertwine are relevant both for inferring spring flow dynamics in the past and predicting them in the future.

The chapter begins with a description of Florida's aquifers, and in particular the Floridan Aquifer, lifeblood for the vast majority of Florida's springs. Following this, I take a step backward to sketch the evolution of the Florida Platform, the geologic structure on which the modern Florida peninsula resides. I focus on the formation of the vast carbonate platform that comprises the Floridan Aquifer, and the sands, silts, and clays that entomb it over much of the state.

Having outlined the formation of the aquifer's raw material, I turn to the transformation of this carbonate platform through a discussion of the geomorphology and hydrology of karst terrain. I review the processes by which water sculpts these landscapes and becomes stored in carbonate aquifers. I then examine the dynamics of water within these aquifers: the means by which it enters, flows through, and ultimately exits the aquifer through springs and other discharge points, and the factors that drive this movement.

With this understanding in place, the following section examines the changing climatic conditions of Florida over the course of the late Pleistocene and Holocene, as global climate transitioned after the last glacial period and modern regimes became established. Of particular relevance are sea-level changes and fluctuations in precipitation, both of which have the potential to augment or retard spring flow.

The final section ratchets down from a statewide scale to the St. Johns River basin itself, the setting for much of what follows. I review the hydrology and geomorphology of the basin, including a discussion of its formational history. I then close with a discussion of the geographical distribution of springs in Florida generally and the St. Johns River valley specifically.

Springs and Aquifers

Over 1,000 springs have been recorded in the state of Florida, the largest concentration of springs in the world. Broadly, a spring may be defined as a point on the landscape where groundwater—water stored in rock, soil, or sediment—flows, or discharges, onto the surface of the earth (including the bottom of the oceans; Copeland 2003). Typically springs flow from aquifers, that is, concentrations of groundwater in sufficient quantity that water can be extracted for human use (Knight 2015:14; Lane 1986:9). The amount of water available in an aquifer depends in part on the porosity and permeability of the rocks, in other words, the presence of voids in the rock that can hold water and accessibility and interconnectedness of those spaces. This water is typically derived from precipitation that percolates down through overlying materials. Groundwater in aquifers may also come from water that has infiltrated from adjacent aquifers or, in coastal zones, intruding seawater.

Aquifers may be either *confined* or *unconfined* (Lane 1986). Unconfined aquifers are typically near the surface and are under only normal atmospheric pressure. As a result they are often referred to as *surficial* or *water table* aquifers. Springs flowing from these unconfined aquifers are referred to as *seep* or *water table* springs. In the following discussions, water table spring is preferred, as seep spring has a specific utilization in Florida (Copeland 2003). Water table springs occur when water percolating through surficial soils and sediments encounters an impermeable layer. The water moves laterally along this layer until it reaches a point of lowered elevation, such as at the base of hills or in a topographic depression, where the land surface drops below the elevation of the aquifer surface (i.e., the water table).

Confined, or *artesian*, aquifers are often deeply buried, and separated from surficial aquifers by less permeable materials, such as clay, that restrict the flow of water (Lane 1986). This layer is referred to as a *confining* or *semi-confining* unit, depending on the degree of impermeability.[1] Recharge of water in confined aquifers occurs in upslope areas where the confining unit is thin or absent. Upslope recharge and the weight of water entering a confined aquifer place it under hydrostatic pressure. This pressure creates the necessary conditions for artesian flow, wherein water will rise to a higher elevation than the top of the aquifer itself when tapped by a well. The elevation that the water rises to in a tightly cased well, where the water pressure is in equilibrium with atmospheric pressure, is referred to as the *potentiometric level*. Pressure within a confined aquifer varies over space and time and is visualized across its extent as a *potentiometric surface*.

Springs that flow from a confined aquifer are referred to as artesian springs. They occur at places on the landscape where the confining unit overlying an aquifer is absent or has been breached and where the pressure within the aquifer is sufficient to push water up onto the terrestrial surface, that is, where the potentiometric level of the aquifer is higher than the ground elevation (Lane 1986; Scott et al. 2004).

The vast majority of springs in Florida are artesian springs that discharge from the Floridan Aquifer System, an extensive source of groundwater that underlies all of Florida, much of Georgia and South Carolina, and portions of Alabama and Mississippi, with an aerial extent of over 250,000 km² (Figure 2.2; see Miller 1986, 1997; Williams and Kuniansky 2015). The Floridan Aquifer is the primary source of freshwater for agricultural irrigation, industrial, mining, commercial, and public supply in Florida. In 2010 over four billion gallons per day were pumped from groundwater aquifers in Florida, supplying potable water for 17.3 million people, or 92 percent of Florida's population (Marella 2014:9). Most of this groundwater was extracted from the Floridan Aquifer.

The Floridan Aquifer is a thick sequence of highly permeable carbonate rocks that are bounded above and below by confining units. The aquifer

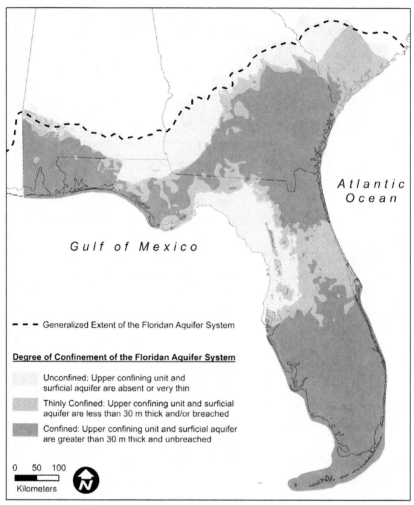

Figure 2.2. Generalized extent and degree of confinement of the Floridan Aquifer System, following Williams and Dixon (2015).

itself is at least 10 times more permeable than these confining units (Hine 2013:113) and ranges in thickness from less than 60 m in the panhandle to over 1,100 m thick in the central and southern peninsula (Williams and Kuniansky 2015:47). The upper confining unit consists of mid- and late Miocene deposits composed principally of interbedded sands, silts, and clays (Miller 1986; Williams and Kuniansky 2015:38). In northeast Florida, the upper confining unit consists almost exclusively of Hawthorn group sediments and measures approximately 120 m thick (Brown 1984). The lower confining unit, typically low-permeability late Paleocene to early Eocene rocks, forms the base of the Floridan Aquifer (Scott 2011:22).

The Floridan Aquifer can be divided vertically into an upper and lower aquifer, which are separated by a middle confining or semi-confining unit. The Upper Floridan Aquifer is the source of most of the springs in Florida and is tapped extensively as a source of potable water. It consists largely of late Eocene to middle Oligocene carbonates measuring up to 200 m thick (Miller 1997; Scott et al. 2002:10; Scott 2011:2). The porosity and permeability, elevation, stratigraphic position, and degree of confinement of the Upper Floridan Aquifer vary considerably across the state. The Middle Confining Unit separates the upper and lower portions of the Floridan Aquifer. This is a discontinuous zone of relatively impermeable micritic and dolomitic limestone. The Lower Floridan Aquifer is not as thoroughly studied, due to its deep burial and the presence of saline water (Miller 1986). It varies from a relatively thin zone of carbonate rocks in northwest Florida to a thick, complex sequence of thin permeable zones separated by thick semi-confining units in southeastern Florida. The Lower Floridan Aquifer is generally composed of early to middle Eocene carbonates and reaches over 950 m in maximum thickness (Scott 2011:22).

Two major aquifers overlie the Floridan Aquifer:[2] the Intermediate Aquifer and the Surficial Aquifer (Miller 1986; Reese and Richardson 2008; Scott et al. 2004). These aquifers are usually separated from the Floridan Aquifer by confining units (e.g., clay or limestone) that prevent, or at least limit, transmission of water. However, in some places they are in communication with the Floridan Aquifer to varying degrees. The Surficial Aquifer consists of sands, silts, shell, and occasional limestone and sandstone overlying the Floridan Aquifer. This aquifer is as thick as 120 m in some areas but is completely absent in portions of northwest Florida, where the Floridan Aquifer is unconfined at the surface (Reese and Richardson 2008). The Intermediate Aquifer extends from the base of the Surficial Aquifer to the uppermost confining unit of the Floridan Aquifer, primarily in southwest Florida. This aquifer similarly consists of sands, silts, clays, and carbonate rocks and is likewise discontinuous across the state.

Ultimately, the presence and distribution of springs is controlled by the physiography and geologic framework of Florida and the productivity of the Floridan Aquifer. Understanding the spatial heterogeneity of the Floridan Aquifer and the abundance of springs in Florida requires a brief foray into the geologic history of the peninsula, and a discussion of the conditions under which the Floridan Aquifer was formed.

GEOLOGICAL HISTORY OF THE FLORIDA PENINSULA

The Florida Platform is the geologic structure on which the state of Florida resides. This includes not only the emergent portion of the Florida peninsula, but also submerged portions of the continental shelf and slope. Approximately 50 percent of the Florida Platform is submerged under the Atlantic Ocean and Gulf of Mexico. The platform is bounded to the west, in the Gulf of Mexico, by the West Florida escarpment, to the north by the Georgia Channel System, to the east by the Straits of Florida, and to the south by the passive tectonic margin between the North American and Caribbean plates (Hine 2013:12; Scott 2011). The Florida Platform is a product of the seas, and its geologic history one of marine processes, as seas continually rose and fell, and the platform alternately was submerged and emerged (Schmidt 1997). The Florida Platform has three basic components—basement rocks, carbonate rocks, and siliciclastic sediments—that reflect differing geological processes and histories. The latter two are the most relevant for an understanding of Florida springs, and so I touch only briefly on the first.

Florida Basement

The basement rocks of the Florida Platform are igneous and metamorphic rocks that are exogenous to North America and became sutured onto the continental plate as a result of tectonic processes. These basement rocks are highest in north-central Florida, dipping to the south, east, and west from 915 m to over 5,000 m below mean sea level (Scott 2011:17). Prior to approximately 475 million years ago (Ma), Florida's basement rocks (along with the Yucatán and Bahamas) were a constituent of the continent Gondwana, which included much of the land masses of today's Southern Hemisphere continents (Hine 2013; Smith and Lord 1997). The Florida basement rocks were situated between what is now South America and northwestern Africa and were part of the African continental plate. By 250 Ma the supercontinent Pangaea had formed, welding the Florida basement rocks onto Laurentia, the ancestral North American continent. Twenty-five million years later, tectonic rifting led to the breakup of

Pangaea and the opening of the North Atlantic, Gulf of Mexico, and Caribbean Sea basins. As a result of this rifting, Florida was separated from Gondwana and remained attached to Laurentia as exotic terrain. Rifting at that time also resulted in the formation of the South Georgia Rift—a rift valley across southern Georgia that isolated the Florida Platform from the rest of North America (Smith and Lord 1997:24). Following the creation of the Florida basement, several factors converged to promote the deposition of carbonate sediments and the formation of a thick sequence of carbonate rocks, the second major component of the Florida Platform.

Carbonate Platform

The basement rocks of the Florida Platform provided a broad, relatively flat surface ideal for the deposition of carbonate sediments (Hine 2013; Randazzo 1997; Scott 2011). These sediments would eventually form a thick sequence of carbonate rocks that today house the Floridan Aquifer, the source of the water issuing forth from Florida's springs. The following offers a brief primer on the production and deposition of carbonate sediments before outlining the formation of Florida's carbonate platform.

Carbonate sediments are formed from the skeletal materials of a wide range of lifeforms, including plants, animals, and micro-organisms (Hine 2013:56). As a result, carbonate sediments themselves are highly diverse and reflective of the organisms from which they are derived and the environments in which they were deposited. Carbonate sedimentation occurs most readily in clear, shallow marine environments where light penetration is sufficient to stimulate photosynthesis. However, slight variations in physical and chemical parameters favor different assemblages of organisms. On an emerging carbonate platform, factors such as elevation, water depth, salinity, and wave and current energetics form an array of microhabitats that vary across space. As a result, the organisms and carbonate sediments produced on a carbonate platform can be varied and horizontally stratified (Hine 2013:57–59). The spatial heterogeneity of carbonate sediment production is augmented by the action of waves and currents, which can rework and redistribute sediments after their formation.

The end result is a diversity of sedimentary facies that vary both horizontally, with microhabitat diversity, and vertically as sediments accumulate and conditions change through time, for example, as a result of sea-level fluctuations. Once these sediments are buried, they become fused together through a process called *cementation*, creating carbonate rocks. Cementation occurs as water fills interstitial spaces in the sedimentary matrix. This water contains dissolved carbonate minerals that, under the right conditions, precipitate out to fill these spaces. The cementation process can be quite rapid, often occurring over a matter of decades, or can be ongoing for centuries (Hine 2013:60).

The Florida basement rocks provided a broad, elevated surface that was shallowly submerged during sea-level high stands. Because of both its shallowness and its geographical position at low latitude, the seawater covering the Florida basement was relatively warm. These were ideal conditions for the deposition of a carbonate platform. Carbonate rocks composing the Florida Platform measure as much as 6 km thick. But, as discussed above, carbonate sediments form in relatively shallow (< 50 m) seawater. This would seem to preclude formation of such a thick carbonate platform. But a fortuitous combination of factors allowed for the continued accretion of carbonate sediments that ultimately formed the Florida Platform: tectonic subsidence and sea-level rise.

After the breakup of Pangaea, the newly formed continental margin of North America cooled and began subsiding rapidly, creating space for carbonate sedimentation on the submerged Florida basement. The accumulation of carbonate sediments, in turn, propagated subsidence by increasing the lithostatic load on the plate margin. Sea-level rise likewise propagated tectonic subsidence by increasing the hydrostatic load on the plate, and favored continued carbonate sedimentation (Hine 2013:62–63). Thus, the Florida basement sank while the level of the sea rose, continually creating space for the production and accumulation of carbonate sediments. Importantly, the space created by subsidence and sea-level rise was relatively persistent and kept pace with, but did not outstrip, carbonate deposition. If either subsidence or sea-level rise had proceeded too quickly, water depth would have increased to such an extent that the carbonate "factory" would have been drowned.

So, in sum, the broad elevated surface of the Florida basement rocks provided an ideal substrate for the formation of a carbonate platform. The thickness of this platform was afforded by tectonic subsidence and persistent sea-level rise. Sea-level oscillations and concomitant variations in microhabitat during this overall rise formed laterally and vertically heterogeneous carbonate deposits and unconformities that ultimately resulted in a diversity of carbonate deposits on the Florida Platform.

But this suite of ideal conditions could not persist indefinitely. The Florida carbonate platform accreted early and rapidly, peaking at approximately 140 Ma. As the rifted continental margin migrated away from the spreading ocean basin, subsidence slowed exponentially (Hine 2013:63). Sea-level rise likewise attenuated after approximately 100 Ma. Carbonate deposition continued, albeit at a reduced rate, through the Eocene and into the Oligocene. Following this, a fundamental shift in sedimentation and depositional regimes occurred over Florida. These new regimes formed the third major component of the Florida Platform.

Siliciclastic Sediments

The carbonate platform described above ultimately formed the limestone bedrock of Florida. But this bedrock is not generally visible on the surface. With the exception of the Everglades and Keys, the entirety of the Florida carbonate platform is now covered by a mantle of siliciclastic sediments composed primarily of quartz sands, along with some silts and clays. Typically, this sand is a few meters thick, but in localized areas it may be absent or considerably thicker. This sediment is derived not from a local source, but from the weathering and transport of nonlocal igneous and quartz-rich metamorphic and sedimentary bedrock (Hine 2013:137). The closest source of these rocks is the southern Appalachians and Piedmont of Georgia and the Carolinas.

Over the past 250 million years, the Appalachians have been subjected to extensive weathering and erosion. This has reduced the height of the mountain range by some 7,000 m and produced a vast amount of sediment (Hine 2013; Scott 1997, 2011). These siliciclastic sediments have been transported by streams and rivers to the sea. Along the way they were reworked and deposited by fluvial processes to build up the coastal plain, continental shelf, and continental slope of the lower Southeast.

Until approximately 30 Ma, the Florida Platform was isolated from this sediment source by the Georgia Channel System, a remnant of the South Georgia Rift that formed during the Triassic (Scott 2011:19). Currents in this channel prevented the progradation of deltaic deposits that might otherwise have increased turbidity and negatively impacted carbonate formation. However, prolonged sea-level low stands after 30 Ma reduced current velocity in the Georgia Channel System. This was coupled with uplift of the eroding Appalachians, which increased the siliciclastic sediment supply (Scott 2011:25). The combination of increased sediment load and decreased current velocity in the Georgia Channel System resulted in its gradual infilling with sediments. These sediments eventually reached the Florida Platform, precipitating the demise of carbonate production in Florida.

During sea-level high stands, these sands migrated southward by longshore transport along relict shorelines, visible now as elevated inland ridges oriented parallel to the Atlantic and Gulf coasts (Hine 2013; Schmidt 1997; Scott 2011). During low stands, nascent rivers and drainage systems carved through these ridges, reworking sediments and moving them from the interior onto the emerged continental shelf. In this way water transported siliciclastic sediments south, east, and west, covering the carbonate platform and extending onto the continental shelves off Florida's Atlantic and Gulf coasts.

These three components of the Florida Platform—basement rocks, carbonate platform, and siliciclastic mantle—all play a role in understanding Florida's aquifers and springs. The basement rocks provided the necessary conditions for carbonate deposition—a broad, elevated platform covered by shallow seas and isolated from deltaic deposition on the North American mainland. These carbonate rocks, in turn, provide the structure that composes the Floridan Aquifer and houses the freshwater that feeds Florida's artesian springs. Likewise, the siliciclastic mantle overlies the Floridan Aquifer, forming confining units, surficial aquifers, and surface topography, and in other ways facilitating or hindering access to it. With this understanding of the structures in place, the following section addresses the processes that sculpted the platform to form karst terrain and the carbonate Floridan Aquifer.

Karst Terrain in Florida

Carbonate rocks, like those of the Florida Platform, are subject to a variety of weathering processes that form a distinctive topography referred to as karst. Karst terrain is characterized by numerous surface and subsurface solution features—such as sinkholes, caves, springs, sink-rise streams, conduits, and fractures—that impart a characteristic hydrology. The term "karst terrain," broadly defined as "terrain that has been shaped by dissolution of the underlying carbonate rocks" (Lane 1986:1), is derived from the Karst region of the former Yugoslavia (now encompassing portions of Serbia and Montenegro). This locale is the model karst system, featuring significant subsurface drainage through limestone rocks perforated by numerous conduits and caverns. Within the United States, karst terrains can be found in southern Indiana, central Kentucky and Tennessee, New Mexico, and the Appalachian Mountains, but perhaps the most extensive and well-known karst region is found in Florida (Lane 1986).

The Evolution of Karst Landscapes

The primary geomorphic agent in karst terrains is water, particularly through the chemical weathering of carbonate rocks. This weathering is controlled by 1) the presence of slightly acidic water and 2) a mechanism for transporting that water across and through the rock. As water cycles through the atmosphere, it absorbs carbon dioxide to form small amounts of carbonic acid. When this water reaches the surface as precipitation, it percolates through soils and sediments (if present) to reach underlying carbonate rocks. In doing so it mixes with additional carbon dioxide derived from soil microbial activity, further enhancing acidity (Lane 1986).

On reaching carbonate rock, movement of this acidic water is directed by the porosity and permeability of rocks and the surrounding sedimentary matrix (Lane 1986) and driven by gravity and gradients in temperature and pressure. Porosity refers to the relative number of pores or voids within a rock or sedimentary deposit,[3] whereas permeability more specifically references the ability of water to move through those pores. Thus, while a high degree of porosity is a necessary precondition for high permeability, it is not sufficient in itself. Numerous factors may limit the permeability of a porous material, such as a lack of interconnection between pore spaces, or the presence of fine materials (e.g., clays or organic matter) within interstitial voids. Limestone, like that of the Floridan Aquifer, is typically characterized by both high porosity and high permeability, attributable to its granular structure and the presence of fine fractures and bedding planes.

As water passes through the rock, its weakly acidic nature causes some of the carbonate to dissolve, enlarging preexisting fractures, bedding planes, and voids. As this process progresses, fluid transmission pathways are enlarged and may form interconnected conduits that facilitate the movement of water. Carbonate dissolution is greatest in areas of high groundwater circulation (Hine 2013:124), so this becomes a self-sustaining cycle whereby dissolution begets greater groundwater transmissivity, which further enhances dissolution and concentrates networks of conduits and caverns.

In coastal karst zones, such as along the perimeter of Florida, dissolution is enhanced at the contact between salt and freshwater (Hine 2013:118–119). Freshwater is less dense than salt water and, as a result, floats above it. If both water bodies are saturated with respect to calcium carbonate, they will be unable to dissolve additional carbonate rock. However, in the "mixing zone" the water is brackish and becomes undersaturated with respect to calcium carbonate. Thus carbonate rock can be dissolved within the mixing zone, and this dissolution propagated deep within the aquifer.

In areas where porosity is concentrated and larger cavities form, the dissolution of underlying rock can eventually lead to the collapse of overlying deposits. This typically begins deep within the carbonate structure, where faults and fractures are concentrated. With each collapse a new void for groundwater circulation and carbonate dissolution is formed. In this way, collapse propagates upward through a process called *dissolution tectonics* (Hine 2013:125). Upon reaching the surface, this collapse causes regional subsidence in the form of broad topographic depressions, with underlying fold and sag structures.

The dissolution of carbonate rock and karstification of the landscape produces a variety of surface and subsurface features. As dissolution progresses through time, these become increasingly prevalent and well developed. A variety of names and definitions are applied to karst landscape features in different regions of the world. The following is borrowed from the definitions of the Florida Geological Survey (FGS; Copeland 2003). Where carbonate rock is exposed at the surface, a variety of weathering features are formed, collectively referred to as *karren*. These are formed by dissolution of the rock at the surface. In Florida these typically consist of pinnacles and depressions in the rock, now buried beneath overlying sediments.

More typical in Florida are caves—openings and passages large enough to be entered by humans—and sinkholes—depressions caused by the dissolution of underlying materials (sometimes referred to as *cenotes*, *dolines*, or sinks). Three types of sinkholes are generally recognized: *solution*, *subsidence*, and *collapse*. The mechanism of their formation depends broadly on the thickness of confining units and sediments overlying the carbonate rock (Kindinger et al. 1999; Schiffer 1998). Collapse sinkholes often result in the formation of *karst windows*, openings that reveal portions of subterranean flow in the aquifer.

Another common karst feature, particularly in northern Florida, is a *sinking stream* or *river-rise* system. These occur where channeled surface water disappears into a karst depression called a *swallow hole* (also called *ponor* or *swallet*). The water flows underground for some distance, where it then reemerges onto the surface, usually at a lower elevation. Although these are generally considered to be springs, they are not technically so, as surface water constitutes a significant portion of the resurging water (Copeland 2003).

The features described above are formed by the interaction of water and carbonate rock. Carbonate minerals that have been dissolved in the water are moved in solution through the system, eventually exiting when the water discharges into the oceans. In Florida it is estimated that this dissolution occurs at a rate up to 4 cm per 1,000 years (Hine 2013:115–116). The following section examines the forces that impact the hydrology of karst aquifers and direct this movement of water through the system.

Karst Hydrology

The dissolution of carbonate rock and the formation of a network of water-bearing voids is the mechanism by which the Floridan Aquifer formed and the reason it is so productive. These same processes are also responsible for the karst features visible on the surface—sinks, springs, sink-rise streams, and the like. These features, in turn, are critically important for controlling the movement of water into and out of the aquifer. The hydrologic cycle of karst aquifers entangles processes unfolding over divergent time scales and rhythms but can be conceptually divided into recharge, flow, and discharge (White 2002). Although these will be discussed separately below, each process is intricately tied to the others.

Recharge

Precipitation is the main source of recharge, or water input, to karst aquifers, driven into the system by the force of gravity. Recharge typically occurs in areas where the confining unit does not appreciably restrict the downward movement of water into the aquifer, that is, where the aquifer is unconfined or thinly confined (Aucott 1988; Miller 1986). Further, regardless of the mechanism, recharge to a karst aquifer occurs only in areas

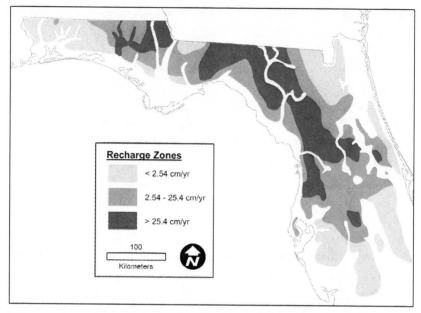

Figure 2.3. Generalized extent of areas recharging the Floridan Aquifer System in Florida. Recharge data from the Southwest Florida Water Management District.

where the potentiometric surface of the aquifer is below the elevation of the land and/or surficial water table (Belaineh et al. 2012). Otherwise, positive pressure within the aquifer prevents the recharge of new water. The areas of greatest recharge to the Floridan Aquifer, then, are areas of well-developed karst that are at relatively high elevation (Figure 2.3).

The surface and groundwater basins that contribute water to a given spring constitute the *springshed* or *spring recharge basin* (Copeland 2003; Scott et al. 2004; Shoemaker et al. 2004; Williams and Kuniansky 2015). Importantly, these are not static boundaries but fluctuate through time with variations in pressure gradients and groundwater flow dynamics.

Flow

The flow of groundwater in karst aquifers is driven by several factors (Lane 1986; Miller 1986; White 2002; Williams and Kuniansky 2015). First, gravity will drive flow from high-elevation recharge areas. If the aquifer is confined, this creates hydrostatic pressure that increases with depth and distance from recharge zones. Recharge water is also frequently warmer than existing groundwater in the aquifer. As a result there are gradients in both pressure and temperature that drive water flow. Finally, convective forces generated by heat deep within the earth, called *Kohout convection*, circulate groundwater and can draw seawater into deep coastal aquifers. This creates a mixing zone, analogous to that described above, but much broader and deeper, that enhances dissolution (Hine 2013:125).

Carbonate karst aquifers are generally considered to have three types of porosity or pathways for water transmission: intergranular porosity in the matrix, small fractures, and large conduits or caverns (Martin and Dean 2001; White 2002). Matrix porosity consists of interstitial spaces in the fabric of the rock or sedimentary structure. Fractures consist of small mechanical apertures, including such features as joints and bedding planes, which range in size from 50 to 500 μm (White 2002). These may be widened by carbonate dissolution up to about 1 cm. Openings or pathways that have been enlarged by dissolution to a size of greater than 1 cm are referred to as conduits or caverns.

The distribution and abundance of these pathways in a given portion of an aquifer can have dramatic effects on permeability and flow. In general, and despite the small size of the voids, matrix porosity is thought to provide much of the water storage within the aquifer. Conduits, meanwhile, provide for the majority of flow (Martin and Dean 2001; White 2002). However, many studies of karst aquifers have focused on areas of dense, relatively impermeable rock. In these karst regions, flow between the matrix and conduits is relatively restricted. As a result springs have been conceptualized as a direct output of subsurface flow through conduits (i.e., "underground rivers"), with little regard given to the potential input from flow through small fractures or matrix pores (Florea and Vacher 2006; Martin and Dean 2001; Moore et al. 2009; Screaton et al. 2004).

Karst can be divided into two main types—*eogenetic* and *telogenetic*—on the basis of age and porosity (Florea and Vacher 2006). Eogenetic karst is young and has not been deeply buried, whereas telogenetic karst is much older, having gone through an intermediate mesogenetic stage of deep burial and subsequent erosion and exposure. These types differ in their physical characteristics, geochemistry, and hydrology. Of particular relevance to karst hydrology are differences in matrix permeability, which decrease roughly with age. As a result of its deep burial and compaction, the matrix permeability of telogenetic karst is reduced by several orders of magnitude relative to eogenetic karst (Florea and Vacher 2006).

The karst of Florida is relatively young, having formed in the Eocene and Oligocene, and has never been deeply buried (Florea and Vacher 2006; Miller 1986; Reese and Richardson 2008). Thus, Florida karst is eogenetic. Although traditional models of karst hydrology minimize the impact of matrix permeability on groundwater flow, it has much greater effect in eogenetic karst (Martin and Dean 2001; Moore et al. 2009; Screaton et al. 2004).

The forces of groundwater flow (e.g., gravity, temperature, pressure, Kohout convection) drive water through the aquifer to points of discharge on the landscape. At the scale of the entire aquifer, the direction of groundwater flow in the Floridan Aquifer is generally from the interior highlands toward the Atlantic and Gulf coasts (Hughes et al. 2009:26). However, at localized scales flow is generally directed from recharge zones within springsheds toward points or zones of groundwater discharge.

Discharge

Springs are the primary discharge point for groundwater in karst aquifers (Scott et al. 2004; White 2002). A variety of classifications are used for springs, which are subdivided on the basis of size, water source, landscape position, or discharge mechanism (Copeland 2003; White 2002:90). The Florida Geological Survey, for example, uses a simple bivariate scheme based on geomorphology that categorizes springs as either terrestrial or marine, with focused or diffuse flow (Copeland 2003).

As noted above, springs that originate from surficial, unconfined aquifers are referred to as water table springs. Those that emerge at the surface as a result of pressure, like those originating in the Floridan Aquifer, are artesian springs. In Florida these are also referred to as karst springs (Copeland 2003). Most artesian springs discharge through a *spring vent*, defined as "an opening that concentrates ground-water discharge to the Earth's surface" that is significantly larger than the pore space of the surrounding rock, often forming a cavern or fissure (Copeland 2003:16; see also Scott et al. 2004:10).

However, not all groundwater discharge is concentrated at focal points such as spring vents. Discharge can also be diffuse, occurring over broader portions of the landscape. Diffuse groundwater discharge (sometime called upward leakage) occurs through the intergranular pore spaces in the aquifer matrix (Scott et al. 2004:10) and thus is more common in the eogenetic karst of Florida than in other karst regions (see above). If

Table 2.1. Spring magnitude and corresponding discharge rate

Magnitude	Discharge (Metric)	Discharge (English)
1	>2.83 m³/s	>100 ft³/s
2	.28–2.83 m³/s	10–100 ft³/s
3	.03–.28 m³/s	1–10 ft³/s
4	6.31 l/s–.03 m³/s	100 gal/min–1 ft³/s
5	.63–6.31 l/s	10–100 gal/min
6	.06–.63 l/s	1–10 gal/min
7	.47–3.79 l/min	1 pint/min–1 gal/min
8	< .47 l/min	< 1 pint/min

this occurs in a relatively restricted area, it is referred to as a *seep*, that is, an artesian spring composed of "one or more small openings in which water discharges diffusely ('oozes') from the ground-water environment" (Copeland 2003:12).

The water discharging from springs is typically contained in a water body referred to as a *spring pool* (Copeland 2003; Scott et al. 2004). Discharge from spring vents can be turbulent, resulting in a notable roiling on the surface of the pool referred to as a *spring boil*. This water can then be channeled to form a *spring run*, or it may drain directly into existing streams, creeks, or other surface water bodies. Springs may also be subaqueous—located beneath existing surface water bodies in the beds of rivers or lakes, or beneath the oceans.

As with recharge, discharge from carbonate aquifers is most common where the confining unit is thin or absent and karst features are prevalent and well developed. Discharge in these areas occurs where the potentiometric surface of the aquifer is higher than the elevation of the land surface and surficial water table. Artesian springs in Florida, then, are most common at low elevations in areas of well-developed karst (Scott et al. 2004:15).

Springs can also be classified on the basis of the amount of water that discharges through them. In Florida, discharge is used to divide springs into eight magnitude classes that encompass a huge range of variation (Table 2.1). The smallest, eighth-magnitude springs, discharge a maximum of one pint of water per minute. This is equivalent to approximately 180 gallons per day. In contrast, first-magnitude springs discharge a minimum of

64,600,000 gallons of water per day, and the largest of these, such as Silver and Wakulla Springs, discharge considerably more (Scott et al. 2004). The intensity of discharge in artesian springs is pressure dependent. This pressure fluctuates both temporally and spatially as a result of several factors that vary within and between individual spring basins, such as precipitation, topography, elevation, soil characteristics, and the physical properties of the aquifer (e.g., permeability, confining unit thickness; Scott et al. 2004).

Current understanding of spring flow dynamics emphasizes precipitation as the main driver of seasonal and annual discharge variation (Knowles et al. 2002; White 2002). However, springs in areas of eogenetic karst, such as Florida, tend to respond differently to precipitation than those of telogenetic karst. They generally have lower amplitude variation in discharge, longer lag time in response to precipitation events, and greater buffering of high-frequency/low-intensity events, which may not substantially recharge the Floridan Aquifer. Rather, high-intensity storms and seasonal, annual, and decadal precipitation cycles appear to exert greater influence on variation in spring discharge (Florea and Vacher 2006, 2007). These differences are caused primarily by the greater contribution of matrix permeability to groundwater storage and flow in eogenetic karst aquifers, which buffers variation and increases aquifer inertia. In addition, deep-water upwelling in the Floridan Aquifer can contribute significant amounts of water to spring discharge (Moore et al. 2009). Discharge at springs includes both water that entered the aquifer relatively recently and much older waters, recharged as much as 30,000 years ago (Plummer 1993; Toth and Katz 2006). At longer temporal scales, fluctuating sea levels, climate change, and groundwater withdrawals can impact hydrostatic pressure in the Floridan Aquifer and, therefore, spring flow. How these factors changed over the course of the late Pleistocene and Holocene, and the concomitant impact on springs, is the subject of the next section.

QUATERNARY ENVIRONMENTS OF FLORIDA AND THE ST. JOHNS RIVER VALLEY

From the perspective of spring flow, the most relevant climatic factors over long periods of time are those that can significantly influence the potentiometric surface of the Floridan Aquifer and the pressure and temperature gradients that drive flow within the aquifer. These are, principally, sea level and precipitation.

Sea level is typically considered to be the lower limit, or base level, for water movement in both ground and surface water systems (Charlton 2008; Knox 1995). Other things being equal (e.g., precipitation and evapotranspiration), a reduction in the base increases the hydraulic gradient. In a surface network, such as a river, this increased gradient generally leads to greater water velocity and down-cutting, or incision, of the river channel (Blum and Törnqvist 2000). Likewise, an increased hydraulic gradient in a groundwater system raises water velocity and, in the case of a carbonate aquifer, increases the rate of carbonate dissolution.

Further, sea level is relevant because the freshwater of the Floridan Aquifer is in communication with the water bodies surrounding it. Although the Floridan Aquifer ends at the coasts, carbonate rocks of equivalent age extend offshore up to 100 km in the Atlantic, and 200 km in the Gulf (Hughes et al. 2009:795). Groundwater discharges diffusely onto the continental shelf in many locales, and submarine springs are well documented in Florida and elsewhere (Fleury et al. 2007; Karst Environmental Services 2008; Lane 2001; Swarzenski et al. 2001). Likewise, submarine karst features (i.e., sinkholes) have been found deep within the Straits of Florida (Land and Paull 2000). Recall that freshwater in the Upper Floridan Aquifer floats atop brackish and saline waters deep within the Lower Floridan Aquifer. This water is circulated through Kohout convection and is also found in isolated pockets within the freshwater of the Upper Floridan Aquifer (Williams and Kuniansky 2015:122). Sea-level fluctuations will raise and lower the mixing zone between fresh and saline water. Again, with other things being equal, under conditions of lowered sea level, this zone would drop and the saline water in the system would gradually be replaced by freshwater. This would also, however, decrease hydrostatic pressure in the deep aquifer, lowering the potentiometric surface and reducing or eliminating artesian flow.

Conversely, under conditions of sea-level rise, hydrostatic pressure in the aquifer will increase, and the elevation of the potentiometric surface will rise. Spring flow would then likely increase, depending on local circumstances. However, sea-level rise would also gradually flush out the freshwater in the system, replacing it with brackish and saline water.

It is clear that sea level has a strong influence on the Floridan Aquifer. However, several factors suggest that the correlation between sea level and spring flow is far from linear or straightforward. Permeability in the aquifer is not uniform, and confining units represent significant impediments to flow and groundwater equilibration (Williams and Kuniansky 2015). For example, hydraulic connectivity with the Atlantic Ocean is restricted in the Upper Floridan Aquifer relative to the Lower Floridan Aquifer (Bennett 2004). Recent efforts to model the response of the Upper Floridan Aquifer to fluctuating conditions indicate that hydrostatic pressure in the aquifer may require up to 1,000 years to stabilize after sea-level rise, depending on the rapidity of change and the local degree of confinement (Hughes et al. 2009). Temperature and chloride stabilization require even longer. This indicates that simplistic models correlating sea-level rise with artesian spring flow potentially mask other relevant factors, while limiting the potential to understand variability among springs.

Similarly, long-term changes in precipitation, particularly over areas where the aquifer receives significant recharge, have the potential to alter the hydraulic gradients and available water within the system. Greater precipitation in recharge areas increases the velocity of groundwater movement, hydrostatic pressure, and spring discharge. However, as with sea level, the relationship between precipitation and spring flow is not linear or direct, particularly in Florida (see above). Both precipitation and sea level have been highly variable over Florida's geologic history. Here I focus on how these have fluctuated since the Last Glacial Maximum of the late Pleistocene, just prior to the migration of humans into Florida.

Late Pleistocene Conditions in Florida

General narratives of late Pleistocene to Holocene climate change in Florida emphasize the gradual inundation of the peninsula as sea level rose and precipitation increased (e.g., Milanich 1994; Miller 1992; Watts and Hansen 1988). This is thought to reflect global- and regional-scale processes as temperatures warmed following the Last Glacial Maximum (LGM; approximately 20,000–22,000 years ago), and oceanic currents and atmospheric circulation accommodated the influx of glacial meltwater. This reconstruction is consonant with the greater American Southeast, which overall experienced an amelioration of climatic conditions following the LGM (Anderson and Sassaman 2012:36–46; Anderson et al. 1996).

A number of sea-level reconstructions have been put forth for the Gulf of Mexico (Balsillie and Donoghue 2004, 2011; Donoghue 2011; Otvos 2004; Simms et al. 2007; Törnqvist et al. 2004; Wright et al. 2005), the western Atlantic (Horton et al. 2009; Toscano and Lundberg 1999; Toscano and Macintyre 2003) and globally (Siddall et al. 2003; Smith et al. 2011). Although there are divergences and disagreements in the models, there is general agreement on the pace and direction of sea-level change. Collectively they indicate that sea level was nearly 120 meters lower than present during the LGM. This magnitude of reduction in sea level exposed vast expanses of the Florida Platform now inundated, particularly in the Gulf of Mexico where Florida's Gulf Coast would have been some 200 km west of its present position (Faught and Donoghue 1997; see also Anderson and Bissett 2015).

The main sources of inference about temperature and precipitation are sediment cores extracted from deep Florida lakes (Grimm et al. 1993; Grimm et al. 2006; Quillen et al. 2013; Watts 1969, 1971, 1975, 1980; Watts et al. 1992; Watts and Hansen 1994, 1998; Watts and Stuiver 1980). During the LGM, winter temperatures in Florida were, on average, 3–4 °C cooler than today (Willard et al. 2007). The Florida peninsula was also considerably drier at the peak of the last glaciation, with less precipitation and reduced surface water availability. Watts (1971) estimated that the water table in north Florida was some 12 m lower than it is today. Only a handful of Florida's deepest lakes held water during this interval, and most of the rivers and wetlands were nonexistent, at least in their current configuration. The combination of sharply reduced hydraulic pressure gradients from the Gulf and Atlantic and lower recharge rates from precipitation no doubt reduced the potentiometric surface within the Floridan Aquifer. As a result, many of Florida's springs likely did not flow. If the caverns and conduits now in place were present at that time, they may have been water-bearing sinks or dry caves (Rupert 1988).

However, the expanse of land exposed by reduced seas likely contained a number of artesian springs. Currently documented submarine springs would have been exposed on land, and others no doubt existed. Faure and colleagues (2002) have hypothesized that these springs formed a "coastal oasis" for flora and fauna during times of lowered sea level. A further consequence of reduced sea level during the LGM was the replacement of saline water in the Lower Floridan Aquifer by freshwater derived from precipitation (Morrissey et al. 2010).

After this apex of glaciation, global climate warmed, and the ice sheets receded. Melting glaciers released water into oceans and reduced the load on the continental land masses, resulting in isostatic rebound and an increase of sea level. However, this was not a uniform or gradual process. Donoghue (2011; also Balsillie and Donoghue 2011) argued that Gulf of Mexico sea-level rise in the late Pleistocene was punctuated by several periods of rapid change caused by glacial meltwater influx and/or global climate change events. The first of these rapid changes in the Gulf of Mexico began at approximately 17,700 cal BP, when the Gulf rose some 12 m over a span of 750 years. Warming of the Florida peninsula followed shortly after this, beginning in earnest by approximately 17,000 years ago (Willard et al. 2007).

The rate of both deglaciation and sea-level rise increased markedly after 15,000 cal BP, during the Bølling-Allerød interval (14,700–12,900 cal BP). Another period of rapid change in the Gulf began at 14,300 cal BP, when sea level rose 24 m over a span of 500 years (Donoghue 2011:22). This was likely caused by an input of meltwater from the Laurentide Ice Sheet, delivered to the northern Gulf of Mexico via the Mississippi River drainage. The available records from Lake Tulane and Lake Annie in southern Florida indicate that Florida was cool and dry during the Bølling-Allerød. However, pollen and ostracod records in Tampa Bay contradict this, indicating rather that central Florida reached warm, moist, near-modern conditions at that time (Willard et al. 2007).

Rising seas during the terminal Pleistocene had several ramifications for the Floridan Aquifer. Notably, this decreased the hydraulic gradient of the system, reducing the velocity of groundwater flow. Consequently, salt water intruded into the Lower Floridan Aquifer, trapping freshwater in the Upper Floridan Aquifer (Morrissey et al. 2010). Springs flowing on the emergent continental shelf were inundated, but the overall potentiometric surface of the aquifer was raised. This elevated water levels in water-bearing sinks on the interior and may have initiated spring flow in new places, again dependent on local conditions.

Following the Bølling-Allerød, the Younger Dryas (12,900–11,700 cal BP) marked an interruption of postglacial warming and a rapid return to cooler, but globally variable, conditions (Broecker 2006; Broecker et al. 2010; Tarasov and Peltier 2005). The onset of this interval coincided with another rapid sea-level rise in the Gulf of 27 m over 600 years, from 12,900 to 12,300 cal BP (Donoghue 2011:22). Evidence for the impacts of the Younger Dryas in Florida is contradictory but suggests the peninsula may be out of phase with the rest of the northern Atlantic. Pollen records from Lake Tulane (Grimm et al. 2006) in southern Florida indicate the dominance of pine at that time and point to deeper lake levels and warmer, wetter conditions than the oak-dominated assemblages of the preceding and succeeding intervals. This is corroborated by the record from Lake Annie. The pollen record from Sheelar Lake (Watts and Stuiver 1980) in northern Florida is likewise dominated by pine from ca. 13,000 to 11,000 cal BP. Rather than an increase in year-round temperature and precipitation, these records indicate increased summer precipitation and winter temperatures. This is primarily caused by warming in the Gulf of Mexico and Atlantic Ocean, which in turn is best explained by changes in atmospheric circulation at the time (Donders et al. 2011). In contrast, the Tampa Bay record indicates progressively drier conditions over the course of the Younger Dryas (Willard et al. 2007). Lack of temporal correspondence and resolution in these records may be to blame for these discrepancies. Or, as Donders and colleagues (2011) suggest, the Younger Dryas may have contained both a warm/wet and cool/dry sub-phase in Florida.

Holocene Conditions

The terminus of the Younger Dryas at 11,700 cal BP marked a return to postglacial warming and the onset of the Holocene. Sea-level rise continued into the Holocene, with pulses beginning at ca. 11,000 and 8700 cal BP (Donoghue 2011; Balsillie and Donoghue 2011). Palynological analysis of early Holocene sediments indicates that upland forests were dominated by oak and grasses, with scattered pines. Whereas different species of oaks can tolerate a variety of moisture conditions, the combination of oaks and grasses indicates a dry oak-scrub with prairie- or savanna-like openings, similar to that found on xeric hilltops and ridges in Florida today.

However, this interpretation is not uncontested. Despite the abundance of grass pollen at Lake Tulane, low $\delta^{13}C$ values of leaf waxes indicate a relative paucity of C_4 plants (Huang et al. 2006). Because most Florida grasses are C_4 plants, this contradicts the pollen evidence and suggests instead a dearth of grasses. Further, the pollen assemblage has relatively low amounts of herbs, such as *Ambrosia*, that are typically abundant in an oak-grass savanna. An alternative scenario, then, is that the grass pollen is derived from emergent or damp-ground grasses on the lake margin and thus overrepresented in the core. The grass pollen is, then, reflective of local conditions and not representative of the regional plant community. If this supposition holds, the uplands may have contained closed woodlands, reflective of moister conditions, and not a dry savanna or prairie.

Regardless, the evidence suggests increasingly wetter conditions as the Holocene progressed. Lacustrine sedimentation in many of Florida's shallower lakes began (or was reestablished) between 10,000 and 9000 cal BP (e.g., Donar et al. 2009; Watts 1969). This is indicative of rising water tables, largely driven by sea-level rise rather than increased precipitation. However, early Holocene water levels were lower and more seasonal than they are today. For example, diatom records from Lake Annie indicate that it was a shallow, seasonal pond by ca. 11,000 cal BP, with a diverse flora surrounding it (Quillen et al. 2013). Water depth and hydroperiod (i.e., the proportion of the year that the lake was inundated) increased slowly over several millennia. Likewise, water became deeper in Little Salt Spring, a 70-m-deep sinkhole/spring in Sarasota County, as the water table rose after approximately 11,000 years ago (Zarikian et al. 2005).

By approximately 8000 cal BP, the rate of sea-level rise attenuated as it approached 8 m below present levels (Donoghue 2011; Balsillie and Donoghue 2011). The available records indicate a broad transition in vegetation and (by proxy) temperature and moisture regimes in the middle Holocene. Forest composition changed from oak-dominated to pine-dominated, prairie herbs declined, and wetlands developed. These changes are indicative of increased moisture and temperature. Time-transgressive trends, from north to south, are apparent in these records (Grimm et al. 2001), with the transition occurring earlier in northern Florida (ca. 8500–7500 cal BP) than in southern Florida (after ca. 6000 cal BP). In northern Florida, pine was well established prior to 8000 cal BP, coincident with an increase in swamp trees and shrubs (Watts and Stuiver 1980). Farther south, Lake Annie witnessed a rapid increase in water depth and pine pollen from 6000 to 5000 cal BP, some 2,000 years later.

Donders (2014) synthesized the evidence for increased precipitation in Florida from multiple lake cores across the peninsula. A clear divide is apparent between the north and south Florida records, both in the timing of increased moisture and the apparent underlying causes. Time-transgressive trends between northern and southern Florida were a consequence of the differential effects of sea surface temperature and circulation patterns in the Atlantic and Gulf (Donders et al. 2011; Enfield et al. 2001; Kelly and Gore 2008). There is little evidence for marked increase in precipitation over the early to middle Holocene in northern Florida. Rather, vegetative changes indicative of greater moisture were likely driven by increasing water-table height resulting from sea-level rise. In contrast, the southern Florida records show a pronounced increase in precipitation from 6000 to 5000 cal BP. This was likely driven by intensification of the El Niño Southern Oscillation (ENSO), which dictates winter precipitation in Florida and extends the hydroperiod of seasonal wetlands, and possibly by a shift in the position of the Intertropical Convergence Zone (ITCZ; see Donders 2014; Donders et al. 2005; Donders et al. 2011; Kelly and Gore 2008).

Increased moisture in southern Florida after circa 6000 cal BP coincides with a further reduction in the rate of sea-level rise as it reached near-modern levels. It is thought that this stabilization of sea level enabled the establishment of productive coastal habitats, such as estuaries (Donoghue 2011). Indeed, peat accumulation began in wetlands across Florida after ca. 6000 cal BP (Gaiser et al. 2001; Gleason and Stone 1994; Scherer 1988; Wright et al. 2005), and by 5,000 years ago the Everglades reached from Lake Okeechobee to the Florida Keys (Willard and Bernhardt 2011).

By 4,000 years ago, the seas were within 2 m of present levels, periodically oscillating above and below modern conditions (Balsillie and Donoghue 2004). Likewise, the intensity and temporality of ENSO events and the position of the ITCZ, reflective of atmospheric and oceanic circulation patterns in the Gulf and Atlantic, approximated their modern configuration (Donders et al. 2005). The depth and condition of many Florida lakes was relatively consistent from 4,000 years ago to the near present, prior to nineteenth- and twentieth-century land alterations (Quillen et al. 2013), although there is some indication that water depth increased at ca. 2500 cal BP (Filley et al. 2001; Watts and Hansen 1994).

Although this summary paints a picture of a gradual shift to modern conditions, this was likely not the case. Mayewski and colleagues (2004) have argued that Holocene climate change was far more chaotic and spatially heterogeneous than previously thought. They identify six rapid climate-change events in the Holocene, through a synthesis of paleoenvironmental proxies (e.g., ice cores, lake varves). These events had global impacts, although they were not equally expressed in every region, and the effects in Florida are unclear. Recent evidence suggests that two, in particular, may have been impactful. The 8200 BP event was a period of rapid cooling, less severe than the Younger Dryas, which elapsed over two to four centuries (Alley et al. 1997; Barber et al. 1999; Kurek et al. 2004). This was likely caused by the final pulse of meltwater from the Laurentide Ice Sheet. A second event at 4,200 years ago has been linked to an interval of severe drought in the mid-latitudes that lasted up to 500 years (Arz et al. 2006; Booth et al. 2005; Magny et al. 2009; Rosenswig 2015). Again, the specific impacts this had on Florida are unclear, but these are only the largest of several intensifications, fluctuations, and reversals of the general trends outlined above.

In sum, and at a broad scale, over the past 20,000 years, the Florida peninsula has witnessed several dramatic changes as glaciers retreated in the Northern Hemisphere and the modern climatic regime became established. A large swath of the Florida Platform was lost to the rising seas. Sea-level rise and increased precipitation likewise raised surficial water tables and pressure within the Floridan Aquifer, resulting in greater surface water availability and spring flow. However, these changes were not gradual, and many reversals—cold snaps, prolonged droughts, sea-level regressions, and the like—are apparent. Further, there was spatial variability in the timing, tempo, and magnitude of these fluctuations that is not reflected in continental, hemispheric, or global reconstructions. This underscores the need for local reconstructions to contextualize these models.

In the following sections I turn from broad-scale climatic reconstructions to a discussion of the St. Johns River valley and the springs of Florida. The St. Johns River valley is the geographic setting for much of what is discussed in the following chapters. Of particular relevance are the hydrology and geomorphology of the valley and the relation of these to the distribution of artesian springs.

THE ST. JOHNS RIVER VALLEY

The St. Johns River is the largest river in Florida and one of the few in the Northern Hemisphere to flow from south to north. It is a broad, shallow, blackwater system that is tidally influenced with an estuary at its mouth (DeMort 1991; Miller 1998; Smock et al. 2005). The St. Johns drains approximately 23,000 km², or roughly one-fifth the land area of Florida (DeMort 1991:97), and is one of the few large rivers in the southeastern United States not impounded by dams. This is primarily because of the low gradient of the river, which drops only 8 m in elevation over a course that meanders for some 500 km from headwaters near Vero Beach to the mouth at Jacksonville. As a result of this low gradient, both water velocity and average discharge are low for a river of this size. The St. Johns also lies at a low elevation, having a maximum floodplain elevation of only 8 m above mean sea level (amsl).

As a consequence of its low elevation and gradient, the St. Johns is particularly susceptible to fluctuations in sea level. The physiography of much of peninsular Florida consists of north–south-trending highlands that roughly parallel the coasts in the northern two-thirds of the peninsula (Scott 2011:28). Like many of the larger rivers in Florida, the St. Johns is situated in a low swale or valley between these upland ridges. These lowlands are generally poorly drained and house isolated wetlands or surface drainage networks (i.e., creeks and streams). The St. Johns basin lies in the Eastern Valley physiographic province (Figure 2.4; following Cooke 1939). This expansive, low-lying area is bordered to the east by the Atlantic Coastal Ridges and to the west by the Osceola Plain, Deland Ridge, Crescent City Ridge, and Duval Upland.

These ridge and swale complexes are the remnants of sea-level high stands in the Pleistocene and earlier epochs (Cooke 1945; Miller 1998; White 1970). It is thought that the uplands are relict barrier islands and/ or beach ridges, and the lowlands were once estuarine or shallow marine environments. The St. Johns River valley was repeatedly inundated during these high stands, to a depth of at least 7.5 m (Alt and Brooks 1965), and formed a system of elongated estuarine bays or lagoons behind barrier islands, connected to the Atlantic Ocean by widely-spaced inlets (Belaineh et al. 2012; DeMort 1991:97–99). When sea level later receded, salt water was drained from the lagoon and the valley transitioned to a freshwater drainage.

The river itself is more reminiscent of a chain of lakes than the sinuous rivers commonly found elsewhere in the Southeast. The main channel of the St. Johns flows through 10 large lakes, and is fed by tributary streams

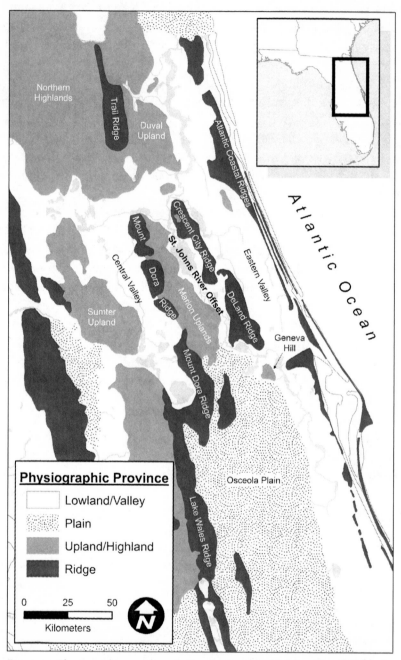

Figure 2.4. Physiographic provinces in the vicinity of the St. Johns River valley, following Cooke (1939).

from at least six more. The river basin can be divided into three primary segments—upper, middle, and lower—that reflect divergent geomorphology and hydrology (Figure 2.5). Since the St. Johns flows from south to north, the upper portion is the southernmost reach of the river. The upper St. Johns stretches for approximately 120 km from the headwaters near Vero Beach to the vicinity of Lake Harney and the confluence with the Econlockhatchee River, a major tributary. The headwaters of the St. Johns are derived from the Blue Cypress Marsh, an extensive floodplain marsh in Brevard and Indian River counties (Brenner et al. 1999; Brenner et al. 2001). The river channel is poorly defined, and sheetflow through these wetlands dominates for the upper 50 km (Kroening 2004). The channel of the St. Johns forms in the vicinity of Lake Hell 'n' Blazes and from there flows through a series of lakes formed by broad, shallow depressions in the floodplain. Unlike other central Florida lakes, which result from solution processes and karst development (Kindinger et al. 1999; Schiffer 1998), these lake basins are remnants of the estuarine lagoon from which the St. Johns River originated (White 1970). The channel becomes more distinct between lakes Windsor and Poinsett, where the bottom transitions from peat-dominated to sandy (DeMort 1991:100). From here the river channel adopts an anastomosing pattern: not a single flowing channel, but a series of lakes, lagoons, and floodplain wetlands, connected by multiple channels separated by islands and bars. The channel is generally shallow, averaging 1–3 m deep, although high-amplitude water fluctuations are common (Smock et al. 2005).

Prior to the twentieth century, the vast wetlands of the upper St. Johns covered approximately 1,800 km² (Brenner et al. 1999). The soils in these wetlands are extremely fertile and well suited to ranching and agriculture. An extensive series of levees, canals, and other water-control structures was installed to drain these soils and render them suitable for human use. By the 1980s approximately 80 percent of the basin had been converted to pasture or other agricultural use, and 70 percent of the wetlands had been drained (Brenner et al. 2001; Kroening 2004; Sterling and Padera 1998). These water-control efforts and the influx of nutrients from agricultural runoff have had numerous impacts on the hydrology and ecology of the region. Restoration efforts were begun in the 1980s by the St. Johns River Water Management District (SJRWMD) and the U.S. Army Corps of Engineers to attempt to mitigate some of these impacts.

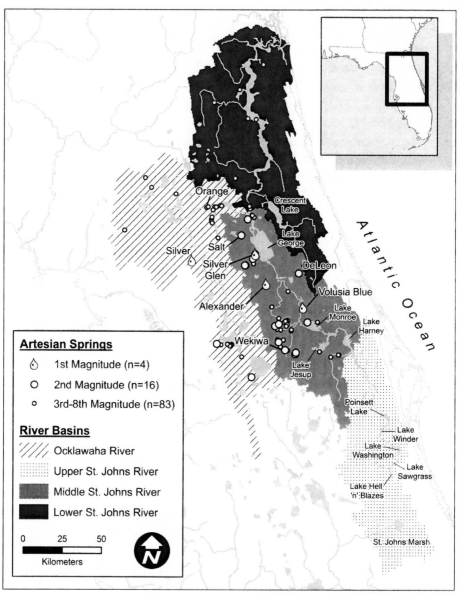

Figure 2.5. Major river basins and surface water features of the St. Johns and Ocklawaha rivers.

The middle St. Johns River is sometimes referred to as the St. Johns River Offset. The course of the St. Johns jogs west from Lake Harney to Lake Monroe, near Sanford, where it resumes its northward course on the western side of the Crescent City and Deland ridges. The river jogs back to the east just south of Palatka. This is contrary to what would be expected from fluvial dynamics and the physiography of the region. In a headward-consequent course, the river would be expected to flow from the headwaters to the mouth in a relatively straight line, following the late Pleistocene ridges adjacent to the Eastern Valley. However, as the river makes its westward jog, it flows around a block fault and passes between the DeLand Ridge and Geneva Hill, into a geologically older valley (Belaineh et al. 2012:4–75; Pirkle 1971). As a result, the channel is constrained on both sides by ridges and uplands—the Crescent City and Deland Ridges to the east and the Marion Uplands and Mount Dora Ridge to the west—before returning to the Eastern Valley.

It is thought that the middle St. Johns formed earlier than the segments above and below it (White 1970). The most likely scenario is that the middle St. Johns captured the headwaters during an early Pleistocene sea-level low stand, diverting them from an eastern course into the western offset. Crescent Lake, then, is probably a remnant of the St. Johns channel that was abandoned when the river switched to its current configuration (Miller 1998).

As a result of this diverging geomorphological history, the middle St. Johns also features distinctive hydrology. In places the floodplain is more constrained, and the river quickens as it meanders between well-defined, elevated banks, sometimes forming multiple, braided channels (DeMort 1991:101). In other places the channel flows through expansive, shallow lakes, including the aforementioned lakes Harney and Monroe, Lake Dexter, and Lake George. Unlike the lakes of the upper St. Johns, these reside in basins formed, at least partially, as a result of karst development. For example, seismic profiling of the northern portion of Lake George revealed the presence of subsidence sinkholes beneath several meters of recent lacustrine deposits (Kindinger et al. 1994).

The Ocklawaha River is the largest tributary of the St. Johns, draining an area of over 7,400 km² (Livingston 1991:85). Like the St. Johns, the headwaters of the Ocklawaha are a series of wetlands and a chain of lakes (Lakes Apopka, Harris, Eustis, Dora, Yale, and Griffin). The Ocklawaha

River lies to the west of the St. Johns in the Central Valley physiographic province. It roughly parallels the St. Johns over much of its 113-km course. The Ocklawaha receives significant input from artesian springs and receives overflow from Orange Lake by way of Orange Creek. The spring-fed Silver River, a major tributary, provides approximately half of the streamflow in the Ocklawaha (Livingston 1991:88). The river follows a northerly course, winding through extensive floodplain wetlands before making an eastern turn and debouching into the St. Johns downstream of Lake George.

The lower (northern) St. Johns River begins at the confluence with the Ocklawaha River,[4] and, after returning to the Eastern Valley, is bounded to the west by the Duval Upland. The channel of the lower St. Johns widens rapidly, expanding from 1.5 km wide at Palatka to 5 km wide near Jacksonville, and remains in a single channel without extensive intervening lakes (DeMort 1991:101). On reaching Jacksonville, the river makes an abrupt turn to the east, and the channel narrows, essentially forming a drowned estuary reaching to the Atlantic Ocean at the mouth of the river. Both salinity and tidal influence increase as the river approaches the Atlantic Ocean, with high tides causing daily flow reversals. Tidal influence routinely reaches Lake George, some 160 km upstream, and can occasionally have an impact as far south as Lake Monroe, especially when low river flow and particularly high tides coincide (DeMort 1991). Likewise, a wedge of saline water commonly reaches 40 km upriver, sometimes penetrating 90 km or more (Smock et al. 2005).

Springs of Florida and the St. Johns River

As of 2011 the inventory of springs recorded by the Florida Department of Environmental Protection (FDEP) included 1,014 entries (FDEP 2012). This inventory does not exclusively record artesian springs discharging from the Floridan Aquifer. A small number of water table springs and relict man-made wells are included. Further, the list collapses some springs with multiple, distinct vents into spring groups, whereas others are recorded individually. In many cases these vents are hydrogeologically independent, drawing water from different portions of the aquifer and relying on different recharge basins, and so it is questionable whether they should be grouped together (Scott et al. 2002). Finally, the list includes some karst features that are not technically springs, such as river-rise segments

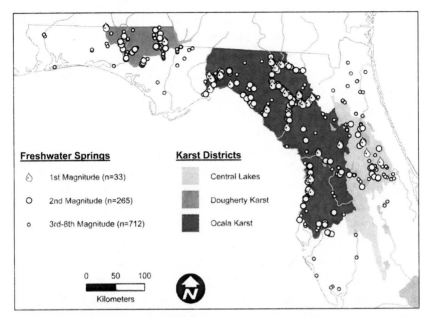

Freshwater Springs

◊   1st Magnitude (n=33)

O   2nd Magnitude (n=265)

o   3rd-8th Magnitude (n=712)

Karst Districts

Central Lakes

Dougherty Karst

Ocala Karst

0   50   100
Kilometers

Figure 2.6. Distribution of karst districts (following Brooks 1981) and freshwater springs in Florida. Karst geographic data provided by the Florida Geographic Data Library. Springs data from the Florida Department of Environmental Protection (2012).

and karst windows. As a result, the exact number of springs in the state is somewhat nebulous. It is also ever evolving, as new springs are documented and new hydrogeological research refines the grouping of spring vents.

Within the state of Florida, most artesian springs are found in areas of well-developed karst, where the Floridan Aquifer is near the surface and overlying sediments are thin or absent (Figure 2.6). Within these regions springs tend to be located at lower elevations, such as river valleys and coastal reaches, where the potentiometric surface of the aquifer is higher than the land elevation and surficial water table. Springs are most frequent in the Ocala Karst District, a broad area encompassing most of northwest peninsular Florida (Scott 2011; Scott et al. 2002). This area, sometimes referred to as the Ocala Uplift District (e.g., Brooks 1981), is an area of karst plains where the Floridan Aquifer is unconfined, with limestone at or near the surface. Springs are also found in abundance in the Dougherty Karst and Central Lakes districts. The Dougherty Karst District is located in northwest Florida and, like the Ocala Karst District, is an area of well-developed karst where the Floridan Aquifer is unconfined. The Central Lakes District lies to the east of the Ocala Karst District, where xeric sandhills thinly confine the Florida Aquifer. This is an area of active sinkhole development that encompasses a portion of the St. Johns River basin (Brooks 1981:6).

The St. Johns River Water Management District maintains an independent digital springs inventory (SJRWMD 2015a). Combined, the inventories of the SJRWMD and FDEP document 205 springs in the basins of the St. Johns and Ocklawaha Rivers (Figure 2.5). This tally includes 14 water table springs that will be excluded from further discussion. It also includes cases where a number of spring vents are documented individually, despite constituting a recognized spring group. For the sake of convenience, I collapse these in the following discussion. Treating spring groups as single entities trims the total to 103 springs. Of these, the majority (60 springs, or 58 percent of the total) feed into the middle St. Johns River basin. A further 32 discharge into the Ocklawaha River, and 11 into the lower St. Johns River. No springs have been documented in the upper portion of the St. Johns River basin.

The preponderance of springs in the middle St. Johns is a function of geography and geology. The Hawthorn Formation that confines the Floridan Aquifer in northeast Florida varies in thickness across the St. Johns River valley (Belaineh et al. 2012; Scott 1983, 1988). Recall that the middle St. Johns is offset to the west of the upper and lower thirds. This offset places the river within the Central Lakes District in a geologically older lowland valley surrounded by uplands and ridges. In this valley the Hawthorn Formation has been uplifted by faulting and warping, exposing it to erosion. As a result, it is considerably thinner in the middle St. Johns (~15 m) than either the upper or lower segments, where it is up to 150 m thick. The thickness of the Hawthorn Formation in the upper and lower St. Johns limits diffuse groundwater discharge and explains the relative lack of springs in these reaches (Connor and Belanger 1981; Spechler 1994). Further, incision of the river during Pleistocene sea-level low stands cut through the thin Hawthorn Formation in segments of the middle St. Johns River (Stringfield and Cooper 1951). The incised channel has since infilled with sediments (Kindinger et al. 2000), but it nevertheless enhances connection to the Floridan Aquifer in this portion of the valley.

Finally, uplands rise 10–20 m above the middle St. Johns River valley and are significant recharge areas for the Floridan Aquifer (Belaineh et al. 2012). The river valley itself is a significant discharge area for both diffuse leakage and spring flow, as the potentiometric surface is typically 3–6 m above the level of the St. Johns River. This high recharge to the east and west coupled with discharge within the valley creates a positive hydraulic gradient that drives groundwater circulation into the valley from both sides (Phelps and Rohrer 1987). Many springs are located near the contact between the upland recharge zone and lowland discharge zone.

The inventory of springs in the St. Johns basin includes some of the largest in Florida, such as the first-magnitude Alexander, Silver Glen, and Volusia Blue springs, and second-magnitude Salt, DeLeon, and Wekiwa. There are 13 additional second-magnitude and 83 third- or lower magnitude springs. Several of these springs feed spring runs that form major tributaries of the St. Johns River (e.g., Alexander Creek, Wekiwa River). Taken together, groundwater from the Floridan Aquifer constitutes a significant portion of the water flowing in the river, particularly in the middle St. Johns. Miller (1998:67) estimates that flow from the largest springs in the region (i.e., first and second magnitude) makes up one-third the water flowing in the St. Johns River. Similarly, groundwater flow modeling conducted for the St. Johns River Water Management District (Motz and Dogan 2004:41) suggests that direct discharge of groundwater from spring flow and diffuse upward leakage into the river channel accounts for 25 percent of the total stream flow in the St. Johns and Ocklawaha rivers.

As outlined in chapter 1, the abundance of springs in the St. Johns River valley and their substantial contribution to the flow of the river are important factors in Miller's (1992, 1998) model of climate and culture change in the region. This model posits that, prior to the establishment of near-modern climatic regimes some 6,000 years ago, the majority of springs in the St. Johns River valley could not have been flowing. Without this groundwater input the St. Johns itself did not exist in any recognizable configuration. Therefore, the cultural changes evidenced by the construction of freshwater shell mounds, middens, and the like were predicated on the onset of substantial artesian flow in the region. Indeed, they are a direct consequence of it (Miller 1992, 1998).

This chapter has reviewed the geological context, history, and physical parameters of spring flow, the evidence for climatic changes in the late

Pleistocene and Holocene, and the environmental framework of the St. Johns River valley and its springs. I have done this to provide a platform for the discussion that follows and to highlight the enormous geological and hydrological complexity of springs issuing from the Floridan Aquifer. Springs are entangled in myriad ways with processes and events unfolding over a wide range of spatial and temporal scales. The complexity of this entanglement underscores the deficiency of models that use global or hemispheric paleoenvironmental reconstructions to infer the hydraulic status of Florida springs. Also unsatisfactory are archaeological arguments that posit lockstep stimulus-and-response dynamics to complex human–ecological systems in the past. In the next chapter I unpack this model, evaluating it through multiple lines of evidence and setting the stage for a revised understanding of Florida springs archaeology.

SPRING ORIGINS

In central Polk County, a half kilometer west of the Peace River, a spring sits at the edge of a wooded swamp. The former owner of the spring, Dr. R. H. Huddleston, opened it to the public as a recreational retreat and health spa in 1883 (Figure 3.1). He installed bath houses, cottages, a diving platform, and a small hotel (Bair 2011; Brown 1991:283). Originally known as DeLeon Mineral Spring, Huddleston renamed it Kissengen, after a Bavarian spa town renowned for its medicinal springs. At its height in the early twentieth century, Kissengen Spring drew as many as 10,000 picnickers, swimmers, and revelers on a single summer day. The spring basin held a pool of water some 60 m across, with water flowing from a cave 6 m beneath the surface. In 1898 the rate of discharge was measured at 20 million gallons of water per day, making it what we would now call a second-magnitude spring (Ferguson et al. 1947:140).

The vulnerability of Kissengen Spring became apparent in the late 1920s. At the time it was thought that the Florida Platform might contain untapped oil and gas deposits (Hine 2013:107). In July 1927 drilling began on an oil test well less than 100 m from the spring. The drill had penetrated 70 m into the surface when it intercepted the groundwater flow feeding Kissengen Spring. The spring's water level dropped alarmingly, and the pool was nearly drained. The well was quickly capped, restoring spring flow, and further testing was moved away from the spring (Peek 1951).

A decade later the water again began dropping in Kissengen Spring. Not suddenly, but slowly and persistently. Drilling was no longer the culprit; by this time oil prospectors had largely lost interest and moved on to greener pastures. The problem was resource extraction of another kind. Kissengen Spring lies in the heart of the Central Florida Phosphate

Figure 3.1. Kissengen Spring, Polk County, Florida, in 1894. Courtesy of the State Archives of Florida.

District, one of the most productive phosphate deposits in the world[1] (Hine 2013:157–158). Phosphate mining has many unfortunate side effects. Metallic monstrosities known as "draglines" strip-mines phosphate ore located beneath the surface sands, resulting in the release of radon gas and the accumulation of waste products in massive phosphogypsum stacks. Further, vast amounts of water are consumed during the chemical processing that transforms phosphate into phosphoric acid and, ultimately, fertilizer.

The rate of groundwater withdrawal in Polk County began increasing progressively after 1937 (Peek 1951). Nearly 70 percent of the water used at that time went to phosphate mining. The output of Kissengen Spring declined in step with this until, on a winter day in 1950, the final trickle of water pulsed from the spring. What had once been a popular gathering spot for residents and visitors alike was transformed into a stagnant puddle, choked with dog fennel (Figure 3.2). And so the death of a spring is not unknown: Kissengen became the first major spring in Florida to cease flowing as a result of groundwater withdrawals (Peek 1951; Rosenau et al. 1977:307). But what of the birth of a spring? How does a spring come into being, for example, as pressure increased in the Floridan Aquifer over the late Pleistocene and Holocene? The birth of a spring, or rather of springs writ large, is the subject of this chapter.

As discussed in chapter 1, the onset of the Mount Taylor period in Florida's St. Johns River valley is demarcated by the appearance of large shell mounds on the banks of the river some 7,400 years ago (Beasley 2009; Endonino 2010; Randall 2013, 2015; Wheeler et al. 2000). These constructions are generally taken to be an index for the inception of a riverine adaptation and more sedentary settlement (Milanich 1994:87). It has been argued that shell mounds and the practices that gave rise to them were predicated on a "natural" event: the initiation of artesian flow from the numerous springs that today feed the St. Johns River (Miller 1992, 1998). Although surface water gradually increased over the course of the early and middle Holocene, the St. Johns River likely did not attain its modern configuration until it began receiving fresh groundwater from artesian springs. Under this model, the inhabitants of the region would have mapped on to the emerging aquatic habitats, exploiting shellfish as a food resource and depositing their shells on the banks of the river. Miller (1998:97) views this as a rapid change in the landscape: "the flooding of the St. Johns River Basin around 5,000 years ago must have been a sudden

Figure 3.2. Kissengen Spring in 2006. Courtesy of the U.S. Geological Survey.

event, in geological time. Because the artesian flow of a spring is a step function . . . either on or off, there would have been little warning that the river basin was about to double in size." Interpreted in this way, the initiation of spring flow appears as an ecological founding event—a rapid restructuring of the landscape that provided the necessary and sufficient conditions for a specific adaptive strategy.

Intuitively this explanation makes sense. People could not collect and deposit shells if the habitats for shellfish were not present. However, there are several problems with this hypothesis. First, it perpetuates a perception of hunter-gatherers as ahistorical and reactionary. That is, change in human cultures is reduced to a process of adaptation to external stimuli with no consideration of internal dynamics as the driver of stability or change (e.g., sociopolitical or ideological factors). Second, this explanation assumes that shell mounds are simply middens, the palimpsest refuse of many small meals. By corollary it denies any intentionality or foresight to the shell mounders themselves and imposes onto the past our own biases about what constitutes trash. Third, it simply has not been empirically tested. The onset of spring flow is hypothesized to follow Holocene sea-level rise and initiate changes in aquatic ecology and human interactions with the river. But the timing and synchronicity of these events and the implications of a sudden influx of freshwater to the system have not been investigated.

Recent archaeological work at several springs in the St. Johns River valley is casting light on these questions and causing us to rethink environmental and cultural histories of the region. In this chapter I discuss the results of both field investigations and hydrological modeling of the onset of artesian spring flow in the region. Mounting evidence calls into question the "eventfulness" of these changes in hydrology and ecology, in terms of both the tempo with which they unfolded and, more importantly, the human response they elicited.

In the following I first review the archaeology of the Mount Taylor period, with emphasis on the changing form of shell constructions through time and the association of these sites with artesian springs in the St. Johns River valley. After this I discuss the notion of "events" as the term is used here. This is important to clarify because the eventfulness of artesian and cultural changes in the region is at issue. Miller posits the onset of spring flow as a (geological) event, but it is not altogether clear whether this is commensurate with commonsense understandings of the term or if it can be addressed with archaeological evidence.

With this background in place, I then turn to a GIS-based model of spring flow in the middle St. Johns River basin. This model examines how springs at different landscape positions would be affected by a reduced potentiometric surface of the Floridan Aquifer. The model begins with aquifer pressure reduced to such an extent that spring flow would be absent in the middle St. Johns basin. The potentiometric surface is then incrementally increased until predevelopment levels are reached. The model is a heuristic device and not intended to mimic the reaction of the Floridan Aquifer to specific sea-level or precipitation changes. Rather, it allows me to evaluate whether the onset of spring flow valley-wide might have been a sudden and widespread event.

The implications of this model are evaluated with empirical evidence from two archaeological sites. Site 8MR2322 surrounds Salt Springs in the western portion of the valley. Investigations conducted in 2009 of a subaqueous Mount Taylor midden in the spring channel provide insights into both the timing of initial spring flow and the changing spring-side practices of Mount Taylor people. Fifteen kilometers south of Salt Springs are a plethora of archaeological deposits surrounding Silver Glen Springs. I focus here on Locus A at site 8LA1-W, a Mount Taylor shell ridge paralleling the spring run that is the subject of ongoing field investigations. Recent archaeological evidence points to pre–Mount Taylor activity, and cores extracted from the wetland adjacent to Locus A provide data pertinent to changing hydrological conditions in the spring.

I close with a discussion of the implications of these data to the hypotheses described above. Was the onset of spring flow in the middle St. Johns River rapid and widespread? Was it an event that precipitated changes in the lifeways of local inhabitants? I argue that it was not and set the stage for an alternative explanation, developed in the following chapters, that springs were critically important for people inhabiting the region, but not for reasons traditionally offered.

The Mount Taylor Period in Northeast Florida

The Mount Taylor archaeological culture encompasses a suite of material objects and practices centered on the St. Johns River valley (Figure 3.3).

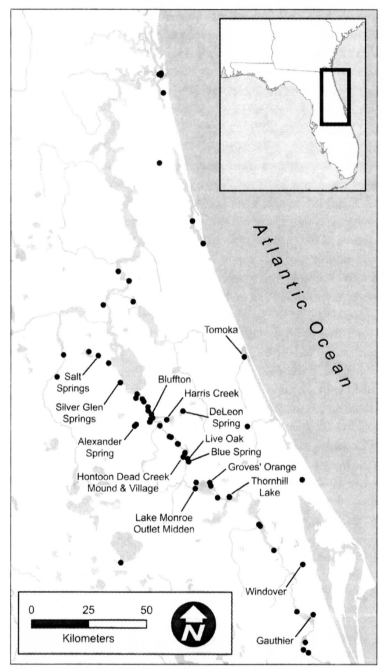

Figure 3.3. Distribution of Mount Taylor era sites in the St. Johns River valley, highlighting locations mentioned in the text. Also shown are two pond burial sites, Windover and Gauthier.

Regionally, it falls within the Archaic period of the American Southeast (Anderson and Sassaman 2012; Sassaman 2010). The Archaic has long been characterized as a transitional era of mobile, egalitarian hunter-gatherer bands gradually adapting to postglacial conditions and leading a simple lifestyle that remained relatively unchanged for some 8,000 years (e.g., Smith 1986; Steponaitis 1986). The Archaic is generally divided into Early (11,500–8900 cal BP), Middle (8900–5800 cal BP), and Late (5800–3200 cal BP) sub-periods (Figure 3.4). These divisions are recognized largely on the basis of shifts in technology, although the precise timing

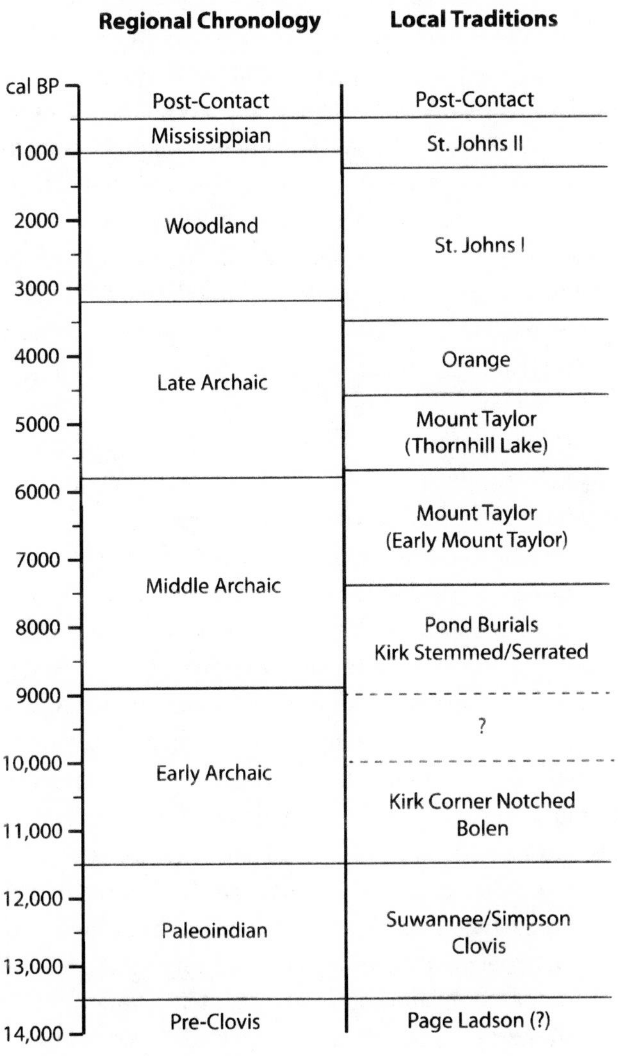

Regional Chronology	Local Traditions
cal BP	
Post-Contact	Post-Contact
1000 Mississippian	St. Johns II
2000 Woodland	St. Johns I
3000	
4000	Orange
5000 Late Archaic	Mount Taylor (Thornhill Lake)
6000	Mount Taylor (Early Mount Taylor)
7000 Middle Archaic	
8000	Pond Burials Kirk Stemmed/Serrated
9000	?
10,000 Early Archaic	Kirk Corner Notched Bolen
11,000	
12,000 Paleoindian	Suwannee/Simpson Clovis
13,000	
14,000 Pre-Clovis	Page Ladson (?)

Figure 3.4. Culture-historical chronology of the southeastern United States (after Anderson and Sassaman 2012) and local traditions of the St. Johns River valley.

of these changes varies considerably both throughout the Southeast and within the state of Florida. Broad brush strokes generally paint a picture of increasing population, reduced settlement mobility, and subsistence specialization as communities adapted to ameliorating environmental conditions. However, this picture of gradual adaptation is being overturned by recent research that emphasizes the importance of sociality, interaction, identity, and history to Archaic communities (e.g., Claassen 2010; Emerson et al. 2009; Gilmore 2016; Randall 2015; Sassaman 2010).

Investigations into the Early Archaic period typically focus on environmental changes at the Pleistocene to Holocene transition, and concomitant human adaptation to new climatic regimes. The Early Archaic is recognized by a shift in the form of diagnostic hafted bifaces, as lanceolate forms, characteristic of the earlier Paleoindian period, ceased to be manufactured by approximately 11,000 cal BP (Anderson and Sassaman 2012:71–72). In their place appear a variety of side- and corner-notched forms and bifurcate-based hafted bifaces. The most common of these in Florida are the Kirk and Bolen types. Early Archaic communities in Florida were likely highly mobile and may have been tethered to sources of freshwater and toolstone. Dunbar (2002, 2006, 2016) has argued that a multicentury dry spell termed the Bolen drought, spanned the Paleoindian to Early Archaic transition ca. 11,500–10,800 cal BP. However, both sea level and precipitation increased over the course of the early Holocene, so the constraint posed by freshwater availability likely lessened, opening up new areas for exploitation (Donoghue 2011; Milanich 1994:62–63).

Similarly, Middle Archaic cultural developments have been explained by reference to a warming and drying trend variously referred to as the Hypsithermal, Altithermal, or Mid-Holocene Climatic Optimum (e.g., Anderson et al. 2007; Brown and Vierra 1983; Marquardt and Watson 2005). After ca. 8000 cal BP there was an increased focus on aquatic resources across the Southeast, as evidenced by the appearance of shell middens and mounds along the coasts and interior river valleys (Dye 1996). Middle Archaic earthen monuments were constructed in the Lower Mississippi River Valley and Florida, the first of their kind in the region (Piatek 1994; Russo 1994; Saunders et al. 2005). This period is marked by the disappearance of notched hafted bifaces and the appearance of stemmed varieties. Kirk stemmed or serrated is perhaps the earliest of these, in use by approximately 9,000 cal BP in Florida (Faught and Waggoner 2012). Following this are a variety of local variants (Levy, Alachua, Putnam,

Marion) grouped under the rubric "Florida Archaic Stemmed" (Bullen 1975). This period also saw the inception of the pond-burial tradition, best known in Florida from the Windover archaeological site in Brevard County (Doran 2002) where at least 168 individuals were interred in saturated peat deposits sometime between 9000 and 8000 cal BP. Archaic pond mortuaries have been documented at other locations in Florida as well (Clausen et al. 1979; Purdy 1991:167–177; Wharton et al. 1981).

The onset of the Late Archaic period is marked by the end of the Hypsithermal and establishment of near-modern climatic regimes and sea level (Anderson and Sassaman 2012). This interval is characterized by long-distance exchange and interaction centered on Poverty Point, Louisiana (Gibson 2001; Kidder 2010). The Late Archaic also witnessed technological innovations, notably the initial dissemination of pottery in the region, which appeared by ca. 4600 cal BP in Florida (Gilmore 2016; Sassaman 2004). This pottery, among the earliest in North America, was tempered with Spanish moss (*Tillandsia usneoides*) fibers and is referred to as the Orange series. Despite the addition of pottery, little else seems to differentiate the Orange period in Florida from what came previously (Milanich 1994). Settlement and subsistence patterns were largely similar, with a continued focus on the aquatic resources of the coasts and interior rivers and wetlands. However, a handful of locales in the middle St. Johns River valley became the focal points for massive gatherings that drew people from across the Florida peninsula (Gilmore 2016; Randall et al. 2014).

The focus of this chapter is the preceramic Archaic Mount Taylor period of northeast Florida. Mount Taylor was originally defined by Goggin (1947, 1952) as one of the earliest recognizable cultural complexes in the region. Dating from ca. 7400–4600 cal BP, it spans the Middle and Late Archaic periods and is traditionally defined by the inception of large, complex deposits of freshwater shell[2] (Beasley 2009; Endonino 2010; Randall 2013, 2015; Wheeler et al. 2000). The dominant species of mollusk in these deposits is the banded mystery snail (*Viviparus georgianus*). Remains of the apple snail (*Pomacea paludosa*) and freshwater bivalves (*Unionidae* sp.) are commonly present as well, often in discrete deposits.

A suite of artifact types is characteristic of Mount Taylor assemblages, although to some degree these crosscut boundaries with the preceding Early Archaic and subsequent Late Archaic Orange period. It is rather the appearance of shell sites that delimits the onset of the Mount Taylor period, and the appearance of pottery that signals its terminus. Mount

Taylor assemblages are typified by bone, shell, and antler tools, with varying amounts of lithic materials (Wheeler et al. 2000). Where present, lithic hafted bifaces are largely consistent with the Newnan Horizon and Florida Archaic Stemmed cluster (Bullen 1975). Bone and antler tools include both decorated and undecorated forms, such as awls, pins, socketed projectile points, and net fids (Byrd 2011; Wheeler and McGee 1994). Marine shell was transformed into receptacles, beads, and woodworking tools (e.g., axes and adzes). Later Mount Taylor assemblages often contain items that originated far from the St. Johns River valley, such as soapstone and greenstone from the interior Piedmont, Queen conch (*Strombus gigas*) from southern Florida, and stone beads that evidence connections as far away as Mississippi (Endonino 2009, 2010).

Recent work in the middle St. Johns River valley has clarified our understanding of Mount Taylor material culture and chronology. A recent development is the definition of two phases within the Mount Taylor period (Beasley 2009; Endonino 2009, 2010): the *Early Mount Taylor* phase (7400–5700 cal BP) and the *Thornhill Lake* phase (5700–4600 cal BP). This division is based primarily on the recognition of changes in mortuary and exchange practices. Randall (2013) has further refined this chronology, delimiting three "episodes" of shell deposition that vary in content, context, and form. The first two of these correspond to the Early Mount Taylor phase, and the third is commensurate with the Thornhill Lake phase.

The Early Mount Taylor Phase (7400–5700 cal BP)

The Early Mount Taylor phase began with the onset of intensive freshwater shell deposition in the St. Johns River valley at approximately 7400 cal BP. Again, Miller (1992, 1998) attributes this practice to sea-level rise and the onset of artesian flow in the St. Johns River valley. Although the hallmark of the Mount Taylor period is the building of large shell mounds and ridges, measuring as much as 200 m long and 5 m high, the earliest shell deposits were less conspicuous on the landscape. These have been studied both in isolated contexts and beneath larger ridges. The evidence to date indicates that at the onset of the Early Mount Taylor phase, shell deposits consisted of habitation spaces arrayed, perhaps in a linear fashion, along waterways. For example, the Hontoon Dead Creek Village (8VO215) comprises a series of small, regularly spaced shell nodes, interpreted as house mounds, fronting a relict channel of the St. Johns (Randall 2007, 2015).

These nodes range from 13 to 25 m in maximum dimension and 50 cm in height, and consist of thin layers of crushed and whole shell that likely correspond to periods of occupation and abandonment. The material inventory is consistent with habitation activities, as food remains, ash, charcoal, and shell tools are abundant.

Beginning approximately 7,200 years ago, some of these domestic spaces were apparently covered over and transformed into linear or crescentic shell ridges. These imposing sites were once abundant along the middle St. Johns, numbering in the dozens, if not hundreds, prior to twentieth century mining for road fill and fertilizer. Only a few remain relatively unscathed, but those that do attest to dramatic transformations in depositional practices (Randall 2015; Sassaman 2012, 2013; Sassaman and Randall 2012). The Hontoon Dead Creek Mound (8VO214) is a teardrop shaped ridge, 140 m long with an offset summit approximately 5 m high (Randall and Sassaman 2005:83–106). The nearby Live Oak mound (8VO41) is similarly arrayed, measuring 120 m long and 5 m high (Sassaman 2003a:69–90). Both ridges are located on former channels of the St. Johns that have since been abandoned. The presence of buried shell deposits beneath a meter of muck adjacent to these ridges attests to rising water levels and wetland aggradation over the past seven millennia. Although these are discrete sites, their constituents are strikingly similar, and I discuss them collectively below.

The basal components consist of midden deposits that are partially or wholly saturated today. These are the only portions of either ridge that exhibit evidence of domestic or habitation-related activities. Their disposition beneath the water table hampers recovery and interpretation, but they appear to be similar in content and form to the house mounds of the Hontoon Dead Creek Village. These basal middens were subsequently covered with a thick (1.5–2 m) deposit composed largely of clean, whole *Viviparus* shell. This shell layer has a conspicuous dearth of both non-shell matrix and artifacts. These thick shell layers are interpreted as intentional "capping" events that sealed off former domestic spaces and marked a transition in site use (Sassaman and Randall 2012).

Upon this massive cap are diminutive layers of unburned and burned shell. These alternating light and dark layers, or "couplets," are reminiscent of stacked living surfaces documented elsewhere, but indicators of daily living (e.g., vertebrate faunal remains, lithic or shell tools, charcoal) are sparse. This, combined with their relatively rapid construction and a lack of indicators of significant depositional hiatuses (i.e., pedogenesis), has led to the conclusion that these couplets result from a series of restricted, but repeated, communal events aimed at renewing mound surfaces and drawing on these places as historical resources to confront unanticipated change (i.e., changing hydraulic conditions evident in the abandonment of the river channel; Sassaman and Randall 2012).

These practices constitute Randall's (2013) Episode I deposition and persist until approximately 6350 cal BP. Episode II (6350–5700 cal BP) shell deposition entails the abandonment of earlier sites, likely coincident with wetland aggradation and channel migration facilitated by the relative stabilization of sea level prior to 6000 cal BP. Episode II shell sites take on two divergent forms. The first of these are dedicated mortuaries constructed of shell and sand. Neither the Live Oak nor Hontoon Dead Creek mounds have produced evidence for mortuary use, although mound cores were not penetrated, and Episode I mortuary practices remain unknown. However, Episode II mortuary practices have been well documented at the Harris Creek site (8VO24) on Tick Island. The site was first visited by C. B. Moore in the nineteenth century and subsequently excavated by Ripley Bullen in 1961 (Aten 1999; Jahn and Bullen 1978). Aten (1999) reconstructed the complex depositional history of this site, which includes multiple shell fields and ridges covering five acres. Over 180 Mount Taylor burials were recovered from the largest shell ridge at the site, which measured 10 m in height. These burials, likely a small fraction of the total, were found in two discrete mortuary deposits (Aten 1999:170). Like the ridges described above, Harris Creek began as a residential space that was subsequently capped with shell and repurposed (Randall 2015:222–228). The major mortuary feature is white sand that was used to inter burials emplaced atop and within the shell deposit. Above this is a charcoal-rich layer with postholes and other features indicative of a charnel house (Aten 1999:147). A second mortuary component with multiple interments lies atop this and in turn is capped with deposits of shell and earth. Isotopic analysis indicates that the individuals interred in the mound included some who were local to the St. Johns region and others hailing from as far away as Tennessee and Virginia (Quinn et al. 2008; Tucker 2009).

The second major site type documented for Episode II consists of shell ridges that are similar in form and scale to earlier Episode I ridges but contain ample evidence for daily habitation. These have been documented at sites such as the Silver Glen (8LA1-W) and Thornhill Lake complexes

(8VO58–60) and occur along extant bodies of water, rather than relict channels. Locus A at 8LA1-W is the remnant of a Mount Taylor shell ridge some 200 m long (Randall 2015; Sassaman et al. 2011; Sassaman and Randall 2012). Although much of the site was destroyed by twentieth-century shell mining, surface relief and subsurface exposures have revealed 4 m of intact, stratified deposits. Three macro-units have been defined, similar to those of Episode I ridges (Sassaman and Randall 2012). Once again this ridge began as a domestic or habitation space that was subsequently capped. However, in this case the cap was not shell but relatively homogeneous brown sand. The upper deposits above this cap consist of alternating layers of shell and earth, interspersed with crushed shell surfaces and occasional pit features. These are similar in form and content to the shell nodes documented at Hontoon Dead Creek Village, containing numerous vertebrate faunal remains and tools of bone, stone, and shell. Notable in these assemblages is the inclusion of marine-shell vessels and substantial quantities of lithic debris and tools, both of which are lacking in Episode I deposits (Randall 2013).

In sum, the Early Mount Taylor phase is characterized by changing patterns of shell deposition and landscape use over 1,700 years. Initial habitation spaces were repeatedly capped and conscripted for new uses. During Episode I (7400–6350 cal BP), this transformation entailed cyclical, communal events of mound surface renewal. Over relatively short periods of time, these new depositional practices built up imposing shell ridges along abandoned, relict channels of the St. Johns. During Episode II of shell deposition (6350–5700 cal BP), earlier shell ridges were abandoned as loci for emplacing shell, and new ridges were formed. In Episode II ridges, basal domestic spaces were likewise transformed toward diverging ends. In some cases these became loci for interment of the dead, in others for the ongoing sustenance of the living.

Thornhill Lake Phase (5700–4600 cal BP)

The Thornhill Lake phase is coincident with Episode III shell deposition (5700–4600 cal BP) and, like the earlier transition from Episode I to II, marks the abandonment of some earlier shell ridges and the establishment of new shell sites (Randall 2013). Shell deposition was apparently restricted to fewer locales than previously, but the resulting mounds and ridges tend to be larger and more complex, a trend that would reach its apogee in the subsequent Late Archaic Orange period. Continuity is evident in the arrangement of domestic spaces, reliance on aquatic resources, and use of a similar tool set. The primary distinguishing feature of the Thornhill Lake phase is a novel mortuary tradition involving the construction of sand burial mounds and the widening of exchange networks to encompass much of the lower Southeast (Beasley 2009; Endonino 2009).

Thornhill Lake mortuary practices contrast with earlier interments in shell, like those at Harris Creek. Conical sand mounds built during this phase are the earliest earthen monuments in the region. Well-studied examples include the Bluffton burial mound (8VO23) and mounds A and B at the Thornhill Lake complex (8VO58–60). At Bluffton a single individual was interred in a conical mound some 20 m in diameter and 5 m in height. The mound was composed of brown sand and shell beneath layers of organic muck and redeposited shell midden (Randall and Tucker 2012; Sears 1960). No artifacts or other inclusions were associated with the burial. A single radiocarbon assay places the burial early in the Thornhill Lake phase, at 5660–5320 cal BP (Randall and Tucker 2012).

As documented in recent excavations by Endonino (2009, 2010), the Thornhill Lake Complex consists of multiple shell ridges and at least two conical sand mortuary mounds. The shell ridges began accumulating during Episode II, between 6300 and 5600 cal BP. The mortuary mounds, a later addition, were initially excavated by C. B. Moore (1894a, b), who noted a lack of pottery but significant quantities of nonlocal items accompanying burials. The larger Mound A (3.4 m high) contained at least 42 burials in alternating lenses of brown and white sand. Mound A was constructed late in the Thornhill Lake phase, likely postdating 4840 cal BP. Mound B was built directly atop an Episode II ridge and is composed of brown sand with sparse shell. It contains seven burials and was constructed sometime after 5600 cal BP.

Long-distance relationships with denizens of the interior Southeast are indicated by the inclusion of items that originated in far-flung locales. These items appear in both mortuary and non-mortuary contexts in the middle St. Johns River valley. At Thornhill Lake these included bannerstones, polished stone beads and pendants, and marine shell beads. Stone items were produced of materials not available in the Florida peninsula (e.g., greenstone, steatite, jasper). Whereas the bannerstones likely originated in the Piedmont region of northern Georgian and Alabama (Endonino 2009:157–158; Sassaman and Randall 2007), polished stone beads are reminiscent of those produced in Mississippi (Randall 2015:140–145). The Thornhill Lake mortuaries thus contrast with the Bluffton Burial Mound in that they encase multiple individuals and exotic grave inclusions and were apparently used over a longer period of time. A similar earthen mortuary, roughly coeval with Bluffton and Thornhill Lake, has been documented at the Tomoka Mound Complex (8VO81). Nonlocal items were also recovered there, notably a cache of bannerstones (Piatek 1994).

Randall (2010:317–321) has suggested that many Thornhill Lake phase mortuary mounds were constructed in a single stage over few individuals, thus contrasting with Early Mount Taylor mounds not only in terms of the principal construction medium, but also with regard to the temporality and sociality of mound construction. That is, whereas earlier shell mortuary and ceremonial mounds were apparently communal, integrating affairs erected through cyclical acts of deposition, later Thornhill Lake sand mortuaries appear more eventful and exclusionary, and may have been less labor intensive.

Sassaman (2012, 2013) has further argued that changing Mount Taylor ritual practices are underlain by a common thread, a historical ontology that viewed water as both the source of life and a medium of renewal. Taking the position that water was an important symbolic medium in past ritual practices, Sassaman argues that the shift from Archaic pond burials to shell burials occurred at a time when sea level was still rising rapidly, and changes in the local hydrology (i.e., inundation of the valley) would have been perceptible over the course of a human lifetime. This may have been at odds with elements of cosmogony that held that earth and life emerged from water (i.e., the earth diver myth), and had a profound impact as pond mortuaries became inaccessible under rising waters. The Early Mount Taylor practice of ritualized shell deposition is interpreted as a response to the contradictions of rising water, inasmuch as it represents a conversion of ponds into mounds. Shell, in this sense, is metaphorical water. Capping mortuaries with shell may have recapitulated the emergence of earth and life from water. The couplets of clean and burned shell witnessed at Hontoon Dead Creek and Live Oak mounds reenacted this cosmogonic myth at a smaller scale. Ritual action involving shell was thus a strategy for imposing greater control over unpredictable yet symbolically charged water and became an important medium for community building.

The second transformation of mortuary practices, involving the use of sand, occurred as rates of sea-level rise attenuated and hydrology became more stable (Sassaman 2012, 2013). Water levels were thus more predictable, and environmental change no longer perceptible at the generational time-scale. Shell was no longer needed as a ritual medium to intervene against erratic hydrology. In addition to the shifting ritual media, mounds became smaller in scale and more eventful in their construction, in that they no longer evidence repeated ritual depositions. Further, Sassaman suggests that the inclusion of nonlocal items indicates contact with diverse groups of "outsiders." Thus, shell and earth may have become signifiers of original/native and newcomer/non-native, respectively.

Mount Taylor Historicity

Several observations can be made about the history of Mount Taylor shell deposition outlined above and the role played by springs in the onset of this practice. First, the underlying theme throughout the Mount Taylor period is the covering over of prior habitation spaces and the establishment of new depositional regimes atop them. This indicates a persistent concern with places as *historical* resources that were drawn upon in the siting of locales for communal mortuary or renewal rites, or the reestablishment of everyday dwelling (Randall 2015).

Second, at least in the case of Episode I ridges like Hontoon Dead Creek and Live Oak mounds, the triggering event that precipitated the mounding of shell was not the *birth* of ecological productivity drawing people to the river, but rather the *demise* of places. Rising waters, wetland aggradation, and channel migration stranded existing habitation spaces and inundated existing mortuary spaces (i.e., pond burials; Sassaman 2012, 2013; Sassaman and Randall 2012:73). As a result, new dwelling spaces were required for both the living and the dead. It is unclear whether similar processes or events preceded the erection of later Episode II shell ridges, or if some other factor was at play. But the Mount Taylor concern with history persisted, as preexisting habitation spaces were capped with shell or sand prior to renewed habitation or the interment of the dead. This cap marked a transition, the end of one stage in the history of a place and the beginning of another. We currently lack the data to say with certainty whether these habitation sites were in use at the time of their capping, or if they were abandoned and then transformed at a later juncture.

Finally, it is notable that Episode I Mount Taylor shell ridges have not been documented proximate to springs in the St. Johns River basin. This could be explicable if springs were not yet flowing, but if so this undermines the hypothesis that shellfish exploitation is dependent on spring flow. Or it may be that springs were flowing but people did not visit them, perhaps because their flow was intermittent or unreliable. This again undermines hypotheses that characterize spring flow as eventful, precipitating a rapid transformation in the ecology of the St. Johns. Data pertinent to these hypotheses will be brought to bear below. But first the following section explores the concept of "event" and clarifies how I conceive of events here.

EVENTS AND NON-EVENTS

Studying events in the deep past is tricky business. The distortion of time and the palimpsest nature of the material world conspire to blur the residues of past happenings. Or rather, they blur the totality of events that might make up a thick history of a given people, time, or place. Where discrete events have been identified and studied, they are typically broad transformations in material culture that have the appearance of rapidity. Often these are correlated with changes in climate at the local or regional scale that assume a causal role in explaining the eventful changes in human behavior.

When considering events in the past, our commonsense understanding is often tacitly invoked. An event is generally considered to be an occurrence or happening that is recognized as having significance. To paraphrase Sahlins (1985:xiv), an event is a happening interpreted and imbued with meaning. Typically we conceive of events as having a finite duration, though their boundaries can be difficult to define. Events may happen rapidly, even instantly, or they may unfold over a protracted interval. The spatial scale of events and the number of people who experienced them also vary, as does their materiality, with some events leaving little trace of their passing and others significantly more. But regardless of scope, it is recognized that something of consequence transpired; it was affective to those who experienced and/or interpreted it. Further, the affective quality of events extends them through space and time; their repercussions give them life beyond the immediate experience (Sahlins 1985, 1991; Sewell 2005). And if the event itself varies in scale and extent, so too do the consequences.

In contrast to events are what Fogelson (1989) refers to as "non-events." Again a commonplace understanding is a useful starting point. To indicate that an occurrence was a non-event is to assert that nothing of consequence transpired. Whatever fallout may result is nondescript and insignificant. But if an event is a happening interpreted, what, then, is a non-event? Can we say that a non-event is a happening not interpreted? This clearly cannot be the case. Non-events are interpreted happenings as well. They may be happenings that are dismissed, ignored, or simply overlooked, but whatever the case, they are interpreted. However, in the case of the non-event, the happening is deemed inconsequential.

Fogelson discusses several ways that non-events come into being. First, for any given happening some may recognize an event where others do not. Similarly, though there may be agreement that an event transpired, the significance or consequences of the event may be debated. Another form of non-event is the *imagined event*. This is an event that could or should have happened but did not. These nevertheless impact individuals' actions and understandings, either because they are asserted to have happened in the past or are anticipated in the future. A subtype of imagined events is the *epitomizing event*, "narratives that condense, encapsulate, and dramatize longer-term historical processes" (Fogelson 1989:143). These often provide compelling historical explanations, although they are fictions in the sense that the events recounted did not "actually" occur. A fifth form of non-event is the *latent event*, an event that has been overlooked because it does not fit into existing questions or narratives. Finally, *denied events* are events that are so traumatic that their recollection is repressed, and they are deliberately forgotten.

The important point of Fogelson's scheme is not the typology of non-events, but rather his illustration of the multiple vehicles, justifications, and circumstances that contribute to the interpretation of any happening as significant or insignificant, and thus as eventful or non-eventful. This highlights the relational quality of events and non-events, as both are constructed in the interplay between objective conditions and subjective perception and interpretation. The significance of an event is derived from its appropriation and interpretation in a given cultural order

(Sahlins 1991:45) and thus is dependent on cultural and historical context. The eventful is not solely dictated by what "actually happened," but neither is it plucked out of the ether. Events, then, are an emergent quality of the human-inhabited world.

It is important to emphasize that the interpretation of incidences as significant or insignificant involves a certain perspectivism, such that "events may be recognized, defined, evaluated, and endowed with meaning differentially in different cultural traditions" (Fogelson 1989:135) or by different individuals or sects within a tradition. These may be contemporaries with competing interests and differentials of power that dictate their ability to interpret occurrences. Or the observers may be separated in space or time, as in the distinction between events recognized by observers who lived through them and those recognized by researchers or analysts looking in (or back) from the outside (discussed as "experiential" and "analytical" events by Gilmore and O'Donoughue [2015:7–8]). The more pertinent question, then, is not whether some occurrence was eventful or not, but rather for whom was it an event or a non-event?

This highlights that non-events can become events retrospectively and thus are influenced by subsequent happenings. The distinction involves an attribution of meaning. What we recognize as events in hindsight may not have been interpreted as such by those who experienced them. If we are to avoid grafting our understanding of events onto the past, then it is insufficient to simply demonstrate that some happening transpired over a relatively short interval of time (i.e., perceptible within a human generation or two). Rather, it is necessary to demonstrate if and how that happening was acknowledged by and incorporated into existing cultural traditions. These distinctions, then, of event/non-event and experiential/analytical events help disentangle events that may be recognizable at the geologic time-scale from those recognizable at the human perceptual scale.

All of this redoubles the challenge facing archaeologists, who must tease out events from their material residues while continually guarding against the bias of our own subjective understanding of the world and what constitutes a "significant" happening. One approach is to focus solely on *historical events*. As defined by Sahlins (1985, 1991), these are the happenings that cause a rupture in social structures and thus are moments of significant change. To some these are the only events worth considering (e.g., Beck et al. 2007), although there is debate over whether the rearticulation of social structures is limited to moments of existential chaos, or if it can be realized in mundane, daily events (e.g., Gillespie 2007; Gilmore 2015). Further, focusing solely on transformation disregards the eventfulness of structural reproduction, a point Sahlins (1991) recognized but did not resolve.

Lucas (2008) takes a slightly different approach, arguing that archaeologists should focus on the materiality of events. However, Lucas refers not simply to the surviving objects or elements of an event, but rather to the material organizations of things as *assemblages*. He characterizes assemblages on the basis of two salient features—*reversibility* and *residuality*. The reversability of an assemblage is the ease with which it can be reorganized or reconfigured. In contrast, residuality refers to the potential of an assemblage to leave material traces. Lucas argues that the material organization of most events is not preserved in the archaeological record because they have high reversibility and low residuality. Those events that are most accessible to archaeologists consist of changes in material organizations that are entrenched and carry great inertia—they have high residuality and low reversibility. The reconfiguration of such an assemblage constitutes an archaeological event and is apparent in the material record.

From this perspective the construction of large shell mounds and ridges by Mount Taylor people was an event inasmuch as it was the establishment of a material assemblage characterized by high irreversibility. The act of emplacing shell in particular locales along the river fundamentally altered the material circumstances of subsequent occurrences at those places (Barrett 1999). Once established these deposits could not be easily disassembled and they structured future material organizations and practices. Similarly, we might argue that the onset of spring flow was eventful if it significantly altered the local and regional ecology (i.e., the assemblage of beings, places, and objects). However, it is insufficient to assume that this phenomenon would be interpreted as significant, and hence eventful, by those who experienced it.

In the remainder of this chapter, I investigate whether the onset of spring flow was an event, either archaeologically or experientially, to the inhabitants of the middle St. Johns River valley. Below I present a GIS model of the onset of artesian spring flow in the region to explore the temporal and spatial patterning of this process. I then turn to a discussion of recent archaeological evidence and hydrological reconstructions from two major springs in the region.

SPRINGS CHRONOLOGY I: MODELING

As detailed in chapter 2, Florida is home to one of the largest concentrations of freshwater springs in the world. In the middle St. Johns River valley alone, 60 springs have been documented. The bulk of these springs discharge water from the Floridan Aquifer. As discussed in the previous chapter, artesian flow in springs is dependent on pressure within the aquifer. Aquifer pressure fluctuates over space and time as a result of several factors, such as variations in precipitation, topography, and physical properties of the limestone. This pressure is measured and displayed as a potentiometric surface, defined as the level to which groundwater will rise in a tightly cased well.

There are essentially two requirements for spring flow at any given point on the landscape. First, the potentiometric surface of the Floridan Aquifer must be higher than the ground elevation. In other words, there must be sufficient pressure in the aquifer to force water up and onto the surface. Second, there must be a pathway for the transmission of groundwater to the surface. The Floridan Aquifer is in most places overlain by a layer of relatively impermeable materials. Where present, these materials confine the aquifer and prevent the flow of groundwater onto the surface. Thus, for a spring to flow, this confining layer must be either absent or breached. If there is sufficient pressure, but the confining layer is intact, groundwater will flow to areas of lower pressure within the aquifer. Where the confining layer is breached, but there is insufficient aquifer pressure, closed surface depressions may form, and the area will serve as a recharge zone, rather than a discharge zone.

These criteria are obviously satisfied at the springs of the region today. However, it is unclear how long this has been the case. Given that fluctuations in sea level, precipitation, and evapo-transpiration can all impact aquifer pressure, spring flow has likely fluctuated significantly in the past. There were probably few, if any, springs flowing during the Last Glacial Maximum (LGM), when both sea level and, concomitantly, aquifer pressure were considerably lower. Or rather, few springs would have been flowing in the locations they do today. However, it is possible, if not likely, that numerous springs were present on portions of the Florida Platform that have since been inundated (Faure et al. 2002; Scott et al. 2004:13). Regardless, as sea level rose over the course of the late Pleistocene and the Holocene, aquifer pressure rose with it, reaching a point at which springs began their flow. If the argument put forth by Miller is correct, and spring flow was a prerequisite to both the establishment of extensive wetland biomes and the appearance of shell mounds in the region, then we should expect that the onset of spring flow was relatively rapid and synchronous across the St. Johns River basin.

To explore the tempo of these changes, I constructed a model of spring flow in the middle St. Johns River basin under conditions of decreased pressure in the Floridan Aquifer. This model carries several caveats. First, it assumes that the configuration of the aquifer has not been drastically altered over the course of the Holocene. That is, there have not been significant structural geologic changes that shifted the flow of groundwater. Second, it assumes that changes in the potentiometric surface of the aquifer would be realized uniformly over the study area. Third, the model is not linked to specific reductions in sea level or precipitation, as these do not correlate in a linear or simplistic manner with reductions in aquifer pressure. The individual effects of these variables and others (e.g., soil permeability, thickness of overlying sediments) are complex and difficult to disentangle. But reduction in either has essentially the same effect—a net reduction of the pressure in the aquifer, and thus lowered potential for spring flow.

I constructed the model using a digital elevation model with 15-m resolution developed by the Florida Geologic Survey (Arthur et al. 2005). The locations of springs in the region were provided by the St. Johns River Water Management District (2015a). Groundwater withdrawals for domestic, agricultural, and industrial uses have altered the potentiometric surface of the Floridan Aquifer, so this model uses predevelopment estimations of the potentiometric surface produced by the U.S. Geological Survey (Bush and Johnston 1988). A hydrologically correct raster was interpolated from the potentiometric isolines and laid over the digital elevation model. The elevation of the ground surface was then subtracted from the elevation of the aquifer's potentiometric surface on a cell-by-cell basis. The potential for spring flow exists where this differential is greater than zero (i.e., where the potentiometric surface is higher than the ground surface). This procedure was repeated for progressively lowered potentiometric surfaces to explore the conditions under which contemporary springs could have begun their flow, thus indicating the pattern of the onset of spring flow in the region.

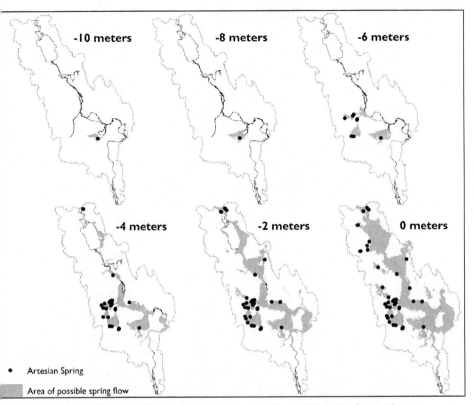

Figure 3.5. Results of the GIS model, showing areas of potential spring flow in the middle St. Johns River valley under reduced potentiometric surfaces of the Floridan Aquifer. Reprinted from *The Archaeology of Events* by permission of the University of Alabama Press.

The model produced several interesting results (Figure 3.5). First, there is a high degree of variability, as the differentials at contemporary springs range from .5 m to over 12 m. This indicates that even a small reduction in aquifer pressure could cause some springs to stop flowing, whereas others would be much more resilient. It follows too that there would be significant differences in the onset of flow at different springs.

The model indicates that it is unlikely that any springs would have flowed if the potentiometric surface of the aquifer was in excess of 12 m lower than present. This is equivalent to the water table reduction hypothesized by Watts (1971) for north Florida during the LGM. At 10 m below present, a single spring, Clifton Springs on the southern shore of

Lake Jesup, could potentially flow. However, it would remain the only flowing spring in the region until the potentiometric surface increased to 6 m below present. Several additional springs would begin flowing under these conditions, but most would not begin flowing until the potentiometric surface increased to 2 m below present. There is some regularity to the pattern of spring initiation in that the earliest flowing springs are in the southern portion of the middle St. Johns River basin (e.g., Clifton, Wekiwa, and Rock springs) and are relatively small. Springs in the northern portion of the study area wouldn't begin to flow until the potentiometric surface was much closer to present conditions. Indeed, some of the largest springs in the area (e.g., Silver Glen, Blue, and Alexander) would have been among the last to begin flowing.[3]

I am not suggesting that this model precisely predicts the sequence of spring initiation in the region, but it does provide several points to consider regarding the eventfulness of spring flow. The GIS model suggests that the onset of spring flow was not a wide-scale occurrence that suddenly inundated the valley with groundwater. It is therefore also unlikely that the regional hydrology and ecology were rapidly restructured as a result of spring flow. Given that the springs of the region vary with regard to elevation, conduit depth, and the localized expression of the potentiometric surface, initial artesian flow was probably heterogeneous and time transgressive.

Further, it is difficult to know how the birth of a spring would be manifested. Many may have been dry caves or groundwater-fed ponds that spilled over their banks as pressure increased. Alternatively, conduits may have been plugged with sediment that required significant pressure to flush, or were covered by thin limestone ceilings that collapsed suddenly. There are other possible scenarios as well, and this was no doubt highly variable, since the ways that spring flow could begin are dependent on preexisting structural conditions at different locales. Regardless, the point is that whereas spring flow at any single spring may have begun rapidly, the regional-scale pattern is decidedly more complex.

Although the model indicates that all of the springs of the middle St. Johns River valley did not begin flowing simultaneously, it is possible that groups of geographically proximate springs came on line in rapid succession. This may have been the case for the springs feeding into the western shore of Lake George (Figure 3.6). These six springs have differentials within 2 m of one another. Thus, other things being equal, these springs

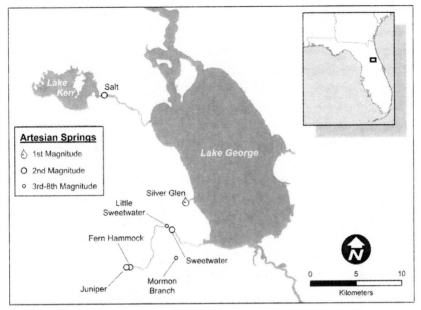

Figure 3.6. Lake George and the artesian springs that feed into it.

would have responded to increases in aquifer pressure roughly contemporaneously. However, the question remains what the timing of this was and whether it had significant ramifications for those who experienced it. Fortunately, recent archaeological investigations along several springs in the Lake George watershed have generated data relevant to these questions.

Springs Chronology II: Archaeology and Hydrology

The complex of archaeological sites and water bodies surrounding Lake George provides an ideal laboratory for investigating the timing of increased water availability in the middle St. Johns River valley and the human response to these dynamic conditions. Lake George itself is the second-largest lake in Florida, covering an area of more than 190 km² (Stewart et. al 2006). The lake sits in a broad, shallow basin bordered on the west by high relict dunes. The eastern flank of Lake George is lower and seasonally flooded (DeMort 1991:101). Average depth in the lake is only 2.5 m, outside of the dredged navigation channel. It is thus heavily influenced by wind action, resulting in a well-mixed water column with little thermal or chemical stratification.

As part of the St. Johns River, Lake George is a flow-through lake with an average turnover time of 84 days (Stewart et. al 2006). Tidally induced reverse flows are periodically experienced because of the low gradient of the river. Seismic profiling of the northern portion of Lake George has indicated the presence of both subsidence sinkholes and incised fluvial channels beneath several meters of lacustrine deposits (Kindinger et al. 1994). The age of these features is unknown, but their presence suggests that the infilled lake basin was once an open prairie with both sinkholes and channelized water.

Abundant fresh groundwater flows into Lake George from six artesian springs on its western margin. These springs lie on the eastern edge of the Ocala National Forest. Juniper and Fern Hammock springs collectively form the headwaters for Juniper Creek, a 15-km-long spring run that winds through extensive wetlands. Sweetwater and Mormon Branch springs contribute their flow to the creek approximately 10 km downstream. Salt and Silver Glen springs are the largest springs feeding Lake George, indeed some of the largest in the entire St. Johns River valley. Both are located in U.S. Forest Service Recreation Areas and are surrounded by significant archaeological deposits. Fieldwork conducted at Salt Springs in 2009 and Silver Glen Springs since 2007 investigated the archaeological and hydrological histories encased in spring-side sediments.

Salt Springs

The Salt Springs Recreation Area is situated in eastern Marion County, in the town of Salt Springs. Lake George is located to the east, connected to Salt Springs by a spring run that meanders for more than 8 km through lowland swamps and wetlands (Figure 3.7). Lake Kerr is just to the west, separated from the spring by a narrow (300 m) isthmus of land. Salt Springs lies at the eastern flank of the Marion Upland, a relatively narrow ridge characterized by Pleistocene sand dunes that extends from the Mount Dora Ridge to the western shores of Lake George. Approaching the spring from the west affords a panoramic view from the edge of the escarpment as the land slopes quickly down to the spring basin.

Salt Springs is aptly named, as the concentration of dissolved salts is several orders of magnitude greater than in most springs in Florida. The spring has been developed as a recreation area, complete with picnic pavilion, restroom facilities, and a campground. Salt Springs itself consists

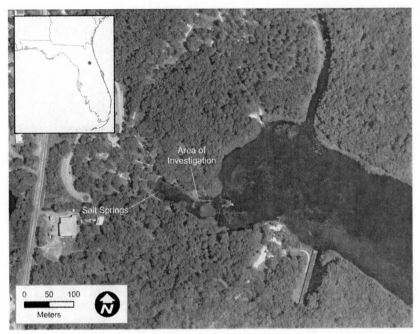

Figure 3.7. Aerial photograph of Salt Springs, showing the area investigated by the University of Florida in 2009.

of a broad, shallow pool approximately 40 × 60 m in maximum dimension, surrounded on three sides by a concrete retaining wall. The water, a relatively constant 23.3 °C (74 °F), issues from several vertical fissures in the pool bottom. The average depth of the water is approximately .5 m (Scott et al. 2004:237–239). Salt Springs is a second-magnitude spring, the fourth-largest in the middle St. Johns River valley, with a mean discharge of 80 ft³/s.

Archaeological Investigations

In 2009 the Forest Service conducted maintenance and repairs on the concrete retaining wall, extending a portion of it along the northern shoreline to replace an existing timber bulkhead. Prior survey work within the recreation area had documented dense archaeological materials in this vicinity, recorded as site 8MR2322, but the depth and integrity of these deposits was unknown (Dickinson and Wayne 1994). To facilitate the repair and replacement of the retaining wall, the Forest Service installed a coffer dam and pumping system. The coffer dam held the spring water away from the

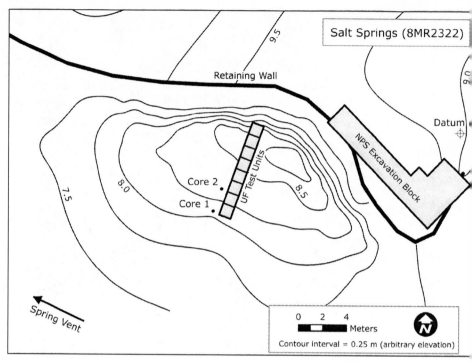

Figure 3.8. Topographic map of the subaqueous portion of the Salt Springs site (8MR2322), showing locations of the University of Florida excavation trench and cores and National Park Service excavation block. Topography derived from a total station survey. Elevation relative to arbitrary datum.

shore while the pumps removed seeping water, effectively drawing down the surface of the water some 2 m in a localized area. The net effect of draining the area behind the coffer dam was the exposure of a saturated midden component in the spring bed. The surficial expression of the midden is a lobe-shaped area elevated approximately 1.5 meters over the surrounding channel bed (Figure 3.8). The elevated area measures roughly 30 × 20 m, with its long axis oriented parallel to the spring run. Historical photographs indicate that this is likely the subaqueous portion of a shell ridge situated on the northern bank of the spring. Twentieth-century land alterations largely obscured this ridge, although intact subsurface deposits are present and were investigated by archaeologists from the Southeast Archaeological Center, National Park Service (NPS) in 2009. The excavation of a construction trench with heavy machinery, and installation of the new section of retaining wall, severed the subaqueous portion of this deposit from its terrestrial component.

The University of Florida's Laboratory of Southeastern Archaeology (LSA) conducted archaeological testing of the saturated midden in 2009 (O'Donoughue et al. 2011). National Park Service testing of the terrestrial component determined that it was largely Mount Taylor aged with well-preserved organic materials. Our excavation strategy was designed to address the histories of anthropogenic and fluvial deposition and relate them to fluctuating water levels and shoreline transgression. To this end, a 1-×-8-m trench was laid out near the center of the subaqueous midden deposit. Testing of this orphaned midden remnant was facilitated by the Forest Service coffer dam and pumping system, which kept the test units relatively free of standing water until the drawn-down surface of the water table was intercepted. Excavation of the trench was halted when this surface was reached and standing water began to accumulate.

The material recovered from Salt Springs is rife with evidence for daily habitation. Organic preservation was excellent in the saturated deposits, with abundant botanical and vertebrate faunal remains. The faunal assemblage is well preserved and diverse, with an emphasis on aquatic resources (Blessing 2011). The botanical assemblage is likewise varied and includes a number of economically important species (e.g., bottle gourd, squash, passionflower, grape, and blackberry [Talcott 2011]). The most ubiquitous taxon recovered was elderberry, likely used for its medicinal properties. Few pottery sherds were recovered, and those that were came from the uppermost excavation levels. Marine shell, sharks' teeth, lithic debitage and tools, and modified bone were found throughout the trench but were typically more frequent in the southern half.

Four stratigraphic units were identified in the trench excavations. These are grouped into two macro-stratigraphic units. Stratum I consists of shell-bearing deposits in the upper portion of the midden. Stratum II encompasses an underlying shell-free midden. Stratum I is composed of three substrata (IA-1, IA-2, IB), with subdivisions based primarily on changes in both the shell content and non-shell matrix.

The basal unit in the trench consisted of organically enriched sands largely devoid of shell (Stratum II). This unit contains contorted layers of stacked and interdigitated sand lenses, varying in color from grey to black. These sands are often stained with colloidal organic matter and contain moderate amounts of vertebrate faunal remains, lithic debitage, and both charred and uncharred botanicals (e.g., wood, hickory nut, seeds, and charcoal). The top of Stratum II is undulating and dips away from the shore. Stratum IB is a relatively thin (5–15 cm) layer of grey sand and shell that lies unconformably over these midden sands. Overlying Stratum IB is Stratum IA, a shell midden deposit more than 50 cm thick that contains very-dark brown to grey organically stained sands with abundant *Viviparus* shell and localized lenses of bivalve shell. Apple snail shell was relatively rare, but several concentrations were encountered. Stratum IA was divided into Stratum IA-1 and IA-2 on the basis of color and textural variations in the matrix. Stratum IA-2 is slightly darker and finer than Stratum IA-1. The contact between the two is diffuse in places but dips noticeably away from the shore, suggesting that Stratum IA-2 was deposited partially over and to the south of Stratum IA-1.

Chronology and Depositional History

Well-preserved organic materials in near-shore anthropogenic deposits generally indicate permanent saturation (Bleicher and Schubert 2015). Thus, the abundance of organic materials, particularly in the lower levels of the trench, points to deposition directly in the water. The morphology of Stratum II lends further credence to this interpretation, as the constituent sand lenses have a contorted or rippled appearance, consistent with their mobilization and deposition in an active open-water environment. However, the presence of concreted shell, coupled with a lower frequency of organic remains, in the uppermost levels indicates that some portions of the midden were subject to periodic aerial exposure and drying as water levels in the spring fluctuated.

Six AMS radiocarbon assays were obtained to investigate the chronology and depositional history of the midden. Two were selected from each of the major stratigraphic units defined in the trench (i.e., Strata IA, IB, and II). To investigate the sequence of deposition within each stratum one sample was taken from the shoreward (northern) side of the stratum and one from the springward side. Based on 2-sigma calibrated ranges, the anthropogenic deposits investigated in the trench were emplaced over a period of some 400 to 900 years in the interval 6640–5750 cal BP. The radiocarbon sequence obtained from the trench bears out the inferred order of deposition. Although there is slight overlap at the 2-sigma range, none of the dates are out of sequence. Samples from the lowest deposits exposed in the trench, Stratum II, returned the oldest dates: 5710 ± 50 BP (6640–6400 cal BP) and 5610 ± 50 BP (6480–6300 cal BP). Slightly younger dates were obtained from Stratum IB, the lowermost shell-bearing deposit, at 5460 ± 50 BP (6400–6130 cal BP) and 5230 ± 50 BP (6180–5910 cal BP). Stratum IA, the uppermost unit, was dated to 5150 ± 50 BP (6000–5750 cal BP) and 5130 ± 50 BP (5990–5750 cal BP). The terminus of deposition is not known, as dates were not obtained from the upper portions of Stratum IA. However, several radiocarbon assays from the terrestrial portion of the site excavated by the NPS have a 2-sigma range of 5450–4850 cal BP, pointing to at least three additional centuries of occupation (Michael Russo, personal communication 2010).

Comparison of the radiocarbon assays between stratigraphic units confirms the observed vertical sequence of deposition. Within each unit, the date obtained closer to the shore is older than that obtained closer to the spring. Taken together, these data suggest that these anthropogenic deposits prograded outward, away from the shore. This progradation was followed by the establishment of a new depositional regime closer to the shore, atop the previous deposits. This pattern is most strongly expressed in Strata II and IB, where overlap between the dates is less than a century. The two dates from Stratum IA are virtually contemporaneous. However, as noted above, the position of Stratum IA-2 relative to IA-1 is indicative of progradational deposition. Thus, the tightly clustered dates of Stratum IA may indicate an increase in the tempo of deposition rather than a change in its mode.

To recap, the depositional history revealed in the trench began with the aggradation of a shell-free midden deposit prior to the emplacement of shell sometime after 6300 cal BP. With regard to the eventfulness of spring flow and the changes it precipitated, this is relevant for two reasons. First, it shows that the initial occupation of the spring did not involve shell deposition. Spring flow is inferred at this time from the character of the deposits, and thus the conditions for shellfish exploitation are presumed to have existed, but this exploitation is not reflected in local practices. Second, this shell-free midden postdates shell sites elsewhere in the St. Johns River valley. Recall from above that massive accumulations of shell are evident by 7400 cal BP at places like Hontoon Dead Creek Mound and Live Oak Mound. But at Salt Springs shell deposition did not begin until a millennium later, coincident with the onset of Randall's (2013) Episode II. Thus, people were visiting the spring without depositing shell, despite a 1,000-year history of doing so in the St. Johns River valley. Clearly, cultural practices, if not hydro-ecological conditions, were diverse in the region.

Hydrological History

We also explored the hydrological history of Salt Springs, through the extraction of three percussion cores. These were emplaced directly in the spring bed, penetrating the anthropogenic deposits and documenting alluvial sediments beneath. Two cores were successfully recovered (Core 1 and 2), but the third was lost during extraction (Core 3). The sequence of deposits observed in the cores offers insight into deposits that could not be reached during trench excavations (Figure 3.9).

Sub-midden deposits were delineated as Strata III–VI. They appear to represent water-lain sediments that are largely lacking anthropogenic inputs. Variations in the fluvial regime at Salt Springs are registered by changes in these deposits, which are broadly composed of layers of clean, light grey sand alternating with more heterogeneous layers. Organic materials (i.e., faunal and botanical remains) are well preserved throughout these deposits, but they are markedly more abundant in Strata III and V. Stratum V also exhibits fine laminations and a slightly silty texture consistent with quiet, slack-water deposition. Meanwhile, Strata IV and VI, which are largely clean deposits of light grey sand, may reflect periods of increased flow from the spring and the consequent flushing of organic matter and fine sediment.

Two AMS assays were obtained from Core 1, which was adjacent to the southern end of the excavation trench. A large wood fragment at the juncture between Strata V and VI at 110 cm below surface (cmbs) was uncharred, organically stained, and well preserved, indicating that it was deposited underwater. This sample returned a date of 8320 ± 40 BP (9460–9140 cal BP). Charcoal from the basal shell deposit (Stratum IB; 35 cmbs) in Core 1 returned a date of 5300 ± 40 BP (6190–5950 cal BP). Thus, 72 cm of fluvial sediment were deposited over the course of some 3,000 to 3,500 years, yielding an average sedimentation rate of 2.0–2.4 cm/ century. Although this evidences relatively slow, gradual accumulation of sediment, it is not outside the range of variation recorded in other fluvial settings in North America (Ferring 1986) and can be explained by the minimal sediment load being carried by the spring as it emerges from the aquifer (Vernon 1951).

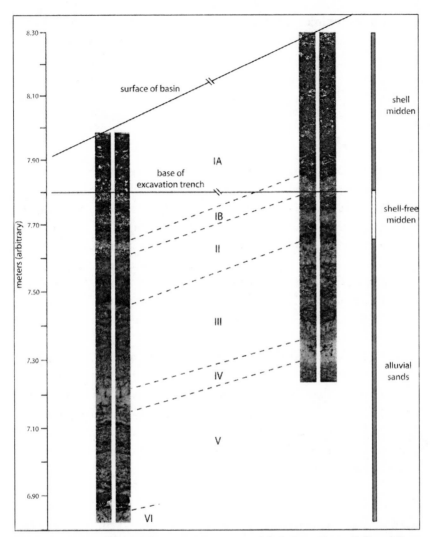

Figure 3.9. Deposits observed in percussion cores at Salt Springs, Core 1 (*left*) and Core 2 (*right*), in relation to trench stratigraphy. Elevation relative to arbitrary datum. View is upstream, facing northwest.

These results indicate that water was available at Salt Springs over 9,000 years ago. This is more than three millennia earlier than hypothesized by Miller (1992, 1998) and well before sea level stabilized in a near-modern regime. Although we recovered no evidence of contemporaneous human activity, wood associated with a hafted end scraper in the terrestrial portion of the site was radiocarbon-dated to ca. 8500 cal BP (Michael Russo, personal communication 2010). This suggests a significant lag between the onset of spring flow and initial shell deposition, indicating neither a rapid nor a dramatic exploitation of the purported ecological ramifications of spring flow. This is compelling, but it is only a single data point. For corroborating evidence we can turn to Silver Glen Springs.

Silver Glen Springs

The Silver Glen Springs Recreation Area is in eastern Marion County, approximately 14.5 km southeast of Salt Springs. Like Salt Springs, Silver Glen lies adjacent to the eastern edge of the Marion Upland. Lake George is located to the east, connected by a short (1.2 km) spring run that that averages 60 m in width, with a maximum depth of approximately 3 m (Pandion Systems, Inc. 2003). Silver Glen is a first-magnitude spring, one of the largest in Florida, with an average discharge of 102 ft³/s. The spring consists of a large pool, measuring 200 × 175 m in breadth, with water discharging from two main vents and numerous smaller vents both adjacent to and within the spring run.

The main vent of Silver Glen Springs sits at the base of a conical depression beneath 5.5 m of water, near the center of the spring pool. A second vent, referred to as the "natural well" (Plate 4), lies at the southwestern edge of the pool. This is a 12-m-deep vertical shaft, or chimney, measuring 4.5 m in diameter. An extensive system of caverns and conduits has been mapped at Silver Glen Springs, extending over 600 m from the main vent (Springs Eternal Project 2013).

Archaeological Overview

Numerous archaeological sites surround the pool and run of Silver Glen Springs (Figure 3.10). These are referred to collectively as the Silver Glen Complex and have been investigated since 2007 by the LSA and the University of Florida St. Johns Archaeological Field School, both under the direction of Ken Sassaman (Sassaman et al. 2011). This fieldwork has uncovered a dense archaeological record and generated numerous technical reports, dissertations, and other publications (e.g., Gilmore 2014, 2016; Randall 2010, 2015; Randall et al. 2011; Randall et al. 2014; Sassaman et al. 2011; Sassaman and Randall 2012).

The Silver Glen Complex includes as many as four Mount Taylor shell ridges, Thornhill Lake phase mortuary mounds, two massive U-shaped

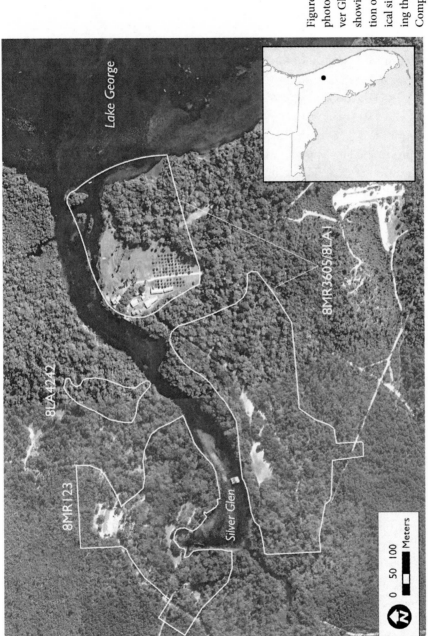

Figure 3.10. Aerial photograph of Silver Glen Springs, showing the location of archaeological sites composing the Silver Glen Complex.

Lake George

8LA4242

8MR123

Silver Glen

8MR3605/8LA1

0 50 100
Meters

N

shell mounds constructed during the Orange period, Orange- and St. Johns era habitation sites, and a St. Johns burial mound. Few of these components are spatially isolated, but rather occur in overlapping deposits at various locations in the watershed. Evidence for late Pleistocene and early Holocene occupation in the vicinity is also present, if ephemeral. The Silver Glen Complex is discussed in detail in the following chapter. For present purposes I focus on the evidence for the onset of both spring flow and shell deposition.

The best-documented Mount Taylor shell ridge at Silver Glen Springs is 8LA1-W Locus A. Locus A is located approximately 500 m downstream from the pool of Silver Glen Springs, on the southern shore of the spring run. Immediately across the run from Locus A, on the northern shore, lies another shell ridge, dubbed the Silver Glen Run North site (8LA4242). Little is known about this site, as it has only recently been documented. Based on its size and configuration (185 m long by 85 m wide, in a teardrop shape parallel to the run), it is likely a Mount Taylor shell ridge (Randall et al. 2011). Additional Mount Taylor shell ridges are suspected at other locations, notably beneath later U-shaped shell mounds surrounding the spring pool (8MR123; Randall et al. 2011) and at the confluence of Silver Glen Run and Lake George (8LA1-E; Sassaman et al. 2011).

Shell Deposition at Locus A

Locus A of site 8LA1-W is the remnant of a Mount Taylor shell ridge measuring some 200 m long by 75 m wide (Randall 2010:330–335, 2015:228–233; Sassaman et al. 2011:121–170). Much of the ridge core was destroyed by mining operations in 1923, leaving behind a halo of discontinuous elevated deposits that mark the outline of the ridge. The pre-mining height of the ridge is unknown, but 4 m of intact deposits remain. Locus A parallels Silver Glen Run but is separated from it by a hydric hammock to the north. A linear embayment, possibly a relict seep spring, marks the eastern extent of Locus A.

Stratigraphic testing in 2007 and 2008 was designed to expose intact vertical profiles along mining escarpments (Sassaman et al. 2011). Six 2-×-2-m test units spread across three areas of Locus A exposed 12 m of profiles and 24 m² of plan excavation. Later block excavations in 2012 and 2015 exposed an additional 29 m² in plan and over 50 m of profiles. The stratigraphic sequence exposed by these excavations is complex, with individual test units revealing as many as 28 discrete stratigraphic units.

However, broad trends in deposition are apparent, allowing these units to be grouped into macro-stratigraphic units (Randall 2013; Sassaman and Randall 2012; Sassaman et al. 2011).

The initial deposition of shell by Mount Taylor inhabitants of Locus A did not involve mounding, but rather the emplacement of shell in a number of large pits (Randall 2014a; Randall and Sassaman 2012). These pits are typically large and straight-walled, measuring 1 to 1.5 m wide and up to 1 m deep. Heavily oxidized sand at their bases suggests that they were used for roasting shellfish before being infilled. Pit fill typically contains multiple species of shellfish, a diverse vertebrate faunal assemblage, and tools of bone and marine shell.

Sometime between 6300 and 5940 cal BP a cap of fine brown sand up to 40 cm thick was emplaced over the entirety of the ridge (Randall 2013). Atop this is an upper deposit of shell, composed of accretional layers of earth and shell alternating with surfaces of crushed and burned shell. Like the underlying pit fill, these shell deposits contain ample material indicative of daily living—food remains, ash and charcoal, and bone, stone, and marine shell tools at multiple stages of manufacture and use. In form and content, these deposits are not dissimilar from shell nodes interpreted as house mounds at the Hontoon Dead Creek Village, discussed above. It is likewise similar to Salt Springs, in both content and timing, albeit in a terrestrial rather than a subaqueous setting.

Recent excavations have also recovered evidence for pre–Mount Taylor activities at Locus A (Randall 2014a; Randall and Sassaman 2012). The pits that mark the onset of intensive shell deposition intrude into a lower deposit of organically enriched soil with small amounts of vertebrate fauna and shell. This deposit is not accretional or pedogenic, but rather is an amalgamation of large pits. These pits measure, on average, 1 m in diameter and depth and have no evidence of burning. The contents of their fill replicate that of the upper pits, but in considerably lower density.

The function of these lower pits is, as yet, unclear. However, they attest to a history of low-level shell deposition that preceded intensive shellfish processing and the building up of the ridge. Radiocarbon determinations from several of these lower pits place them in the ninth millennium before present, with three assays ranging from 8170 to 8980 cal BP. Additional testing indicated that these pits are restricted to the footprint of Locus A. In other words, the shell ridge that was erected some 2,000 years later is isomorphic with the distribution of these pits.

Hydrological History

Excavations at Locus A are pointing to an increasingly long history of shellfish exploitation in the St. Johns River valley. But how this relates to the onset of flow from Silver Glen Springs is not clear from the archaeological evidence alone. Given the proximity of Locus A to Lake George, it is conceivable that aquatic resources, such as shellfish, could be obtained without water input from the spring.

To reconstruct the hydrological history of Silver Glen Springs, six vibracores were emplaced in the hydric hammock intervening between Locus A and Silver Glen Run. The hammock is teardrop shaped, widest at the northeast and tapering to the southwest, and measures approximately 300 m long by 60 m in maximum width. These vibracores were extracted along two transects aligned roughly perpendicular to the axis of the spring channel (Figure 3.11).Transect BC was located near the eastern margin of the hammock, where the channel of the run widens proximate to the relict seep spring. Two cores along this transect were compromised by rodding—that is, the core penetrated but did not capture unconsolidated materials—as indicated by short and discontinuous sedimentary records. Transect EF was placed near the middle of the hammock, proximate to the western margin of Locus A. Cores from this transect have greater integrity and are thus the focus of discussion below.

Observations at similar locations adjacent to wetlands (e.g., Hontoon Dead Creek Mound) and springs (e.g., Salt Springs) indicated that shell deposits are frequently found beneath wetland sediments. As water levels rose in the mid- to late Holocene hydroperiods also stabilized. Thus, surface water inundated the aprons of shell ridges, and organic sediments accreted atop anthropogenic deposits. It was thus expected that our cores would reveal intact portions of Locus A buried beneath the hammock deposits. However, this was not the case. Strata observed in the cores are devoid of shell or other anthropogenic sediment inputs (Figure 3.12). As many as 12 stratigraphic units were observed, differentiated on the basis of color, clastic particle size, and abundance and degree of decomposition of organic material. These are grouped into two macro-stratigraphic units: an upper layer of organic soils and sediments (i.e., muck and peat) overlying basal siliciclastic deposits (i.e., sand). Intervening between these was a thin (5–10 cm) zone of mucky sand or intercalated muck and sand.

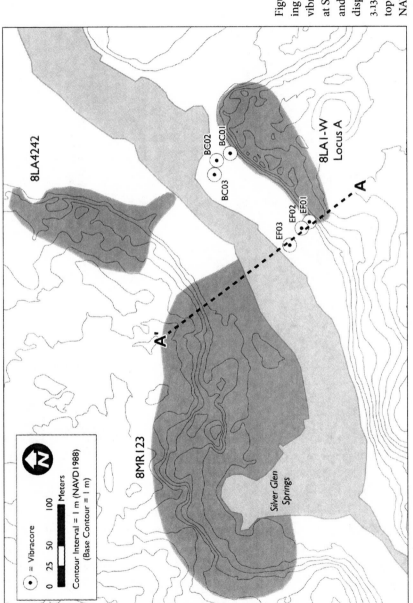

Figure 3.11. Map show-
ing the location of
vibracores extracted
at Silver Glen Springs
and the cross section
displayed in Figure
3.13. LiDAR-derived
topography relative to
NAVD 1988.

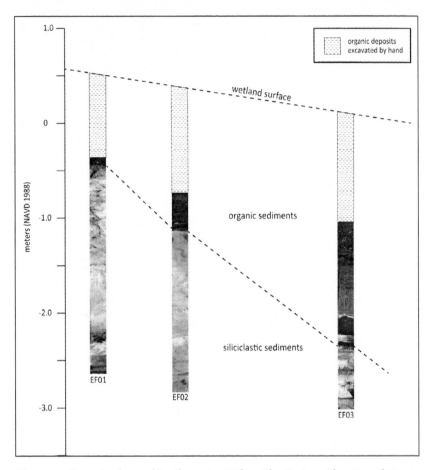

Figure 3.12. Deposits observed in vibracores at Silver Glen Springs. Elevation relative to NAVD 1988. View is upstream, facing southwest.

Organic soils and sediments ranged from dark reddish brown peats with many visible fragments of vegetal matter to black muck with few visible fibers. Basal sands were typically grey to greyish brown beneath the contact with organic deposits. These lightened in color and grew finer in texture to white fine sand at the base of most cores. One core, EF-02, penetrated a pale brown, loamy sand with striations reminiscent of clay lamellae at its base.

The shift from mineral to organic sedimentation reflects a change in the hydrology of Silver Glen Springs. The deposition of peat and muck indicates a relatively quiet, slackwater environment on the margins of the channel. The underlying sands are likely colluvium from the surrounding uplands, deposited in a terrestrial setting when water in the spring run was lower. The sand deposits are largely devoid of preserved organic materials, supporting this inference. The shift to organic sedimentation is thus indicative of rising water that drowned terrestrial deposits and favored the preservation of organic detritus. Presumably this registers the onset of flow from Silver Glen Springs, but it could represent channel migration or an increase in the stage of an already flowing spring. Regardless, the timing of this transition provides a minimum age for the onset of spring flow.

A cross section of the spring run and surrounding terrain along core transect EF is presented in Figure 3.13. Organic deposits were absent at higher elevations adjacent to the remnant shell ridge of Locus A and gradually increased in thickness, extending as far as 2.8 m below surface at the distal end of core transects, adjacent to Silver Glen Run. Likewise, sandy deposits underlying organic sediments were at a higher elevation proximate to Locus A and dipped toward the spring run.

Two radiocarbon assays were obtained from Cores EF-02 and EF-03. These assays were run on basal samples of organic sediment to date the transition to organic sedimentation and, by implication, rising waters. In core EF-03, at the far end of the transect, a sample taken from the base of the organic sediments (278–280 cmbs) returned an assay of 7750 ± 30 BP (8590–8450 cal BP). Core EF-02 was located approximately 25 m inland of Core EF-03. Here, the base of organic sediments was at 170 cmbs. A sample taken 2 cm above this juncture returned an assay of 5170 ± 30 BP (5950–5905 cal BP). Taken together, these results indicate that roughly 125 cm of wetland sediment accumulated over 2500–2685 years, or 4.65–5.0 cm per century. This is a considerably higher rate of accumulation than at Salt Springs, but they are in different sedimentary environments. The cores from Salt Springs were extracted directly from the spring bed. Mineral sediments were deposited there in an actively flowing channel of variable energy. Deposition at Silver Glen was characterized by the accumulation of organic sediments in a low-energy wetland environment.

The hydric hammock fronting Locus A formed as organic detritus accumulated in a basin with basal sands. This basin contains the channel of Silver Glen Run and wetlands along its margin. The sands likely accumulated as colluvium prior to inundation. Water levels began to rise no later than 8450 cal BP. This corresponds with the ninth millennium before

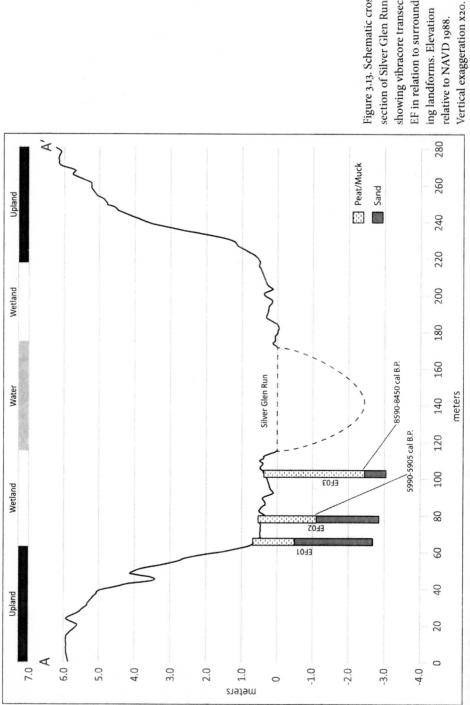

Figure 3.13. Schematic cross section of Silver Glen Run showing vibracore transect EF in relation to surrounding landforms. Elevation relative to NAVD 1988. Vertical exaggeration x20.

present pit digging described above and corroborates the dating of spring flow at Salt Springs, albeit with a gap of some 700 years.

SPRING FLOW AND SHELLFISHING IN THE ST. JOHNS RIVER VALLEY

To summarize, the hypothesis that intensive shell deposition in the St. Johns River valley was predicated on spring flow has several implications. As put forth by Miller (1992, 1998), the onset of spring flow is expected to have followed the stabilization of sea level after ca. 6000 cal BP and to have been widespread and rapid in the valley. Shell deposition should follow the onset of spring flow with minimal delay, as inhabitants mapped onto burgeoning aquatic resources and populations grew.

Minimally, the evidence from cores at Salt and Silver Glen springs pushes the chronology of spring flow initiation back several millennia. Salt Springs was apparently flowing by 9140 cal BP, and Silver Glen no later than 8450 cal BP. I cannot say with certainty that these dates mark the onset of continuous spring flow, which may have been ongoing for centuries prior to this. Indeed, it is likely that both Salt and Silver Glen springs began as sinkholes or depressions that were water-bearing but did not flow onto the surface. But by the mid-ninth millennium before present, water was present in both locations, with sufficient depth and duration that wetland deposits began aggrading.

Likewise, the antiquity of shellfish exploitation in the region has been pushed back significantly. Prior work by Sassaman, Randall, and others has shown that intensive shell deposition in the region began as early as 7400 cal BP at places like Hontoon Dead Creek and Live Oak mounds. The evidence from Locus A at the Silver Glen Complex underscores the need to discriminate between different modes and intensities of shell deposition. The earliest shell deposits documented thus far point to low-level shellfish exploitation and deposition underground, in pits. These practices may have been in place as early as 9,000 years ago and predate intensive shell deposition by over a millennium.

These results perhaps indicate a long interval of gradual change, wherein both spring flow and shell deposition began as intermittent, low-level affairs that slowly increased in intensity over the course of several thousand years. But if all that has been accomplished here is a pushing back or stretching of the chronology of these changes, it would add little to our understanding of either springs or the archaeology of the region. Closer examination reveals not gradual change, but rather a series of disjunctures that appear gradual only when one draws straight lines between them.

The available evidence demonstrates that some springs were flowing on the landscape of the middle St. Johns River valley long before they became a locus for the intensive deposition of shell. This is not to say that springs have been static. The configuration of springs, intensity of their flow, and quality of their waters have undoubtedly fluctuated. Further, while contemporary experience can inform us on the death of a spring, it is difficult to know how the birth of any given spring would unfold and how it would be received by local residents. Indeed, each spring has a unique ontogeny and history, both hydrologically and culturally. Modeling this history indicates that although the initiation of spring flow appears significant and eventful in retrospect, it was not a synchronous event throughout the St. Johns River valley. Even proximate springs, such as Salt and Silver Glen, have divergent and discontemporaneous histories. This underscores that we cannot uncritically apply the results from any one spring to others in the region.

Spring flow within the Lake George watershed was initiated prior to 8500 cal BP, coinciding (or preceding) locally with the excavation of large pits adjacent to Silver Glen Springs and regionally with the pond burial tradition best known from Windover. However, we know little of what transpired at either Salt or Silver Glen Springs in subsequent centuries, from ca. 8200 cal BP to 6500 cal BP. Likewise, the archaeological record is sparse across the region until 7400 cal BP, when intensive shell deposition began at the Hontoon Dead Creek and Live Oak mounds (i.e., Episode I). Thus, the earliest evidence of shell deposition (next to springs) is followed by a gap of at least 800 years, after which intensive piling up of shell began (away from springs). Shell mounding adjacent to springs lagged behind a further 1,000 years, beginning coincident with the onset of Episode II.

Add to this picture the presence of basal shell-free deposits at Salt Springs, which indicates that Mount Taylor habitation adjacent to springs did not always involve the deposition of shell. This is evident elsewhere in the valley as well, outside the Lake George watershed. At Volusia Blue Springs (8VO43), Thornhill Lake phase deposits were encountered, dating to ca. 5300–4600 cal BP (Sassaman 2003a). These consist of a basal, shell-free midden beneath a modest shell-bearing deposit. Abundant faunal remains, charcoal, and occasional lithic and marine shell tools attest to intensive daily habitation in this locale, both before and after the inception of shellfishing.

Future fieldwork will no doubt begin to fill in these gaps, but the work reviewed above calls into question the eventfulness of spring flow initiation. Spring flow does not appear to have precipitated a rapid reorganization of subsistence and depositional regimes (i.e., shell mounding) that we might recognize as an archaeological event (*sensu* Lucas 2008). But I do not mean to suggest that springs were uneventful. Simply that what appears to be significant and eventful to us—the onset of spring flow and the ecological potential this brought about—did not have observable consequences with respect to shell mounding and the Mount Taylor tradition. It was thus rather non-eventful. We can instead recognize a *series* of events—for example, the digging of pits, capping of earlier deposits, and accumulation of living surfaces—that had material ramifications and structured future activities. The transformation of places evidenced by the building up of shell was predicated not on spring flow, but on earlier activities that occurred in those same locales. The events of significance at springs, at least in the middle St. Johns River valley, were not instigated by their changing hydrology but were constructed through the material engagements that people initiated on their banks.

It is no coincidence that spring-side shell deposition coincides with the onset of Episode II. This was a time of expanding social geographies, indicated both by the inclusion of items from distant places and by the interment of people foreign to the St. Johns River valley. Springs became focal points for regional gatherings amidst this widening circumference of interaction. The accumulation of shell at springs marks an acceleration of these gatherings that would continue in the Thornhill Lake period, reaching a peak during the Late Archaic Orange period. In the next chapter, I explore the growth and transformation of springs through a more detailed examination of Silver Glen Springs, gathering place par excellence in Florida.

4

SACRED SPRING

Mount Shasta juts from the horizon, ascending to a peak 3,000 m above
northern California's Sacramento Valley. The treeless, glaciated upper
slopes of the volcano are visible for hundreds of kilometers on a clear day
(Figure 4.1; Huntsinger and Fernández-Giménez 2000; McCarthy 2004).
Just beneath the tree line, at an elevation of 2,400 m, Panther Spring lies
within a lush meadow. This spring and others like it are sacred to the
Winnemem Wintu tribe, a relatively small Native American group indigenous to the McCloud River region of northern California (Theodoratus and LaPena 1994; Winnemem Wintu 2015). Springs are important
for healing, cleansing, and purification rituals and serve as potent conduits to the spiritual realm (McCarthy 2004:175; Theodoratus and LaPena
1994:24). Although all springs are important, Panther Spring is preemi-
nent, the genesis place where the Winnemem Wintu (2015) "first bubbled
into the world at the time of creation."

The Wintu are not alone in their reverence of Panther Spring and
Mount Shasta. It has become a popular destination for New Age religious
seekers, spiritual nomads, and vagabonds, all of whom have easy access
to Panther Meadow from a parking lot at the end of Everett Memorial
Highway (Huntsinger and Fernández-Giménez 2000; McCarthy 2004).
Although they claim to venerate the spring, many actions of these pilgrims are disruptive, if not harmful:

> Even the most casual participant . . . could hardly fail to notice an
> unusual use of the meadows and springs. Crystals were placed in
> and near the water, particularly Panther Spring, sacred to the Wintu
> tribe. Prayer flags were tied to tree branches, and pictures and poems
> were left on small rock altars in the meadow and near springs. The

crisscrossing trails led to altars and to the denuded edges of Panther Spring, where many people came to collect water. Nude sunbathing, drumming, and chanting were frequent activities nearby. (Huntsinger and Fernández-Giménez 2000:536)

The physical damage to the meadow, co-opting of Native American symbolism, and desecration of Panther Spring are all understandably distressing to the Winnemem Wintu. But Mount Shasta and Panther Spring lie within the Shasta-Trinity National Forest, under the management of the U.S. Forest Service. The desire of the Wintu to safeguard these sacred places against the threat of New Age tourism underscores the difficulty of managing competing interests, secular or otherwise, on public lands. Despite this conflict, the perceived sacredness of this place by non-indigenous groups was crucial in mobilizing resistance to, and ultimately rebuffing, a proposal to develop a ski resort on the mountain in the 1990s (Huntsinger and Fernández-Giménez 2000).

There are several parallels between the situation of Panther Spring at Mount Shasta and the issues facing springs in Florida. Both have been threatened by development and overuse of public lands and are subject to competing interests from diverse parties. However, whereas development has been successfully rebuffed at Panther Spring, Florida springs conservation has met with mixed results (Knight 2015). What Panther

Figure 4.1. A field of sagebrush at the foot of Mt. Shasta in northern California. Courtesy of the U.S. Fish and Wildlife Service.

Spring illustrates aptly is that the sacredness of a place can congregate the interests of competing parties and buttress conservation efforts.

The previous chapter decoupled spring flow from the regional construction of shell mounds and argued that the use of springs was predicated not (or not solely) on their ecological productivity. It is argued, rather, that springs became foci for extraregional gatherings in the context of expanding spheres of interaction and exchange. In this chapter I develop this line of thought through an examination of Silver Glen Springs. The long-term record of visitation at Silver Glen reveals numerous historical trends and transformations of practices taking place there. I also explore the idea that Silver Glen Springs, and others like it, may have been considered sacred in the past.

In posing questions of sacredness, I do not mean to recapitulate a simplistic dichotomy between sacred and profane that is itself problematic, a product of Cartesian dualism in Western thought that often has little purchase in non-Western societies (Bradley 2005; Brück 1999). Indeed, in many cultures sacredness extends into all aspects of life and encompasses entire geographies, particularly where they memorialize ancestral or mythic persons and events (Basso 1996a; Hubert 1994; Morphy 1995). Certain places are frequently marked out as particularly important, special, or sacred. However, the power or sanctity of these places is not derived solely from their physical features, nor is it entirely imposed by human consciousness. Places are not static, objective arenas for human activity or canvases for the interpretive endeavors of subjective human thought. Places are experienced from a culturally mediated, human perspective. However, this experience of place is not unbound but must confront the affordances and constraints of the material world. Places thus are not given but emerge through mutually constituting relationships with people. Places and people "interanimate" one another (Basso 1996a). This is true of sacred places as well, which *become* sacred through an emergent, historical process. The question is thus less "Was this place sacred?" than "How, or in what ways, was it sanctified?"

Sacred Site, Sacred Spring

The spring rose up from its deep source and smelled of wet earth and the stones at the center of the world. Whatever you believe and whatever God you pray to, a place where clean water rises from the earth is in some way sacred. (Frazier 2006:56)

Is there an inherent sacredness to springs? Does something of their experiential or aesthetic quality elicit awe or reverence in humans? In the words of Celeste Ray (2011:271) "hydrolatry [water worship] is panhuman and sacred wells or springs of some sort can be found around the globe." Eliade considered water to be a hierophany, a physical manifestation of the sacred: "Water symbolizes the whole of potentiality: it is *fons et origo*, the source of all possible existence. . . . Principle of what is formless and potential, basis of every cosmic manifestation, container of all seeds, water symbolizes the primal substance from which all forms come and to which they will return" (Eliade 1958:188). Similarly, Veronica Strang (2005, 2008) has argued that the physical qualities of water, coupled with the cognitive and sensory apparatus common to all humans, override cultural and historical particularities to generate recurring themes in water symbolism and meaning. Notable among these are associations of water "as a matter of life and death; as a potent generative, and regenerative force; as the substance of social and spiritual identity; and as a symbol of power and agency" (Strang 2005:115). Water is intrinsic to all life and life-sustaining activities and, as a result, is frequently implicated in religious ceremonies and ritual (e.g., baptismal rites, anointing with holy water). Water is mutable, always changing, and so is invoked in metaphors for change and transformation. Likewise, the motion of water is drawn upon in tales of mythical journey and metaphors for the passage of time, while water confluences denote a coming together or gathering. Water can be both creative and destructive, as in a flood that can renew agricultural fields or destroy buildings and settlements. Water thus has "vast imaginative potential to carry cultural meanings" (Strang 2008:124).

In a similar vein, Taçon (1999; see also Nash 1997) suggests that certain landscapes are *archetypal* and considered sacred or special regardless of cultural background. Likewise, it has been argued that "there are broad similarities between peoples from various parts of the world . . . over and over again the sacred places are connected with, or are, what the western world classes as 'natural' features of the 'landscape,' such as mountain peaks, springs, rivers, woods and caves" (Carmichael et al. 1994:1). Such "natural" places are often imbued with meaning (e.g., Basso 1996a; Santos-Granero 1998), and Bradley (2000:33–44) argues that greater attention be paid to these places as part of the larger landscape of monuments and other human-modified locales.

Often archetypal places are transitional, or locales where the upper and lower worlds collide with the plane of the Earth. They can be found "where the results of great acts of natural transformation can be best seen . . . at junctions or points of change between geology, hydrology, and vegetation, or some combination of all three . . . where there is an unusual landscape feature . . . [and] places providing panoramic views or large vistas" (Taçon 1999:37). Springs satisfy many of these criteria. They are transformative places where the upper and lower worlds intersect as water flows up and out of the ground, debouching onto the surface. Many are located at the bases of ridges and uplands that offer panoramic vistas, and lie at ecotones juxtaposing differing geologies and ecologies. They also bring together different kinds of water at their confluences with lakes or rivers. Florida springs, in particular, are striking in their contrast with other water bodies in the landscape. Indeed, in many ways springs are an inversion of the sluggish, blackwater rivers or still ponds, lakes, and wetlands more commonly found in the state. Variability in spring flow is comparatively less than the rivers they feed into, like the St. Johns or Suwannee (see chapter 2). Their temperature is constant, and so, relative to other water bodies, spring water is cool in the summer and warm in the winter. The water flowing up from the ground, often rapidly, is crystal clear and hypoxic, and harbors unique and endemic species of flora and fauna.

But identifying a place as striking, unique, or affective is perhaps insufficient. A sacred place is more than a piece of geography. It implies a set of beliefs and rules, regulations, and cultural norms regarding proper behavior at that place and comportment toward the power manifested there (Carmichael et al. 1994; Hubert 1994). Dwyer (1996:163) discussed the geographies of the "visible" and "invisible" worlds, where the visible world consists of "plants, animals and people and the physical media within which or upon which these reside," whereas the invisible world includes "mythological, spiritual and fabulous beings." The denizens of the invisible world are not typically seen but can manifest themselves in the visible world to varying degrees, particularly at potent places. Often, ritualized practices (i.e., formalized and repeated sets of actions, following Bell [1992]) are enacted with the explicit intent of making connections between the visible and invisible worlds.

In many cases, sacred sites are avoided or visited only by certain individuals or sects of society. The activities taking place there conform to norms and standards of proper behavior that may not leave material traces. In some instances, observing ritualized practices and inferring the rules of behavior may be the only way to identify sacred sites (Hubert 1994). Notwithstanding these special cases, many activities taking place at sacred places do leave material traces, traces that can be interpreted by archaeologists. Notable among these are interment of the dead, construction of monuments, and placement of votive offerings (Bradley 2000).

Springs are considered sacred in many parts of the world. Certainly, Panther Spring is relevant here, but there are others as well. In England and in Ireland, countless springs are revered as holy wells. Many were pilgrimage sites in the past and continue to be important for healing and fertility rituals (Brenneman and Brenneman 1995; Gribben 1992; Logan 1980; Rattue 1995; Ray 2011, 2014). In central Kansas an artesian spring, now inundated by a reservoir, once flowed from atop a travertine hill. Waconda, or the Great Spirit Spring, was a "Native American religious shrine . . . where it was possible for humans to communicate with the animal spirits that lived in the underworld . . . it was sacred to all nations of the region" (Blakeslee 2010:3; see also Patrick 1879; Swineford and Frye 1955). The Maya likewise considered springs, cenotes, and caves to be portals to the underworld (e.g., Brady and Ashmore 1999; Lucero and Kinkella 2015; Prufer and Brady 2005; Woodfill et al. 2015). Like springs elsewhere, these were pilgrimage sites where votive offerings were left, human remains interred, and temples constructed. Ethnohistoric accounts indicate that Native Americans in the southeastern United States also viewed features such as caves, waterfalls, and springs as portals or conduits to the invisible world (Hudson 1976:130). But it cannot be assumed that springs were similarly considered to be sacred liminal places, or portals, by ancient Floridians. Fortunately, the archaeological record of Silver Glen Springs offers much that is relevant to this question.

SITUATING THE SILVER GLEN COMPLEX

Silver Glen Springs was introduced in the previous chapter, in the context of discussing the relationship of the onset of spring flow to intensive shell mounding in the region. In brief, Silver Glen is a first-magnitude spring in Marion County, one of the largest in Florida. It is proximate to the western shore of Lake George—a flow-through lake of the St. Johns River and the second-largest body of water in Florida—to which it is connected by Silver Glen Run. As noted in chapter 2, the St. Johns River experiences flow reversals and saline intrusion as far upstream as Lake George, where there is a confluence of upstream tannic water, downstream brackish water, and subterranean freshwater from Silver Glen (and other springs). Terrestrial environs are likewise diverse, as a narrow strip of hydric lowlands fronting the western shore of Lake George abuts xeric uplands that rise rapidly to greater than 25 m in elevation.

The Silver Glen Complex encompasses a diverse array of archaeological deposits surrounding Silver Glen Springs and both the northern and southern shores of Silver Glen Run (Figure 4.2). The Complex straddles the border between Marion and Lake Counties, necessitating the identification of multiple sites to satisfy state recording standards. These divisions are somewhat arbitrary, as there is a near-continuous distribution of archaeological deposits surrounding the spring run. In addition to straddling two counties, the Silver Glen Complex also crosses multiple ownership and jurisdictional boundaries. The land adjacent the spring and along the northern shore of the run is part of the Silver Glen Springs Recreation Area, managed by the U.S. Forest Service. The surface water bodies are under jurisdiction of the Florida Department of Environmental Protection and St. Johns River Water Management District. The southern shore and adjacent land of Silver Glen Run are owned by the nonprofit Juniper Club of Louisville, Kentucky.

The largest recorded site in the Complex is 8MR3605/8LA1 (hereafter 8LA1), confined to Juniper Club lands south of Silver Glen Run. Since 2007 this site has been investigated by the University of Florida, Laboratory of Southeastern Archaeology (LSA) through the St. Johns Archaeological Field School, directed by Ken Sassaman. Additional testing has been conducted by the LSA in cooperation with researchers from the University of Oklahoma. Multifaceted field investigations have involved bucket auger and shovel test survey, coring, surface collection, remote

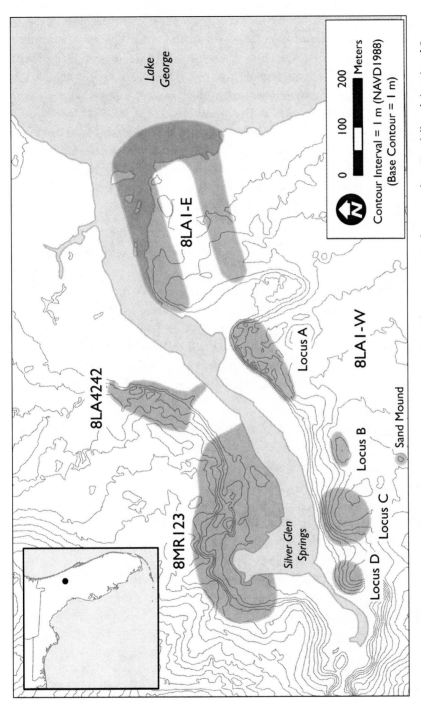

Figure 4.2. Archaeological sites and loci on the landforms surrounding Silver Glen Springs. Site footprints from Randall et al. (2011) and Sassaman et al. (2011).

sensing, and test unit excavation (Gilmore 2016; Randall 2015; Sassaman et al. 2011). To facilitate communication, the site has been divided into eastern and western halves (8LA1-E and 8LA1-W). A linear embayment, or seep spring, intervenes between the two halves. Site 8LA1-W has been further subdivided into four archaeological loci based on the density, age, and character of anthropogenic deposits (Locus A–Locus D).

Beginning in the east, at the mouth of Silver Glen Run, site 8LA1-E consists of the remnant of a large U-shaped shell mound. This mound was noted repeatedly by visitors in the eighteenth and nineteenth centuries. John Bartram (1769:23), for example, described landing "on a shelly bluff amongst thousands of Orange trees, growing so thick we could hardly pass through them." But Jeffries Wyman provided the most detailed description:

> The one last mentioned is much the larger and consists of three portions forming as many sides of a hollow square. The first extending along the shore of the creek, near the mouth of which it has a height of from twenty to twenty-five feet by measurement; the second is on the shore of the lake, and measures from a hundred and fifty to two hundred feet in width, and the third extends inland at nearly right angles to this. Between these ridges is a deep valley, in which the shells are entirely wanting or are only sparingly found. (Wyman 1875:39)

It was the largest shell mound observed by Wyman on the St. Johns River. This mound dates largely to the ceramic Late Archaic Orange period (ca. 4600–3500 cal BP), although, as discussed below, there is evidence that it was founded on earlier deposits (Sassaman et al. 2011).

Just west of 8LA1-E lie the remains of a Mount Taylor shell mound. This is Locus A of site 8LA1-W, described in the previous chapter. Locus A is a linear shell ridge paralleling Silver Glen Run (Randall 2010:330–335; Sassaman et al. 2011:121–170). Shell was emplaced from ca. 6300–5750 cal BP and was thus largely restricted to the Early Mount Taylor phase. A second shell ridge, the Silver Glen Run North Mound (8LA4242) is situated directly across the run from Locus A, on the northern shore (Randall et al. 2011:90–98). Only recently documented, this ridge has been largely destroyed by shell mining, much like Locus A. Subsurface testing has not been conducted at 8LA4242, but its size, its location, and the lack of pottery on the surface indicate that it is likely a Mount Taylor shell mound and may be coeval with Locus A.

Moving farther west, three topographic highs, or ridge noses, overlook the south shore of Silver Glen Run. Site 8LA1-W Locus B occupies a slight topographic rise some 200 m from Locus A (Gilmore 2011, 2016). This portion of the site is well stratified, with both Thornhill Lake phase and Orange period deposits. Locus C of 8LA1-W occupies a ridge nose overlooking Silver Glen Springs, immediately west of Locus B. Secondary refuse and habitation deposits are abundant, dating largely to the St. Johns period (3500–1200 cal BP). The next topographic high to the west is Locus D, a shell-free midden roughly contemporaneous with Locus C.

The western terminus of the Complex includes archaeological deposits surrounding, and within, the pool of Silver Glen Springs. The D.B.'s Cave site (8MR162) consists of lithic and bone artifacts discovered by divers in the early 1960s. These were recovered 30–45 m back inside the cave system of Silver Glen Springs (Dunbar 1990). More recently, a possible dugout canoe was uncovered beneath the sediments of the spring pool (8MR3554 [Porter 2009]). Extensive subaqueous deposits have also been noted along the southern shore of the spring run, including shell, vertebrate fauna, human remains, and both Orange and St. Johns pottery (Seinfeld 2013). Whether these deposits have been disturbed or remain in situ is not presently known.

Terrestrial deposits adjacent to the spring pool have been documented as the Silver Glen site (8MR123). This area was described by Wyman (1875:39) as an "amphitheater" of shell surrounding the spring pool. Although heavily reduced by mining, recent survey and testing has documented the presence of intact deposits proximate to the pool and in the surrounding uplands (Randall et al. 2011). Most shell emplacement appears to have occurred during the Thornhill Lake phase and subsequent Orange period. The mound was crescentic to C-shaped, covering an area of at least 350 × 200 m (Randall et al. 2011:196–197). Shell has been documented 2 m beneath the current water level of the spring, and as much as 4 m above it, suggesting that a vertical shell bluff at one time emerged from the spring to a height of 6 m or more.

The history of Silver Glen Springs is one of repeated alterations of the landscape, over several millennia, as different materials were deposited in different contexts and toward different ends. These landscape alterations register transformations in the occupation and use of the site and its material, historical resources. The following sections detail the various pre-Columbian deposits of the Silver Glen Complex, highlighting these transformations through time.

LATE PLEISTOCENE AND HOLOCENE ANTECEDENTS

The presence of late Pleistocene colonists in peninsular Florida is indicated by diagnostic hafted bifaces. In general, these are lanceolate shaped and may be either fluted or unfluted. The earliest bifaces are generally classified as a variant of Clovis, dating as early as 13,200 cal BP (Waters and Stafford 2007). Other forms include Simpson, Suwannee, and Dalton. The temporal placement of these latter types is uncertain, but they are generally thought to postdate Clovis. However, there is increasing acceptance that an earlier occupation likely existed. Several "pre-Clovis" sites have been reported in the eastern United States, with tool assemblages unlike those of Clovis occupations, and dates older than 13,200 cal BP. Three of these are located in Florida—Page-Ladson, Sloth-Hole, and Wakulla Springs Lodge—and predate Clovis by as much as 1,500 years (Rink, Dunbar, and Burdette 2012).

Several researchers have argued that Paleoindians may have been semisedentary and tethered to freshwater sources, such as first-magnitude springs and large lakes, during the arid late Pleistocene in Florida (Dunbar 1991; Dunbar and Waller 1983; Neill 1964; Thulman 2009). Most Paleoindian sites are located in northwest peninsular Florida, where carbonate bedrock is near the surface and karst terrain well developed (Dunbar and Waller 1983). In contrast, only a handful of Paleoindian sites have been recorded in the St. Johns River basin. These include the Paradise Park site (8MR92) adjacent to Silver Springs (Dunbar and Doran 2010; Faught 2009; Hemmings 1975; Neill 1958), and the Helen Blazes site (8BR27) in the upper St. Johns River valley (Edwards 1954; Rink, Dunbar, Doran, Frederick, and Gregory 2012).[1]

Despite the dearth of Paleoindian sites in the region, Thulman (2009) identified the area from Lake George to the Ocklawaha River as one locale with a high potential for Paleoindian sites, based on the availability of groundwater in the vicinity. The recently documented Lake George Point Site (8PU1470) lends some credence to this. The site consists of over 40 whole or fragmentary lanceolate hafted bifaces, many resembling the Suwannee type (Thulman 2012). These were purportedly recovered by local collectors beneath the shallow waters of northeastern Lake George. Systematic underwater archaeological survey failed to recover evidence of Paleoindian occupation at this locale, although Pleistocene-aged deposits were indicated by the remains of extinct fauna. Thulman (2012) attributed the lack of definitive Paleoindian artifacts to the intensity of collector activity in the area.

At Crescent Lake, some 10 km northeast of Lake George, near-shore survey and analysis of collector assemblages from submerged sites indicated substantial Paleoindian and Early Archaic activity (Sassaman 2003b). Diagnostic hafted bifaces numbering in the hundreds were recovered by collectors along the western margin of the lake, proximate to the Crescent City Ridge. Sassaman (2003b:111) argued that late Pleistocene and early Holocene occupants likely targeted the edge of the ridge, as this provided a panoramic view overlooking the lake basin, likely a productive wetland biome at the time. He suggested revising extant Paleoindian settlement models to include escarpments and ridges overlooking wetlands in northeast Florida. A similar argument was later offered by Thulman (2012), who argued that Paleoindians sought vantage points overlooking broad expanses, such as lake basins, in the St. Johns River valley and elsewhere.

Evidence for Paleoindian and Early Archaic presence at Silver Glen Springs itself is pervasive, if ephemeral. No diagnostic artifacts have been found, but several formal side- and end-scrapers were recovered during survey of the uplands north of Silver Glen Springs (Randall et al. 2011:205; Sassaman et al. 2011:77). In many cases these are heavily patinated, perhaps indicating great antiquity. Lithic debitage, likewise heavily patinated, was frequently recovered below Middle Archaic diagnostic artifacts. Anecdotal evidence from local collectors indicates that Paleoindian fluted, lanceolate hafted bifaces have been recovered from the spring, and several of the artifacts illustrated by Dunbar (1990), recovered from within the cave system of Silver Glen Springs (8MR162), appear to be Paleoindian or Early Archaic forms.

Activities taking place at Silver Glen Springs during the Paleoindian and Early Archaic periods were apparently widespread, based on the distribution of lithic artifacts in shell-free deposits (Randall et al. 2011; Sassaman et al. 2011). However, radiocarbon assays are lacking, and little can be said about the intensity of activities taking place or the nature of those occupations. The potential no doubt exists for a well-preserved site beneath the waters of Lake George, perhaps with associated organic materials that might lend some insight into occupational activities.

The earliest well-documented deposits at the Silver Glen Complex occur at Locus A of 8LA1-W, where a series of pits were repeatedly excavated and infilled for a variety of purposes (Figure 4.3). These Early Mount Taylor deposits were detailed in the previous chapter. But, to review, at least two episodes of pit digging are apparent, one from ca. 9000–8000 cal BP, and a second predating 6300 cal BP. These were eventually capped with sand and a shell ridge emplaced, shifting the pattern of deposition from excavation and infilling to accumulation. Circumstantial evidence suggests that a similar process transpired across the run at the Silver Glen Run North site (8LA4242).

THORNHILL LAKE PHASE

An appreciable transformation of the use of space at the Silver Glen Complex was under way by ca. 5800 cal BP. Regionally, this is coincident with the onset of the Thornhill Lake phase, marked by the abandonment of many earlier Mount Taylor shell ridges, establishment of a new mortuary program, and expansion of regional exchange networks. At Silver Glen this transition manifested itself first with the abandonment of Locus A as a place of daily living by 5700 cal BP (Sassaman et al. 2011:168). Excavations have documented an expansive deposit of sand atop the remnant shell ridge, nearly 50 cm thick. Its position at a high elevation relative to surrounding landforms suggests that this was not the result of natural (e.g., colluvial or alluvial) processes. Likewise, its widespread and uniform occurrence argues against it being a byproduct of shell mining in the vicinity. Rather, it appears that inhabitants of Locus A purposefully capped the shell ridge with sand when it was no longer used as a habitation place.

The practice of capping abandoned habitation sites has deep antiquity in the St. Johns River valley and has historical precedents at the Silver Glen Complex itself. Recall from chapter 3 that places like Live Oak Mound, Hontoon Dead Creek Mound, and Harris Creek originated as habitation spaces that were then capped with deposits of whole shell before being transformed into loci for communal ritual and/or interment of the dead. Similarly, shell-processing pits underlying the Locus A shell ridge were capped with brown sand prior to the accumulation of Early Mount Taylor

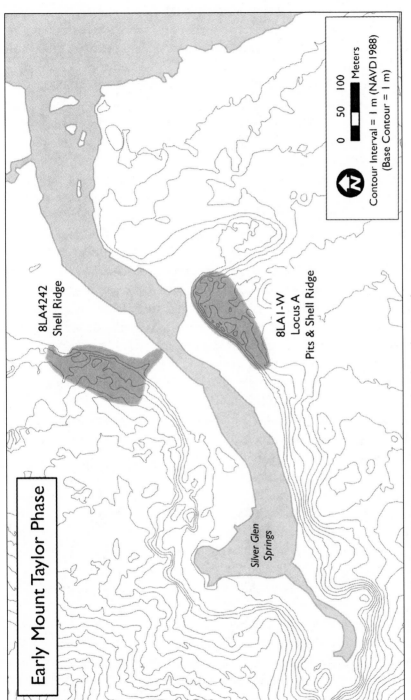

Figure 4.3. Early Mount Taylor phase archaeological deposits at the Silver Glen Complex.

living surfaces and midden deposits (Randall 2013). Whether there was a functional or symbolic difference between shell caps and sand caps is unclear, but, regardless, there was clearly a need or desire to physically mark the cessation of one activity at a place prior to the initiation of another.

After ca. 5700 cal BP, Locus A was no longer the site of significant deposition, whether of shell or other materials, although later Orange- and St. Johns–era artifacts have been recovered in small amounts near the surface. At approximately the same time, inhabitants began transforming previously unmodified portions of the Silver Glen Springs landscape (Figure 4.4). This is evident at Locus B of 8LA1-W, situated a mere 200 m southwest of Locus A. The basal component of Locus B consists of a series of repeated settlements and abandonments spanning the Thornhill Lake phase, from ca. 5800–4600 cal BP (Gilmore 2011, 2016:92). These are evident stratigraphically as a number of stacked, crushed shell habitation surfaces with layers of sterile sand between them. Shell layers are composed principally of crushed bivalve (*Unionidae* sp.) and apple snail (*Pomacea paludosa*) shells, and contain lithic tools and debitage, marine shell, bone tools, unmodified vertebrate fauna, and paleofeces. Many small conical or basin-shaped pits also originate from these surfaces. The intervening layers, in contrast, are devoid of both shell and artifacts and exhibit evidence of pedogenesis. Gilmore (2011:25) estimates that a minimum of four sequences of habitation and abandonment are represented in these deposits. The end result of these practices is an elevated dome of shell, approximately 1 m high, which is reminiscent of the shell nodes documented at the Hontoon Dead Creek Village site.

The habitation-related activities evident in Thornhill Lake deposits at Locus B are not dissimilar from those that preceded them at Locus A. However, coincident with the onset of this deposition at Locus B, inhabitants initiated a radically different transformation of the landscape immediately surrounding the pool of Silver Glen Springs at site 8MR123 (Randall et al. 2011). Although the land surrounding the spring has been heavily modified by twentieth century shell mining and recreational activities, initial testing by researchers from Florida State University documented intact archaeological shell deposits rising 3 m above the modern surface (Marrinan et al. 1990; Stanton 1995). Three radiocarbon assays indicated that the deposits date primarily to the Thornhill Lake phase, ca. 5650–4620 cal BP. Asa Randall's 2010 and 2011 excavations into the mining escarpment approximately 40 m north of the spring pool were expected

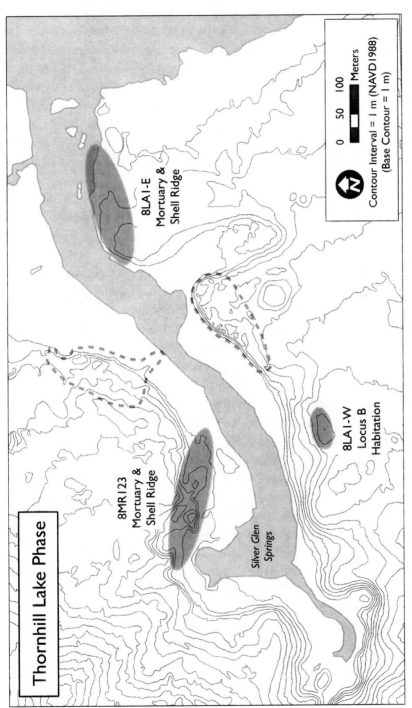

Figure 4.4. Thornhill Lake phase archaeological deposits at the Silver Glen Complex. Dashed lines show the location of earlier deposits.

to document similarly deep shell deposits (Randall et al. 2011:112–121). Instead, only a thin layer of intact shell (Stratum III) was found beneath modern overburden. This shell overlies a deposit of brown and yellow sand (Stratum IV) within which human remains were discovered. The slope and inflection of the contact between these strata suggest that Stratum IV is a portion of a mortuary mound (Randall et al. 2011:116–117). A single radiocarbon assay indicates that this earthen mortuary mound was emplaced between 5850 and 5590 cal BP, early in the Thornhill Lake phase. The shell overlying the mortuary consists primarily of bivalve and apple snails in an ashy matrix with abundant charcoal, deposited between 5590 and 5320 cal BP. Many of the bivalves were closed and paired, indicating that they were not cooked or trampled. Randall and colleagues thus suggest that shell was used to cap the mortuary, either immediately following its emplacement or at a slightly later date.

The mortuary was heavily impacted by mining, and so its original size is unclear. However, this is not an isolated interment (Randall et al. 2011:37). Potter (1935) reported that human remains were found in great numbers when shell was mined from the site. Further, photographs published by Norman (2010) show flexed burials in a context similar to that documented by Randall and colleagues (i.e., in a dark earth matrix beneath shell). Finally, human remains of unknown age and provenance have been documented beneath the water by visitors to the spring and avocational and professional archaeologists (Seinfeld 2013; Willis 1972).

As the mortuary mound at 8MR123 was capped with shell shortly after 5600 cal BP, shell was simultaneously being deposited in two other locations nearby. As noted above, the 1990 Florida State University investigations found 3 m of intact shell deposits, approximately 100 m east of the mortuary (Marrinan 1990). This deposit abuts the terrace edge, but shell was emplaced directly on the ground surface—and not atop a preexisting mortuary mound—perhaps as early as 5650 cal BP. Randall and colleagues (2011) also documented subsurface shell along Silver Glen Run, a further 100 m east. The presence of well preserved, uncharred botanicals indicates that this shell was deposited subaqueously (Randall et al. 2011:88). A radiocarbon assay on nutshell from the base of this deposit was identical to that from the shell cap over the mortuary (5590–5320 cal BP). The implication is that shell was being deposited in three distinct modes—capping an earthen mortuary, atop the ground surface, and within the water—contemporaneously near the onset of the Thornhill

Lake phase. These deposits are arrayed on a line roughly 200 m long that parallels the spring run and thus likely represent basal portions of a nascent shell ridge.

Over the next millennium, shell continued to be deposited, forming a ridge that abutted the terrace edge and prograded into the water, partially or wholly infilling wetlands on the margin of the spring run and reaching a height of 3 m or more (Randall et al. 2011:203, 2014:27–28). How much of this shell deposition was related to daily living, and how much to mortuary activities, is not clear from the available data. However, human remains were encountered in a shovel test proximate to the subaqueous shell deposits (Randall et al. 2011:78–79). Further, there is circumstantial evidence that a second, coeval mortuary existed near the mouth of Silver Glen Run at 8LA1-E, where a single human interment was exposed by erosion amidst densely concreted shells in basal deposits of the U-shaped monument (Gilmore 2016; Randall 2015:184; Sassaman et al. 2011). Although the mound is largely an Orange period construction (see below), concreted shell is frequently found at Mount Taylor period shell ridges. Further, microliths, often associated with Thornhill Lake phase deposits, have been documented at 8LA1-E (Sassaman et al. 2011:79). Finally, the distribution of concreted shell documented on the surface and in subsurface survey is conformant with known Mount Taylor shell ridges, forming a linear expanse approximately 150 m × 50 m parallel to Silver Glen Run (Sassaman et al. 2011:38–42). Taken together, these data suggest that a Mount Taylor period construction, perhaps a mortuary mound, existed at the mouth of Silver Glen Run.

In addition to the deposition of shell in new locales, and for alternative ends, during the Thornhill Lake phase, there is evidence for coeval shell-free deposition in the uplands surrounding the spring (Randall et al. 2011, 2014). Close-interval shovel testing documented at least two concentrations of lithic debitage and tools in the absence of shell. Although datable samples were not recovered, these activities appear to date largely to the Mount Taylor period, as 95 percent of the hafted bifaces recovered were of the Florida Archaic Stemmed variety, and nearly half of the debitage was thermally altered[2] (Randall et al. 2011:205). Whether these remains derive from Early Mount Taylor or Thornhill Lake phase activities is unclear, but a similarly isolated lithic production area was documented at the Lake Monroe Outlet Midden (8VO53), which dates to the Thornhill Lake phase (Archaeological Consultants, Inc. and Janus Research 2001).

In sum, the onset of the Thornhill Lake phase at Silver Glen Springs is reflected in the capping and abandonment of the Early Mount Taylor shell ridges at 8LA1-W Locus A and (presumably) the Silver Glen Run North Mound (8LA4242). Mortuaries of earth and shell were emplaced at both ends of Silver Glen Run—north of the spring pool (8MR123) and at the confluence with Lake George (8LA1-E)—coincident with (or just prior to) the establishment of linear shell deposits in these same locales and a habitation space at 8LA1-W Locus B, halfway down the run.

Near the end of the Thornhill Lake Phase, the habitation space at Locus B was capped with shell and abandoned for a sufficient duration for pedogenesis to proceed on the surface, perhaps a century or two (Gilmore 2011, 2016). The onset of the Orange period brought with it new technology, further landscape alterations, and transformations of the practices taking place at Silver Glen Springs.

ORANGE PERIOD

The onset of the Orange Period (4600–3500 cal BP) is marked by the initial appearance of pottery in the St. Johns River valley and greater northeast Florida. Orange pottery is tempered with plant fibers, typically Spanish moss (*Tillandsia usneoides*), and has affinities to Stallings wares from the Savannah River and Atlantic coast of Georgia and South Carolina (Sassaman 1993). Current interpretations indicate that Stallings pottery spread from the Atlantic Coast along preexisting exchange routes into northeast Florida no later than 4500 cal BP (Sassaman 2004).

Orange pottery is most abundant in northeast Florida, although related fiber-tempered wares have a much broader distribution. Early interpretations of the Orange period suggested that pottery arrived with little fanfare and that life remained largely unchanged from the earlier Mount Taylor period (Milanich 1994:88). Miller (1998:70–71), for example, wrote that "by this time, adaptation to the river environments must have been firmly established, and indeed, despite this new technological development, it is likely that the settled or semipermanent occupation of the Late Archaic hunters, gatherers, and shellfish collectors continued with little change until the introduction of domesticated plants." However, more recent investigations into Orange period developments have revealed several dramatic transformations in settlement patterning, technology, mortuary ritual, and shell mounding (e.g., Gilmore 2015, 2016; Randall et al.

2014; Russo 2004; Sassaman 2010; Sassaman and Randall 2012; Saunders and Russo 2011).

The introduction of pottery to the region brought with it a decline in the use of both lithic and marine shell tools, which are found in much less abundance at Orange period sites than at earlier sites (Gilmore 2011, 2016; Sassaman 2003c). Likewise on the decline were exotic exchange objects, such as bannerstones and beads, which were often interred in Thornhill Lake phase mounds. Instead, ornately decorated pottery appears to have become ensconced as the exchange medium of choice (Gilmore 2016).

Perhaps the most dramatic change is evident in the location and disposition of Orange habitation sites and shell mounds. Whereas Mount Taylor habitations were typically arrayed in a linear fashion and accreted in a tell-like manner to form shell ridges, Orange habitations were arranged in an arcuate or circular pattern and tend to be thin and ephemeral (Sassaman 2003a). The stacked accumulation of living surfaces evident at many Mount Taylor sites has not been documented at Orange period sites. Further, there was a marked concentration of shell mounding. Nearly all Mount Taylor shell ridges were abandoned, and the piling of shell was limited to a few shell mound centers that were considerably larger and more complex than those that preceded them (Gilmore 2016; Randall and Sassaman 2010). Similarly, whereas plain Orange pottery is widely distributed in ephemeral settlements, decorated Orange wares are limited to mound contexts (Gilmore 2016; Randall 2011:138). Four of these complexes have been documented, roughly equidistant from each other along the middle and upper St. Johns River. Each of these was founded upon an earlier Mount Taylor mortuary mound that was used as the base for building massive, multilobed shell complexes. From south to north these are Orange Mound (8OR1), Old Enterprise (8VO55), Harris Creek (8VO24), and the Silver Glen Complex.

Orange period activities at the Silver Glen Complex included both expansion of existing shell ridges and the establishment of new deposits (Figure 4.5). However, not all earlier deposits were treated equally. The two Early Mount Taylor phase shell ridges—8LA1-W Locus A and 8LA4242—continued to be avoided, as they were during the Thornhill Lake phase. In contrast, the Thornhill Lake mortuaries established at the spring pool (8MR123) and the confluence with Lake George (8LA1-E) were significantly expanded to form two of the largest pre-Columbian mound complexes in Florida.

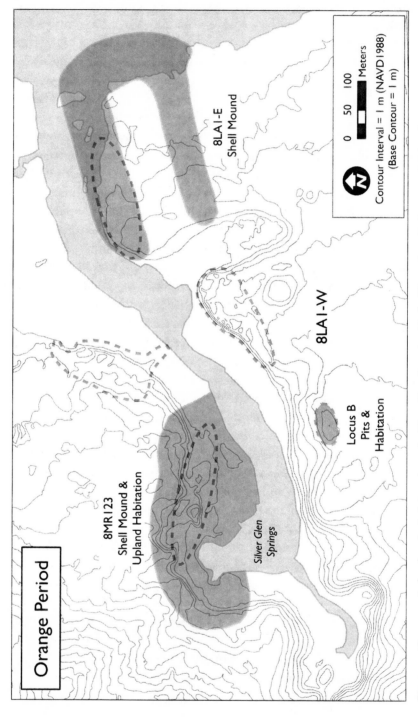

Figure 4.5. Orange period archaeological deposits at the Silver Glen Complex. Dashed lines show the location of earlier deposits.

As noted above, the mound at the mouth of Silver Glen Run, 8LA1-E, was described by Wyman (1875) as the largest shell mound on the St. Johns River. It was a massive U-shaped construction, open toward the west, on the south bank of the run. Although it was largely destroyed by shell mining, subsurface survey effectively documented the footprint of a mound extending some 300 m along Silver Glen Run and 200 m along Lake George (Sassaman et al. 2011). Wyman indicates that the northern ridge of this construction was broader and higher than the southern arm, reaching a maximum elevation of approximately 8 m in the northeast corner. Auger survey along the shorelines in the vicinity of the north ridge indicated that shell, frequently concreted, is present as much as 2.5 m beneath the modern ground surface. Again, these deposits are likely the remnant of a Mount Taylor period mortuary mound that was subsequently covered over by Orange period shell deposition.

Test units excavated in the footprint of the north ridge indicated that near-surface deposits were heavily reworked by mining. Intact deposits were documented but are largely inaccessible beneath the current water table. Artifacts recovered along the surface and in near-shore locales consist of highly decorated Orange wares. Multiple radiocarbon assays on soot adhering to potsherds and Spanish moss fibers on their interiors suggest that this ridge was emplaced relatively early in the Orange period, sometime in the interval 4600–3800 cal BP (Gilmore 2016; Sassaman et al. 2011).

Testing of the smaller southern ridge at 8LA1-E revealed a markedly different depositional history. Intact shell deposits were found to overlie basal sands, indicating that, rather than being emplaced over an existing shell ridge, the southern arm was built *de novo*, directly on the ground surface (Sassaman et al. 2011). The artifact inventory was relatively sparse, but the ceramic assemblage is dominated by plain Orange pottery, in contrast to the predominantly decorated wares from the north ridge. It also appears that the southern ridge was a slightly later addition to the Complex. A basal pit feature was radiocarbon-dated to 4060–3830 cal BP, suggesting that the bulk of the southern ridge was built up late in the Orange period. Importantly, human remains have not been documented at this or any other Orange period shell mound complex, indicating that Mount Taylor mortuary mounds were repurposed.

A second shell mound was also described by Wyman, surrounding the pool of Silver Glen Springs itself (8MR123). Survey and testing by Randall and colleagues (2011) documented the remnant of this mound, which covered an area of 350 × 200 m and reached perhaps 6 m in height. The Thornhill mortuary mound north and east of the pool was, similar to 8LA1-E, renovated and repurposed by Orange inhabitants. That Orange activity here was intensive is attested to by the abundance of decorated Orange pottery collected from the spring pool (Gilmore 2016). Shell-mounding activities during the Orange period were focused on the spring pool, accreting south and west from the Thornhill ridge. Subaqueous shell east of the spring pool, apparently deposited directly in the water, documents the progradation of shell into the spring run during the Orange period. The existing Thornhill shell ridge was expanded some 60 m south, into the spring run, and 40 m west to the edge of the current spring pool by 4520–4240 cal BP (Randall et al. 2011:87). Shell deposits in the same locale, but at a higher elevation, were radiocarbon-dated to 4410–4080 cal BP, indicating that some 2.5 m of shell was emplaced rapidly during the Orange period. This subaqueous shell deposition effectively reoriented the outflow of the spring from a relatively straight, eastward flow to the south-then-east dogleg present today. Shell continued to accumulate, wrapping around the northern and western shore and surrounding the spring to form the amphitheater of shell noted by Wyman (1875:39).

In addition to building up shell at either end of Silver Glen Run, Orange peoples also engaged in subterranean manipulations at multiple locales on the Sliver Glen landscape (Gilmore 2011, 2016; Sassaman et al. 2011). Notably, Locus B was transformed from a habitation site to a specialized shellfish-processing facility. Discussed above, Locus B occupies a relatively flat ridge nose approximately 80 m south of Silver Glen Run (Gilmore 2011, 2015). Deposition began during the Thornhill Lake phase and eventually formed a small, crescentic shell node. Prior to the Orange period, a thin mantle of shell was emplaced, and Locus B was abandoned until, sometime after 4600 cal BP, the directionality of deposition shifted from building up to digging down.

Initial Orange period deposition at Locus B involved the excavation of scores of massive pits geared ostensibly toward shellfish roasting (Gilmore 2011, 2016:102–108). These pits are densely concentrated at Locus B, frequently intersecting and overlapping one another, and forming a complex stratigraphic record. Pits are typically large, ranging from 70–120 cm in diameter and greater than 1 m deep, but their form is inconsistent. Pit fill is likewise variable, with some containing sparse shell, and others abundant shell. The number of shellfish species in pits, the degree of shell crushing and/or burning, and the internal configuration of the pit fill are similarly diverse. After ca. 3900 cal BP, pit digging ceased at Locus B, and a cap of clean, whole *Viviparus georgianus* was emplaced (Gilmore 2016:106–108). This cap, measuring 30–50 cm thick, was largely devoid of artifacts, contained little non-shell matrix, and was coextensive with the pits. This points to rapid deposition that covered over and flattened the pit-pocked surface of Locus B.

Evidence for Orange period habitation or domestic activities is largely absent at Locus B. However, circular arrangements of materials and features indicative of habitation have been documented elsewhere at Silver Glen Springs. At both 8LA1-E and a bait field north of Locus B, ground penetrating radar (GPR) survey located arcuate patterns of anomalies. At 8LA1-E, circular anomalies 5–10 m across were arrayed in an arc that, if projected to a circle, would measure 80 m in diameter (Sassaman et al. 2011). These anomalies were found to be thin subsurface deposits of shell with moderate amounts of vertebrate fauna and plain Orange pottery.

Anomalies in the bait field north of Locus B likewise consisted of subsurface shell deposits, primarily small pits (Gilmore 2016:121–123). Unlike those from Locus B, these pits were small and contained ample evidence for habitation. Two radiocarbon assays indicate that these occupations took place over the interval 4150–3900 cal BP.

Randall and colleagues (2011:206–208) documented a similar arcuate pattern in the uplands north of Silver Glen Springs. However, there was a notable lack of shell at this location. Rather, the distributional pattern of Orange pottery suggested a series of household clusters arranged in a circular pattern around interior plazas. These household clusters were, in turn, arrayed in a circular or arcuate pattern around a larger central plaza.

In sum, Orange period landscape alterations at the Silver Glen Complex included the transformation of two Thornhill Lake phase mortuary mounds into massive U- or C-shaped monuments, the digging of scores of large shellfish-processing pits, and the establishment of several small habitation sites. Gilmore (2016) has argued that the activities reflected in these deposits were a result of massive extraregional gatherings at Silver Glen Springs. He brought to bear technofunctional, petrographic, and elemental analyses of pottery to differentiate locally produced pots from those imported from afar, and to discern patterning in stylistic and manufacturing techniques. These analyses indicated that assemblages from the mounds (8LA1-E and 8MR123) contain an appreciably higher proportion of ornately decorated Orange pottery than any contemporaneous, non-mounded context. Further, mound-centered gatherings frequently involved pottery manufactured in distant locales, perhaps as far as Charlotte Harbor in southwest Florida, over 200 km away. In contrast, pottery from non-mounded locales, such as Locus B, is almost exclusively local and undecorated (Gilmore 2016:210). The mounds, then, are interpreted as the site of ritualized feasts aimed at gathering and integrating participants from across a broad swath of peninsular Florida. Meanwhile, the massive shellfish-processing pits at Locus B likely served to provision these feasts, whereas ephemeral, circular encampments point to intermittent occupation, rather than a sustained resident population. In Gilmore's (2016:210) estimation, the preponderance of decorated and nonlocal pottery at mounds points to the cultural diversity and ritual significance of these gatherings: "Silver Glen's mounds hosted a series of public, ritually charged consumption events that contrasted markedly with the small scale of the routine subsistence practices evinced elsewhere in northeastern Florida during the Orange period."

St. Johns Period

The St. Johns period in northeast Florida is a local manifestation of the regional Woodland (3200–1000 cal BP) and Mississippian (1000–500 cal BP) periods. In the Southeast the Woodland period is generally characterized by an increased reliance on pottery and horticulture and the appearance of widespread mound construction and ceremonialism (Anderson and Sassaman 2012:112–151). The onset of the Woodland in the Southeast is marked by the dissolution of regional interaction networks and a shift from large habitation sites to smaller, dispersed settlements. Fiber-tempered pottery was no longer manufactured by this time, replaced by a variety of wares with differing tempering agents and decorative motifs. The most widespread of these in Florida are the Deptford, Swift Creek, Pasco, and St. Johns series (Milanich 1994:104–274).

In the St. Johns River valley, the Woodland period is termed the St. Johns I period and dates to 3500–1200 cal BP. The dominant pottery type in this period is the spiculate-tempered St. Johns ware, which is frequently undecorated. Florida archaeologists emphasize continuity with the preceding Orange period, despite the fact that the interval 3500–2800 cal BP is poorly documented in the region (Milanich 1994:254; Miller 1998:77–86). This continuity is partially a consequence of the frequent presence of St. Johns I deposits in the same locales as earlier Orange period sites and technological and stylistic overlap between Orange and St. Johns pottery (e.g., spicules in the paste of Orange pottery, St. Johns pottery with Orange decorative motifs [Cordell 2004; Gilmore 2016]). St. Johns I sites are more frequently documented in the region, continuing the trend with earlier periods, and thus population increase is presumed. St. Johns period sites in general are understudied, and little is known about the size or organization of villages and special-use sites.

Following the Woodland period in the Southeast is the Mississippian period. This denotes the era when large, highly stratified societies emerged in the Southeast (Anderson and Sassaman 2012:152–190). Many of these would be classified as chiefdoms or, in some cases, states in cultural evolutionary nomenclature. Individual polities were widespread but were not persistent, and many political centers went through cycles of emergence, florescence, and collapse (Anderson 1994). Maize agriculture was widespread in the Southeast, although the degree to which it was practiced in Florida is debated (Ashley and White 2012). Monumental architecture, with numerous mortuary and platform mounds arranged around plazas, hierarchical settlement patterns, stratified social organization, and regional exchange and interaction, perhaps in the context of shared religious ideology, all characterize Mississippian societies in the Southeast.

The degree to which communities in Florida participated in, or were peripheral to, "Mississipianization" and the socio-political transformations it entailed is unclear. In the St. Johns River valley, the archaeological culture coincident with the Mississippian period is referred to as St. Johns II (Milanich 1994:262–274; Miller 1998:86–87). The shift from St. Johns I to St. Johns II is largely recognized by the appearance of check-stamping as the dominant surface treatment on pottery. Again, in terms of basic lifeways, the St. Johns II period is in many ways characterized by continuity with what came before, but with an increase in population. Despite this continuity, some changes are evident. Hafted bifaces became smaller—as seen in the Pinellas, Ichetucknee, and Tampa types—and may be indicative of bow-and-arrow technology. Burial mounds became larger, and, late in the St. Johns II period, some took the form of large pyramidal mounds, similar to those at Mississippian sites elsewhere in the

Southeast. However, maize agriculture was likely not practiced or was not widespread, and the social structure of St. Johns II communities is poorly understood (Ashley and White 2012).

At the Silver Glen Complex, it is not clear to what extent St. Johns people used or added to the shell monuments that reached their zenith during the Orange period (Figure 4.6). Survey and testing at 8MR123 failed to document evidence of significant post-Archaic alteration. However, a small deposit of shell on the western margin of Silver Glen Springs contained St. Johns plain sherds and elongated specimens of *Viviparus* (Randall et al. 2011:90). The nature of this deposit, and whether it was redeposited by shell mining, is unclear.

In contrast, reconnaissance survey of 8LA1-W documented abundant plain St. Johns pottery, widely distributed across the landform (Sassaman et al. 2011:117–118). However, the densest concentration was at the western edge of the survey tract, and downslope, adjacent to the water of Silver Glen Run. Check-stamped St. Johns pottery was likewise concentrated to the west, particularly at Locus C and Locus D, the two upland landforms (ridge noses) overlooking Silver Glen Springs.

The St. Johns era deposits at the Silver Glen Complex were investigated intensively from 2011 to 2013. Analysis of the materials recovered during these excavations is ongoing (Anderson 2015). Here I present the broad details of these investigations as they relate to the ongoing transformation of the Silver Glen landscape. Locus C is the larger of the two ridge noses, a relatively flat, well-drained promontory with dense midden deposits. Reconnaissance survey in this area documented a ring of shell midden surrounding a shell-free zone approximately 20 × 40 m in plan (Sassaman et al. 2011:114–115). Test-unit excavation supported the inference of a circular St. Johns era occupation that apparently increased in intensity from the St. Johns I to the St. Johns II periods (Anderson 2015:83). Numerous pits were recorded, and a series of postholes arrayed in an arc suggests the presence of circular structures.

Downslope of Locus C, adjacent to the spring run, a dense shell midden was documented (Anderson 2015:84–100). This contains abundant vertebrate fauna, lithic debris, and other indicators of habitation-related activities. The midden apparently accumulated over the course of the St. Johns period, although St. Johns plain pottery is more prevalent than check-stamped. St. Johns pottery has also been documented within the

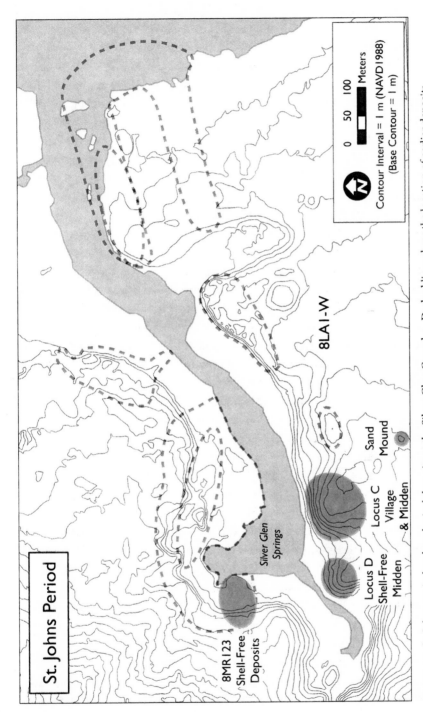

Figure 4.6. St. Johns period archaeological deposits at the Silver Glen Complex. Dashed lines show the location of earlier deposits.

spring run adjacent to the midden (Seinfeld 2013). A basal pit feature dating to the Orange period attests to earlier activities as well.

Locus D of 8LA1-W comprises a smaller ridge nose west of Locus C. This landform is largely devoid of shell, instead housing a shell-free midden. This midden contrasts sharply with the shell-bearing deposits of Locus C. In addition to the absence of shell, pit features documented at Locus D were rich with charcoal and appear to have served a different function from those at Locus C (Anderson 2015:137). No evidence for architecture was recovered, and vertebrate faunal remains were few. Likewise, there is no evidence for St. Johns I occupation. Instead, an abundance of large St. Johns check-stamped sherds indicates that specialized activities took place here during the St. Johns II period. Whether this was a provisioning workshop or a locale for votive or otherwise structured deposition of check-stamped pottery in pits is, as yet, unclear. A single radiocarbon assay indicates that these pits were dug early in the St. Johns II period, possibly predating St. Johns II deposits at Locus C.

An additional deposit, presumably of St. Johns age, lies approximately 150 m southeast of Locus C (Sassaman et al. 2011:103). This small, conical sand mound, measuring 20 m in diameter and 1.5 m high, is similar to other St. Johns era burial mounds in the region. Given the potential for recovering human remains, this mound has not been intensively tested. However, a high density of St. Johns plain pottery was recovered during reconnaissance survey in the vicinity, suggesting that it may have been constructed by St. Johns I people (Sassaman et al. 2011:118).

In sum, St. Johns era deposits have been documented in numerous places in the Silver Glen Complex, but the best-documented are restricted to landforms on the southern shore, opposite the spring. Activities during the St. Johns period apparently did not involve significant shell mounding. This is consistent with shell mounds elsewhere in the St. Johns River valley, which received little additional shell after the Archaic period (Randall 2013). Occupation during the St. Johns I period appears to have been small-scale, with little indication of the extraregional gatherings that characterized the preceding Orange period. St. Johns plain pottery is widely distributed across the Complex, but intensive deposition during the St. Johns I period has been documented in only the spring-side midden. A mortuary mound was established southeast of the spring, possibly early in the St. Johns period. St. Johns II deposits include a circular village-and-plaza overlooking the spring (Locus C), downslope midden deposits, and a special-use site immediately to the west (Locus D) that may have involved votive offerings in pits.

Transformative Histories at Silver Glen Springs

Human use of Silver Glen Springs went through several transformations over the course of some 8,000 years. The evidence for human visitation of the spring during the late Pleistocene and early Holocene is tantalizing but thin. Extant settlement models certainly suggest that Silver Glen Springs would attract people as both a source of freshwater and for the panoramic views afforded from the nearby uplands. However, those early visitors have left few clues to the frequency, duration, and nature of their visits. Lithic debitage, microliths, unifacial tools, and the occasional hafted biface attest to their presence, but they are hardly representative of the richness of life and the suite of activities that likely took place. The presence of Paleoindian-aged hafted bifaces placed more than 30 m back in the cave system (Dunbar 1990) may point to votive offerings marking the spring as special or sacred.

As water rose in the ensuing millennia, people continued to gather at Silver Glen, bringing with them stone from the interior of Florida. By 9,000 years ago, they began to dig into the earth in at least one locale, beneath Locus A. The function of these pits is unclear. They contain the full suite of artifacts found in later deposits, but in much lower density, and are largely devoid of shell (Randall 2014a). Gilmore (2016:126) argues, in the context of later pit digging at Locus B, that, much like springs, the surface of the Earth constitutes a boundary between the present and past, or between upper and lower worlds, in many cultures (see also Knight 1989; Thomas 1999). Digging into the earth transgresses that boundary and the removal and emplacement of materials in the earth, through pit digging and infilling, constitutes an exchange or interaction with the ancestors.

Pit digging continued, likely intermittently, into the Mount Taylor period. At approximately 6300 cal. BP, the pits were capped with a mantle of sand. This sand cap marked the end of *digging down* and the onset of *building up* as a series of shell nodes and associated refuse middens were formed. Over the course of some 500 years, these deposits conglomerated into a linear shell ridge. Atop this ridge is a mantle of sand, possibly emplaced as a cap over earlier deposits (Sassaman et al. 2011:169). This practice of capping a habitation with sand or shell to mark the cessation of inhabitation or to instigate a transformation of use is not uncommon during the Mount Taylor period (see chapter 3). Indeed, as Randall (2013:214) argues, "if there is one theme that courses throughout the Mount Taylor period, it is the replacement of preexisting places of habitation with ceremonial platforms or burial mounds."

This is the striking factor about Locus A, and other Mount Taylor places: later deposits are often isomorphic with earlier ones, mapping onto them (Randall 2010, 2015). The structuring influence of ancient deposits goes some way toward explaining the location of Early Mount Taylor shell ridges at the Silver Glen Complex. That is, why were they not emplaced adjacent to the spring pool but halfway down the run? The shell ridge at Locus A was emplaced atop Mount Taylor–aged pits, which are in turn coextensive with earlier, pre–Mount Taylor pits. Thus, the activities of past inhabitants—several millennia removed—had a profound effect on later depositional practices. This same process may have transpired across Silver Glen Run, at 8LA4242. Whether these two ridges were coeval remains to be determined but seems likely given their disposition and location.

The influence of the past is not limited to Locus A or to the Mount Taylor period. Indeed, material evidence of ancestral activity seems to have been the primary structuring force dictating the projects undertaken across the Silver Glen landscape. The paired Mount Taylor shell ridges along Silver Glen run were avoided after 5700 cal BP, with the onset of the Thornhill Lake phase. In their stead, a small habitation was founded just to the southwest, at Locus B. At the same time, linear mounds were emplaced at the head and mouth of Silver Glen Run. Like the earlier shell ridges, these were paired and on opposite sides of the run, albeit not directly across from each other. In further contrast, these do not appear to have accumulated in a tell-like fashion through repeated or sustained habitation. Rather, as evidenced by 8MR123, they were first constructed as earthen mortuary facilities that were later capped with shell. The ephemeral nature of occupation at Locus B, punctuated by periods of abandonment, suggests that Thornhill Lake occupation of the Silver Glen Complex was intermittent and that mound building likely occurred during periodic gatherings attending mortuary rites. The spatial scale of Thornhill Lake mortuary rites is attested to by the inclusion of extralocal objects in some mortuary deposits. Thus, Silver Glen was transformed from a place of relatively sustained, or at least intensive, habitation of the living during the Early Mount Taylor phase to a repository for the dead during the Thornhill Lake phase. Earlier deposits (i.e., shell ridges) were apparently avoided but no doubt provided historical warrant for the construction of mortuaries.

Near the terminus of the Thornhill Lake phase, a shell cap was emplaced atop the Locus B habitations (Gilmore 2016:92). A period of abandonment followed until the bearers of Orange pottery arrived, encountering a landscape rife with residues of the past. Like earlier Mount Taylor residents, Orange period inhabitants of the St. Johns River valley largely abandoned earlier habitation sites and established residential spaces in new locales. We know little of their mortuary practices, but these apparently did not involve interment in mounds of shell or earth. Rather, the act of emplacing shell was largely restricted to four locales—best exemplified by the Silver Glen Complex—in the context of massive social gatherings that drew people from across peninsular Florida. These gatherings took place at preexisting Mount Taylor mortuary mounds and involved their renovation and expansion into massive, multilobed shell constructs. The cultural diversity and ritual significance of these gatherings is evidenced by the high frequency of nonlocal and elaborately decorated Orange pottery at mounds, relative to contemporary sites (Gilmore 2016:99). Thus, at these gathering places the past was not avoided, but rather "directly and persistently engaged . . . via repeated acts of excavation, circulation, and deposition" (Gilmore 2016:94).

There is a persistent theme of duality in the Archaic constructions at the Silver Glen Complex. As noted above, the Early Mount Taylor shell ridges were paired, as were the later Thornhill Lake mortuary mounds. Whether these reflect a dualistic social organization or the gathering of distinct groups of people is unclear. But these were later renovated into paired U- or C-shaped mounds by Orange folk, adding a layer of complexity and introducing a duality to the internal structure of the mounds themselves. For example, it is known from Wyman's description of 8LA1-E that the northern ridge was larger than the southern ridge. There is also evidence that it may have been constructed earlier, and it has a higher proportion of decorated Orange pottery (Gilmore 2016:99–100). This points to the possible coalescence of two distinct groups of people, perhaps descendant Mount Taylor people indigenous to the river valley and Orange pottery-bearing immigrants from the coast (Sassaman and Randall 2012).

Regardless, and in contrast to earlier Thornhill Lake phase mortuary gatherings that highlighted the status of individuals or groups, Orange period gatherings were integrative affairs. Indeed, the abundant historical resources at Silver Glen Springs—most conspicuously the paired Early Mount Taylor shell ridges and paired Thornhill Lake phase mortuary mounds—were likely an important factor in the siting of Orange gatherings, drawn upon to integrate diverse cultural groups and build communal bonds through the assertion of a shared history or ancestry (Gilmore 2016:216). The liminal qualities of Silver Glen Springs surely played a role as well, particularly when one considers the physiographic diversity in the immediate surroundings. That is, the spring is bordered by dry uplands and feeds into one of the largest water bodies in the state, Lake George. At Lake George, the flow of the river frequently reverses direction as ocean tides push up the river. This brings with it a commingling of fresh river water and saline sea water. Thus, Silver Glen gathers not only people and their attendant artifacts but land both high and low, water dark and clear, fresh and saline.

Historical resources were likewise a significant factor motivating pit excavation at Locus B (Gilmore 2016:112–117). Excavated atop an existing Thornhill Lake phase shell node, these early pits encountered buried residues of the past. Over the course of several centuries, as pits were excavated across Locus B, they began to intercept not only the Thornhill Lake shell nodes but fill from pits excavated decades and centuries earlier. As at Locus A, "as soon as the first pit was excavated and filled . . . it would have exerted a structuring influence on all subsequent digging in that location" (Gilmore 2016:113). Over time the exposure of ancient residues may have become an anticipated result of pit digging. Likewise, pit fill became increasingly complex, combining different species of shellfish in varying conditions (whole/crushed, burned/unburned) in potentially meaningful ways. Gilmore (2016:112–113) argues that these were, in effect, materialized historical narratives; evidence of past feasts and gatherings interred for the benefit of future inhabitants.

After ca. 3500 cal BP, shell mounding appears to have ceased at both Silver Glen Springs and the mouth of Silver Glen Run. The excavation of large pits at Locus B was also discontinued by this time, and Orange pottery was no longer in use (Gilmore 2016:217). Early St. Johns period (i.e., St. Johns I) activities at the site apparently involved small-scale habitation. St. Johns plain pottery is prevalent, but dense midden deposits are restricted to the downslope portion of Locus C. Further, only a handful of the radiocarbon assays from the Silver Glen Complex fall in this interval, suggesting that occupation may have been ephemeral or intermittent. Regardless, Silver Glen once again became an appropriate place for the interment of the dead during the St. Johns I period, as evidenced by the sand mortuary mound southeast of Locus C.

The causal factors at play in these transitions are not altogether clear. There is some indication of increased precipitation and/or sea level at this time, but the evidence is contradictory (e.g., Filley et al. 2001; van Soelen et al. 2012). Within the Silver Glen Complex, it is striking that some St. Johns I deposits contain shells that appear *Viviparus*-like but are markedly more elongated than the typically globular forms (Randall et al. 2011:204). Whether this is a result of shell plasticity in the face of local changes to hydric habitats (e.g., hydroperiod, flow velocity, water chemistry) is unclear. Alternatively, these may be a genetically distinct subpopulation of *Viviparus* with morphological changes resulting from genetic drift, or they may not be *Viviparus* at all, but a distinct species of mollusk. Regardless, additional examples and analysis are needed to confirm the association with St. Johns I deposits and to untangle the roots of these unique shells.

Morphological changes in shellfish populations may point to an ecological explanation for the cessation of shell mounding and the breakdown of extraregional gathering. However, Gilmore (2016:218) has suggested that the roughly coincident ascendance of Poverty Point, in northeast Louisiana, as a gathering place may have disrupted the networks of interaction centered on Silver Glen Springs. Beginning at around 3500 cal BP, Poverty Point was the nexus of a pan-regional sphere of influence that involved the importation of raw materials and finished goods from distant locales including the Great Lakes, the Midwest, the Gulf Coast, and the Appalachians (Gibson 2001; Kidder 2002, 2010; Ortmann and Kidder 2013; Spivey et al. 2015). The presence of St. Johns pottery at Poverty Point implicates northeast Florida denizens in this exchange (Hays and Weinstein 2004), so it is possible that the gatherings taking place at Silver Glen were redirected to Louisiana as people became incorporated into this larger network. Poverty Point appears to have been abandoned by 3100 cal BP. Over the next 500 years, interaction and exchange networks throughout the eastern United States would decline.

Later St. Johns II period deposits at Silver Glen Springs involved the establishment of a circular village and special-use locales. It is possible that the shell-free deposits at Locus D include votive offerings in the form

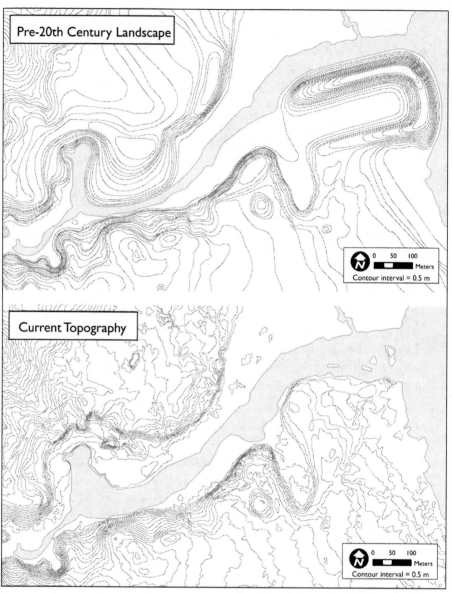

Figure 4.7. Reconstructed, pre-mining topography (*top*) and current topography (*bottom*) of the Silver Glen Complex. Reconstructed topography by Asa Randall (2014b).

of check-stamped St. Johns pottery interred in pits. Locus D is located on a ridge nose directly south of the spring pool and would have faced the opening of the shell amphitheater there. That the placement of the Locus C village was predicated on the location of the spring also seems likely. It lies on a high promontory overlooking the spring pool, but if proximity to the spring at elevation were the primary motivation for the placement of the village, it surely would have been constructed atop the shell mound encasing the spring pool. Rather, the village was placed opposite the spring, at the midpoint of a line connecting the spring and the sand mortuary mound to the southeast. This suggests that the location of the village had less to do with quotidian concerns than with proper disposition with respect to residues of the past.

Silver Glen Springs thus witnessed a succession of alterations and transformations in deposition and use (Figure 4.7). Often these transitions are marked by rapidly emplaced caps of sand or shell that obscure residues of the past, and/or by periods of abandonment. Through a coarse lens, Silver Glen was initially occupied as a habitation space before being converted to a mortuary facility. The mortuary mounds were later co-opted as historical warrants for extraregional gatherings and communal feasts. Following the breakdown of these interaction networks, a conical sand mortuary mound and votive deposits were emplaced, again absent evidence for sustained daily living. Silver Glen again became a locus for intensive inhabitation during the St. Johns II period with the construction of a circular village overlooking the spring. Taken in isolation, many of the pre-Columbian deposits at the Silver Glen Complex can be found at other springs in the region (O'Donoughue 2013). Examples of Paleoindian artifacts, Mount Taylor shell ridges, Thornhill Lake mortuaries, and villages and burial mounds of the St. Johns period are all located adjacent to springs. However, when looked at in its entirety, the Silver Glen Complex is unmatched in the region. It is the gathering of these disparate elements that offers the best evidence for the sacredness of Silver Glen.

Was Silver Glen Springs Sacred?

At the outset I questioned whether springs in the St. Johns River valley may have been considered sacred in the past. That is, whether springs are archetypal places that "invoke common responses in human beings—feelings of awe, power, majestic beauty, respect, enrichment among them"

(Taçon 1999:36–37) regardless of cultural background. Springs have many features in common that distinguish them from other water bodies in the region. The clarity of spring waters lends them certain optical qualities that enhance their strikingness but distort some features beneath the water. This has been extensively remarked upon with reference to Silver Springs—the largest spring in the region, and the subject of the following chapter—where the refraction of light exaggerates the depth of the water and casts iridescent hues over plants, rocks, and animals. Indeed, it is remarkable how many early American visitors refer to Silver Springs as a striking, transformative place. For example, John LeConte (1861:4) remarked that "on a bright day, the beholder seems to be looking down from some lofty airy point on a truly fairy scene in the immense basin beneath him." Or Major General George McCall (1974[1868]:150), who described his impression on first visiting the spring thusly:

> O! how my heart swelled with astonishment as we neared the centre of this grand basin of limpid water . . . in a moment all was still as death. The line of demarcation between the waters and the atmosphere was invisible. Heavens! What an impression filled my mind at that moment! Were not the canoe and its contents obviously suspended in mid-air like Mahomet's coffin?

Granted, it is inappropriate to assume that pre-Columbian visitors to a spring would be so struck by the experience. But one cannot escape the fact that, particularly during the late Pleistocene and early Holocene, Silver Glen Springs must have been an even more visually striking place than it is today, with water emanating from a cave and winding down a valley into the expansive basin of Lake George. This basin may have been an emergent wetland rife with aquatic flora and fauna, or a dry prairie punctuated with channels and sinkholes, each containing water of its own. Particularly if approached from the west, from the xeric scrub of the Marion Uplands, the scene would have unfolded in a panoramic vista.

The construction of shell mounds adjacent to springs added to this strikingness, or alterity, further highlighting the depth of the spring by accentuating the height of the surrounding terrain. Indeed, this may have been a desired outcome. I have argued elsewhere that springs are an unsuitable habitat for large populations of *Viviparus*, and thus the bulk of shell emplaced on their banks likely came from other water bodies

(O'Donoughue 2010). If this is so, then the motivation to gather, transport, and deposit shells from other locales may have been to enhance the visual impact of springs, and create a contrast between high and low. This contrast and diversity is evident in the various deposits that people emplaced along Silver Glen Run—the paired Early Mount Taylor shell ridges, paired Thornhill Lake phase mortuary mounds, the south-facing 8MR123 and west-facing 8LA1-E—again pointing to a coming together of distinct entities.

Votive offerings at springs may also be evidence that they were sacred or special places. Hafted bifaces and carved bone pins were recovered from 30–45 m deep inside the cave of Silver Glen Springs, dating primarily to the Paleoindian and Archaic periods (Dunbar 1990). Whether these are votive offerings is unclear, but it is difficult to imagine anything but purposeful placement, given their position on bare limestone deep within the cave. Later votive offerings, in the form of ornately decorated St. Johns pottery interred in pits, may also be present on the uplands overlooking Silver Glen (Anderson 2015). Dugout canoes have frequently been documented at springs in the region, perhaps purposefully sunken beneath their waters. However, this may be more a function of visibility than intent, as many canoes have also been recovered from non-spring locales (Wheeler et al. 2003).

But if springs writ large are potentially sacred by nature of their qualities, something else differentiates Silver Glen Springs. Perhaps more important than the physical parameters of the place is the 8,000-year history of landscape alteration and construction undertaken by pre-Columbian visitors to Silver Glen Springs. It was the spring's historical resources that exerted such a powerful draw to ancient Floridians and that they manipulated in the context of gatherings for mortuary rites and communal integration. This drawing on the past is not unusual, nor is the modification of such sacred places: "Thus we see a common pattern—human made sacred places modeled on a core set of natural places but embellished with unique artistry to reflect the cultural distinctiveness of given groups of people" (Taçon 1990:40).

Silver Glen Springs is steeped in history, and the entirety of the surrounding landscape is sedimented with the residues of past human presence. The land surrounding Silver Glen Springs was altered repeatedly over millennia in "punctuated moments of intensive occupation"

(Gilmore 2016:126) by people representing multiple cultural groups from a broad geographical expanse. It is the gathering, or entanglement, of so many disparate materials, objects, persons, and qualities—both natural and cultural—that makes Silver Glen unique, that made it sacred.

What is illustrated so well at Silver Glen Springs is the importance of history and sociality in the sanctification of place as social memory is materialized. Although he was from across the continent, Chief Seattle of the Duwamish tribe expressed this sentiment eloquently: "Every part of this land is sacred to my people. Every hillside, every valley, every plain and grove has been hallowed by some fond memory or some sad experience" (quoted in Turner 1989:192). Indeed, the material residues of the past endure and are confronted and accommodated by people as much as the "natural" features of the landscape. These are the medium through which people inhabit and make sense of the world, and not merely a static representation of the past (Barrett 1999, 2001).

Our contemporary engagement with springs is a case in point. We are drawn to these places in part because of the physicality of springs and their cool, clear water. But this physicality is in part the result of past human action—for example, as roads were built, shell mounds cleared, retention walls installed, and parks established. Take Weeki Wachee Spring, with its underwater theater and mermaid shows. Or Silver Springs, where state agencies have invested significant funds to remove artificial features and return it to a more "pristine" state. This is an ongoing, historical process.

Many are also drawn to springs for more intangible reasons, as the place of family gatherings, bellwethers of ecological vulnerability, and icons of an authentic Florida (e.g., Belleville 2011). They are the subject of personal recollections and public narratives. But springs are not merely backdrops that we endow with meaning and significance. It's not what people think, but the things they do—snorkeling in them, painting pictures of them, studying them, protesting their degradation, writing regulations about them—that generate meaning and significance. Springs are nodes in our contemporary social networks, just as they were in the past.

The transformative history of Silver Glen Springs did not end 500 years ago, and chapter 6 will pick up this thread again. But first I want to examine one of the material gatherings manifested at Silver Glen Springs in more detail. Stone used in the manufacture of lithic tools is not found in the St. Johns River valley. Wherever it is recovered in the region, it points to an origin at a place far removed. In the following chapter I turn my attention west, to the gargantuan Silver Springs and the heartland of lithic quarries in Florida. I do so to explore the ways that springs are entangled across the landscape through the movement of humans and stone.

5

SPRINGS ON THE MOVE

In front, just under my feet, was the inchanting [sic] and amazing crystal fountain, which incessantly threw up, from dark, rocky caverns below, tons of water every minute, forming a basin, capacious enough for large shallops to ride in, and a creek of four or five feet depth of water, and near twenty yards over, which meanders six miles through green meadows, pouring its limpid waters into the great Lake George, where they seem to remain pure and unmixed. About twenty yards from the upper edge of the bason [sic], and directly opposite to the mouth or outlet of the creek, is a continual and amazing ebullition, where the waters are thrown up in such abundance and amazing force, as to jet and swell up two or three feet above the common surface: white sand and small particles of shells are thrown up with the waters, near to the top, when they diverge from the centre, subside with the expanding flood, and gently sink again, forming a large rim or funnel round about the aperture or mouth of the fountain, which is a vast perforation through a bed of rocks, the ragged points of which are projected out on every side. Thus far I know to be matter of real fact, and I have related it as near as I could conceive or express myself. But there are yet remaining scenes inexpressibly admirable and pleasing.

WILLIAM BARTRAM, 1774 (1996:149–150)

Springs are defined by motion. As described so poetically by Bartram, many springs arise from the limestone with such force as to roil the surface of cerulean pools. But water's journey began long before this, coursing through subterranean veins from recharge areas many miles distant, where it fell to the surface as rain, working its way down through dry, sandy hills to enter the aquifer below. After emerging from its hidden voyage, water continues, flowing from pools into sometimes lengthy spring runs. And from these runs into lakes and rivers, and from there to the ocean, as at Jody's spring. Springs appear to us as discrete points on the landscape. But they are connected to places near and far by the motion of water both on and beneath the surface.

The places that people establish at springs are likewise defined by motion. Indeed, all places can be thought of as loci where disparate elements are brought together. Places gather a variety of material entities, things, to them. But, as the philosopher Edward Casey (1996:24) wrote, "places also gather experiences and histories, even language and thoughts. Think only of what it means to go back to a place you know, finding it full of memories and expectations, old things and new things, the familiar and the strange, and much more besides." The power of place arises from this gathering together of material and immaterial things that each bring their own temporalities and index their places of origin. This is particularly true of places like Silver Glen Springs, described in the previous chapter. The import of Silver Glen was derived from the aggregating of people and things, both contemporary and historical. Zack Gilmore has convincingly argued that the movement of pottery to Silver Glen Springs in the context of extraregional gatherings, feasting, and mound building contributed to social integration and "the development and maintenance of a regional-scale macrocommunity based on mound-centered interactions" (2016:207).

But pots were not the only things moved into Silver Glen Springs. Massive quantities of shell were mobilized and deposited in pits and mounds adjacent to Silver Glen Springs and its run. Several characteristics of spring water—notably low dissolved oxygen and suspended solids—suggest that shellfish were procured elsewhere and transferred to spring-side mounds. Indeed, shell-bearing deposits are uncommon at all but the largest springs in the St. Johns River valley (O'Donoughue 2010, 2013).

Likewise, the archaeological deposits adjacent to Silver Glen Springs contain an appreciable quantity of lithic debitage and flaked-stone tools. The St. Johns River valley itself is stone poor, and outcroppings of material suitable for the manufacture of tools (i.e., chert) are absent. Thus, whatever lithic artifacts are recovered from archaeological sites in the St. Johns River valley were transported from elsewhere at some point in their history. Chert source areas are located primarily in northwestern peninsular Florida and the panhandle in several discrete deposits (Austin 1997; Endonino 2007; Upchurch et al. 1982). Not coincidentally, these are roughly coextensive with areas of well-developed karst in the state (see chapter 2), and thus with the densest concentration of springs.

The title of this chapter borrows from an article by Barbara Bender (2001) in which she attempts to reconcile diverging anthropological treatments of human movement through landscapes. In her view, anthropologists typically focus either on sociopolitical and historical factors structuring movement or on personal engagement and the affective qualities of place. Lithic materials in the St. Johns River valley were transported from source areas more than 70 km distant. This entailed the movement of people across long distances, and likely through unfamiliar terrains. Discussing the relationship between familiar and unfamiliar places, Bender (2001:85) wrote:

> The rooted, familiar place is never only that, but always surrounded and affected by unfamiliar spaces and attenuated relationships. Moreover, the rooted, familiar places are not necessarily "in place," they may themselves be on the move. Thus some of the nomadic communities in Mongolia create an ego-centred world in which the "centre" moves and the axis mundi—the joining of earth to sky—is recreated through the smoke that rises from the campfire at each resting point along the way.

If being "at home" or "in place" implies a relationship with the unfamiliar or unknown, then being on the move always involves a stance toward, or familiarity, with place. The movement of people involves the movement of things too, and relationships with place are created, in part, by the material practices that people effect there.

Below, I review the results of recent archaeological investigations at Silver Springs, the largest spring in Florida. Silver Springs is located proximate to lithic source areas and is the westernmost spring feeding the St. Johns River. I argue that Silver Springs, and others like it, facilitated the movement of lithic materials to Silver Glen Springs and the greater St. Johns River valley. At the same time the movement of stone effectively entangled people and springs across the peninsula of Florida, contributing to the social integration of gatherings at places like Silver Glen.

SILVER SPRINGS

Approximately 40 km west of Silver Glen Springs, across the upland scrub and wet prairies of the Ocala National Forest, is the famous Silver Springs. Silver Springs is the largest spring in Florida, spilling nearly 500 million gallons of water per day (735 ft^3/s) from the Floridan Aquifer (Munch et al. 2006; Scott et al. 2004). Silver Springs is not a single spring but a group of 30 springs of varying size arrayed along a 1-km-long linear expanse that forms the headwaters of the Silver River (Figure 5.1; see Butt et al. 2006). The main spring, Mammoth Spring, lies at the western edge of this expanse, in a steep-walled pool that measures some 90 m across and 10 m deep (Scott et al. 2004:243–246). Water issues from a 42-m-wide oblong vent in the northeast portion of the pool and accounts for approximately 45 percent of the total discharge of Silver Springs. The Silver River flows for 8 km through cypress swamp to the Ocklawaha River, and from there into the St. Johns River north of Lake George. If springs are gems of the Florida landscape, then Silver Springs is surely the crown jewel.

Silver Springs has been an important destination for tourism and industry since the nineteenth century and is renowned for glass-bottom boat rides over cool, clear waters. Attractions at Silver Springs have included hotels, railway stations, the Ross Allen Reptile Institute and other zoological exhibits, concerts, jungle cruises, and fireworks shows. But the draw of Silver Springs has not been limited to the recent past. Several pre-Columbian archaeological sites have been recorded proximate to Silver Springs (Figure 5.2). Within Mammoth Spring, the Silver Springs site (8MR59) encompasses historic and pre-Columbian artifacts found on the floor and in the main cavern of the spring. This includes a fragment of a Paleoindian-aged Suwannee point and remains of mastodon and mammoth (Neill 1964). Also in the spring run is a canoe (8MR3173) that has been radiocarbon-dated to 920–700 cal B.P. (Wheeler 2001). A pre-Columbian burial mound near Silver Springs, recorded as site 8MR33, was excavated by C. B. Moore in the late nineteenth century (1895:521–525). According to Moore, the mound was located approximately 1.5 km east of the main spring and measured 15 m in diameter and over 1 m high. It consisted of unstratified yellow sand and contained the remains of multiple individuals, numerous pieces of pottery, and lithic debris, as well as items of mica, copper, and shell. The mound was completely excavated by Moore, and so its age and precise location are unknown. A second pre-Columbian burial mound (8MR1081) is also recorded near Silver Springs, but its age and exact location are likewise unknown.

Along the northern shore of the Silver River lie the Franklin 15 (8MR1082) and Lost Arrow (8MR3519) sites. These are expansive, but low-density, lithic and ceramic scatters (Belcourt et al. 2009; Southeastern Archaeological Research 2008). Denser archeological deposits have been recorded along the southern shore. The Paradise Park site (8MR92)

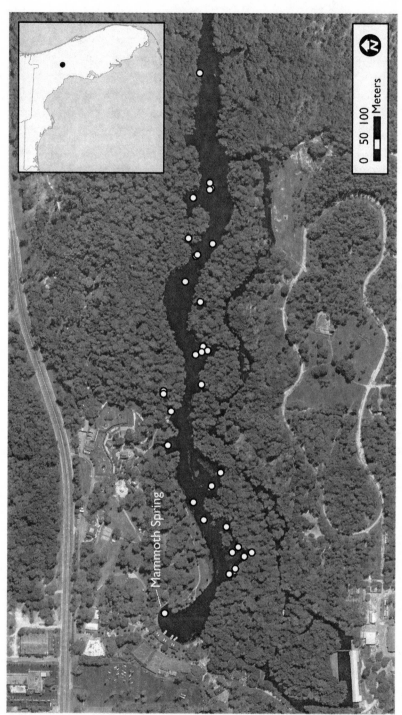

Figure 5.1. Aerial photograph of Silver Springs, highlighting the location of spring vents.

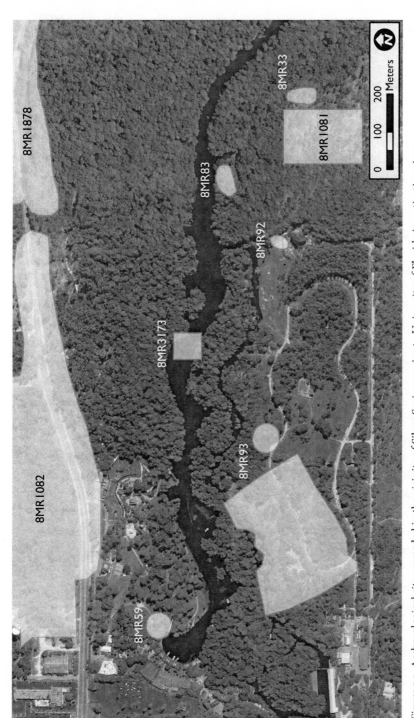

Figure 5.2. Archaeological sites recorded in the vicinity of Silver Springs, prior to University of Florida investigations in 2013.

contains Paleoindian-aged materials beneath more recent deposits. These materials were exposed along the edge of a borrow pit, approximately 150 m long, excavated into an aeolian dune. The site was first investigated in the mid-twentieth century by Neill (1958), who excavated 11 test units into the side of the borrow pit. He recovered fluted and unfluted lanceolate points and lithic debitage nearly 2.5 m below the surface. Two stratigraphic units were recorded: an upper layer of homogeneous sand and a lower layer of sand with clay laminations or lamellae. This site is one of only two known in Florida with fluted points in stratified context.

Hemmings (1975) later revisited the Paradise Park site, assessing its potential for further excavation. He confirmed the stratigraphy noted by Neill but reported fewer artifacts and no organic preservation. More recently, the site has been visited by Faught (2009) and Dunbar and Doran (2010). In 2003 Faught constructed a topographic map of the site and excavated three trenches into the wall of the pit. Although the stratigraphy of the site was again recapitulated, few artifacts were recovered and diagnostic Paleoindian strata could not be identified. Analysis of sediment samples confirmed that the deposit was a relict dune. Dunbar and Doran extracted two vibracores for analysis and OSL dating, but these have not been analyzed. Given that none of the subsequent visits have recovered diagnostic Paleoindian artifacts, Dunbar and Doran (2010:14) speculated that this component of the site may have been completely excavated by Neill or destroyed by mining.

Site 8MR83 was recorded as a possible midden, just east of Paradise Park, adjacent to a dredged pool off of Silver Springs run (Thompson 1964). Recovered artifacts include historic ceramics, aboriginal ceramics, and lithic artifacts in a dark sandy loam. Site 8MR93, initially visited by Griffin and Bullen in 1952, was recorded as diffuse "camping debris" revealed in several garbage disposal ditches. The boundaries of the site were later expanded after a survey conducted by SouthArc in 2002 (Dickinson and Wayne 2002). This survey intercepted a high density of aboriginal artifacts—primarily lithic debris and tools with some ceramics—and further work was recommended to determine the potential significance of the site.

The documented archaeological sites and historical resources indicate a virtually continuous occupation of Silver Springs from the late Pleistocene to the present. It was in this context that the University of Florida, Laboratory of Southeastern Archaeology (LSA), conducted a Cultural Resources

Assessment Survey of an area within Silver Springs Park. This was done in advance of the transfer of park management to the Florida Department of Environmental Protection and the creation of Silver Springs State Park. Although the land was owned by the State of Florida, the park had previously been managed by a variety of private organizations, most recently Palace Entertainment, which negotiated a buyout of its lease in 2013. The reconnaissance survey undertaken by the LSA encompassed an area of approximately 104 acres immediately to the east of the main pool of Silver Springs. The project area was divided into northern (16.5 acres) and southern (87.5 acres) tracts separated by the Silver River (Figure 5.3) and included all or part of four archaeological sites: the Franklin 15 (8MR1082) site in the northern tract, and sites 8MR83, 8MR92, and 8MR93 in the southern tract.

Field operations entailed 25-m-interval systematic shovel testing across the project area. A total of 469 shovel tests were excavated, 85 in the smaller northern parcel and 384 in the southern parcel, 86.5 percent of which were positive (n = 406). The northern parcel has been heavily disturbed by development of the park as a recreational facility. However, in many places the disturbed sediments were shallow with intact sediments below. Modern disturbance in the southern parcel was sparse and discontinuous. Most areas exhibited intact soil profiles beneath the upper 30 cm. Artifacts were found throughout the southern parcel but were most densely concentrated in the northwestern portion of the parcel. Along north–south transects, artifacts were most numerous near the river and decreased in frequency away from the river, to the south.

The amount of material recovered during the survey varied considerably, with some shovel tests containing only a single artifact and others containing several hundred. Artifact density was as high as 4,200 artifacts per m³. By far the most frequently recovered class of artifact was lithic debitage and tools (n = 10,765). Several diagnostic bifaces were recovered, primarily Florida Archaic Stemmed (n = 17), but also individual specimens of the earlier Kirk and Bolen types and later Hernando and Pinellas types. Pre-Columbian pottery was infrequently recovered and was primarily sand-tempered and undecorated, although several check stamped sherds are also present in the inventory. Other types recovered include Orange plain, Pasco plain, and St. Johns plain and stamped. Vertebrate faunal remains were found in only trace amounts.

The abundance of lithic material, preponderance of Florida Archaic

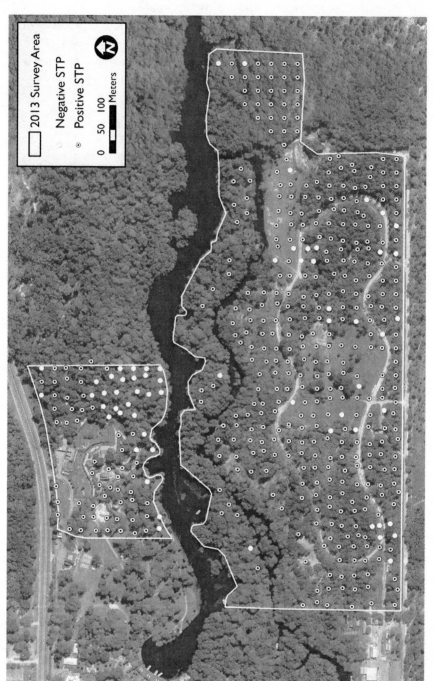

Figure 5.3. Results of the archeological survey at Silver Springs.

Stemmed hafted bifaces, and relative paucity of pottery indicate that the bulk of activity at Silver Springs took place during the Archaic Mount Taylor period. The presence of pottery indicates later visitation to Silver Springs, but the small amount recovered suggests that this activity was intermittent or ephemeral. Likewise, no indication of intensive habitation (i.e., midden deposits) was observed. Notwithstanding the previously recorded sand burial mounds, neither of which could be relocated, mounded deposits of shell or sand were absent as well. Indeed, deposits of freshwater shell of any kind—midden, mound, pit, or otherwise—were lacking, and only a small amount of freshwater shell was documented. Indeed, we recovered nearly eight times more marine shell than freshwater shell (by weight), at a site some 70 km from the Gulf Coast and 100 km from the Atlantic.

The dearth of pottery, vertebrate fauna, and shell in the inventory from Silver Springs is striking. The absence of intensive habitation remains is likewise remarkable, and unique to Silver Springs amongst the largest springs in the region. These patterns could be a consequence of sampling error, but this seems unlikely given that more than 100 acres were surveyed on both sides of the river. If the lack of shell is explicable by the constraints posed by clear, hypoxic spring water detailed elsewhere (O'Donoughue 2010), it is nevertheless the case that all of the other first-magnitude springs, and most of the second-magnitude springs, in the nearby middle St. Johns River valley have substantial shell deposits adjacent to them (O'Donoughue 2013). Further, numerous shell-bearing sites have been documented along the Ocklawaha and Silver rivers, with the closest less than 2 km downstream of Silver Springs (sites 8MR53 and 8MR3266). It seems likely, then, that the absence of shell proximate to Silver Springs is not coincidental but reflective of conscious decisions made in the past with regard to the activities taking place at Silver Springs.

The abundance of lithic artifacts at Silver Springs is even more striking than the lack of other materials. This is apparent when compared to the large springs in the middle St. Johns River valley. Table 5.1 summarizes the results of archaeological survey at Alexander (Willis 1995), DeLeon (Denson et al. 1995), Salt (Dickinson and Wayne 1994), and Silver Glen (Randall et al. 2011) springs and test excavations at Volusia Blue Spring (Sassaman 2003a). Sample volume of surveys was estimated from the number and size of shovel tests excavated and assumes a mean depth of 1 m. At Volusia Blue the sample volume was determined from the number, size, and maximum excavated depth of test units. This estimate was used to calculate the density of lithic artifacts and pottery. Blue Spring is notable for its dense pottery assemblage and relative lack of lithic artifacts. However, these results reflect the testing strategy, which focused primarily on Orange period deposits. The remaining results summarized derive from reconnaissance surveys of relatively broad areas surrounding springs that encountered archaeological deposits of multiple ages. A notable pattern is the high density of lithic artifacts and low density of pottery at Silver Springs. Although the specific densities calculated are likely skewed by the estimated sample volume, differences of this magnitude are unlikely to be attributable to calculation error alone. This supposition is confirmed by the ratio of lithic artifacts to pottery, which disregards excavated volume and thereby bypasses that source of error. With this metric as well, Silver Springs has a considerably greater proportion of lithic artifacts in the assemblage, relative to the other springs.

Taken together, the available evidence indicates that far different activities were taking place at Silver Springs than at springs in the St. Johns River valley proper. These activities were focused on the reduction of lithic materials in the absence of sustained habitation. No radiocarbon dates are available from these deposits, but the material inventory suggests that these activities likely occurred during the Mount Taylor period. As noted in the previous chapter, there is a notable decline in the frequency of lithic artifacts during the succeeding Orange and St. Johns periods, so this is perhaps not unexpected. But, if this is so, then the lack of post-Archaic deposition at Silver Springs is confounding and requires explanation. Alternatively, if these lithic reduction activities are not restricted to the pre-ceramic Archaic but reflect activities taking place in later periods as well, then it is equally confounding that Orange and St. Johns activities would not include intensive deposition of some sort, as they do at other springs in the region.

Regardless of the timing of these activities, it is clear that the primary activity taking place at Silver Springs was the mobilization and reduction of lithic raw materials. This can perhaps be explained by the geographical position of Silver Springs, which is located on the western frontier of the St. Johns River valley, proximate to lithic source areas. Given the density of lithic materials recovered and the connection of Silver Springs to the St. Johns River valley—through the Silver and Ocklawaha rivers—a working hypothesis is that lithic materials at sites along the St. Johns River moved

Table 5.1. Frequency of lithic artifacts at selected archaeological sites adjacent to springs in the St. Johns River valley

Spring Name/Site Number	Lithic artifacts (n)	Pottery (n)	Estimated volume (m³)	Lithic density (artifacts/m³)	Pottery density (artifacts/m³)	Lithic : pottery ratio
Alexander Spring (8LA71)	41	100	4.3	9.6	23.5	.41
Blue Spring (8VO43)	46	4,047	21.0	2.2	192.7	.01
DeLeon Spring (8VO30)	78	82	11.7	6.7	7.0	.95
Salt Springs (8MR2322)	2,025	1,874	137.3	14.7	13.6	1.08
Silver Glen Springs (8MR123)	1,395	762	58.0	24.1	13.1	1.83
Silver Springs (8MR93)	10,776	134	117.3	91.9	1.1	80.42

Note: Sample volumes and artifact density are approximate.
Sources: Denson et al. 1995; Dickinson and Wayne 1994; Randall et al. 2011; Sassaman 2003a; Willis 1995.

through Silver Springs in some fashion. This movement may have been along travel routes from source areas to the St. Johns River valley, as residents acquired lithic raw material directly or as pilgrims brought lithics to the valley in the context of regional aggregation. Alternatively, lithic material may have been acquired through exchange with people at Silver Springs.

This hypothesis, that Silver Springs was a gateway for transporting stone into the St. Johns River valley, was evaluated by comparing lithic assemblages at Silver Springs to sites along the St. Johns River. Data sets comparable to Silver Springs are available for Mount Taylor–aged deposits at Silver Glen Springs (8MR123 [Randall et al. 2011]), the Lake Monroe Outlet Midden (8VO53 [Endonino 2007]), and the Thornhill Lake Complex (8VO58–60 [Endonino 2010]). A combination of debitage analysis, lithic provenance determinations, and least-cost analysis was used to evaluate whether lithics at these sites were acquired by way of Silver Springs, either through direct acquisition or exchange.

Debitage analysis allows inference of the reduction activities taking place at Silver Springs and other locales. If stone was moved from Silver Springs to sites in the St. Johns River valley, then lithic reduction activities occurring at Silver Springs should reflect early-stage reduction and blank preparation. Debitage recovered from sites downstream should be indicative of later-stage tool manufacturing and retouch. Likewise, lithic provenance studies should indicate that assemblages at sites in the St. Johns River valley proper exhibit a similar distribution of source areas as the assemblage at Silver Springs.

An alternative hypothesis is that the lithic materials recovered from each site are dominated by the nearest source area rather than reflecting the redistribution of raw materials from a gateway. However, it is insufficient to use "as the crow flies" distance when determining the most proximate lithic source. Rather, least-cost analysis, taking into account transportation costs and impediments to movement, provides a better indication of the nearest lithic source area. Further, least-cost analysis can provide an indication of the optimal routes from lithic source areas to the St. Johns River valley. If these routes pass through Silver Springs, it would provide further support, and some explanation, for the role of Silver Springs as a gateway.

In the following I begin with the least-cost analysis to establish a baseline for the relative difficulty of transporting lithic materials from each source area to each of the four target sites and to determine the routes by which this transport might have taken place. After this the provenance determinations for lithic debitage and tools are presented and the patterns discussed. Finally, the results of debitage analysis are used to further evaluate the gateway hypothesis.

Least-Cost Paths

As noted above, sources of chert are restricted to northwestern peninsular Florida and the panhandle. Chert is a microcrystalline quartz that typically forms as a replacement mineral. In Florida, chert is found in Lower Oligocene through Middle Eocene carbonates (Scott 2011; Upchurch et al. 1982). The weathering of clay-rich Miocene sediments overlying these carbonates introduces large amounts of silica, dissolved in the groundwater. Under the right geochemical conditions, this silica replaces the calcium carbonate in limestone, forming beds or nodules of chert. Relatively few geologic formations in Florida contain chert deposits that would have been available for human exploitation. Those that do are the Ocala Limestone, Suwannee Limestone, St. Marks Formation, and the Arcadia (Tampa Member) and Peace River formations of the Hawthorn Group (Austin 1997; Endonino 2007; Scott 2001; Upchurch et al. 1982:23).

Nineteen "quarry clusters" have been defined in Florida, extending north in an arc from Tampa Bay, along the Gulf Coast, and into the panhandle. A quarry cluster is defined as "an area known to contain numerous exposures of chert, some of which must have been used by early man, and in which the chert is expected to be relatively uniform in fabric, composition, and fossil content" (Upchurch et al. 1982:9). These deposits are distinctive enough that samples can be discriminated by microscopic examination. The quarry clusters of Florida were originally defined by Upchurch and colleagues (1982), and later revised by Austin (1997) and Endonino (2007). The analysis presented below follows the quarry cluster delineation of Endonino (2007).

Lithic materials from the most-distant quarry clusters have not been documented in the assemblages under consideration here and so are excluded from further discussion. The remaining nine lithic source areas are (from north to south) the Santa Fe, Gainesville, Ocala, Lake Panasoffkee (East and West), Brooksville, Upper Withlacoochee, Caladesi, Hillsborough River, and Peace River quarry clusters. In the following, Lake

Panasoffkee East and Lake Panasoffkee West are treated as a single quarry cluster, because of their proximity and to simplify the analysis.

To explore the hypothesis that lithic materials moved through Silver Springs, it is first necessary to derive an accurate understanding of the proximity to, and cost of, transporting lithic materials into the St. Johns River valley. Although a Euclidean, or straight-line, measure of distance provides one indication of proximity and cost, it fails to consider several mediating factors, such as mode of transportation and terrain heterogeneity (e.g., boundaries, elevation, and land cover). A more realistic model of proximity and travel cost can be derived through least-cost analysis.

Least-cost analysis is a spatial analytical technique for determining optimal travel routes over a terrain (Bell and Lock 2000; Connoly and Lake 2006; Howey 2007; White and Surface-Evans 2012). Typically this is done within a geographic information system (GIS) using a variety of environmental inputs. Calculation of least-cost paths is essentially a three-step process. The first step is to develop or define a *cost of passage* or *friction surface* that approximates the cost of traveling across a terrain. This is usually a raster surface with each cell value representing the cost of traveling across that cell. The second step uses this friction surface to derive a *cost surface* that models the cumulative cost of traveling outward from an origin point. The final step is to trace the path of least cost from a destination or destinations back to the origin point. Accuracy of the final model depends on both the user-defined input (the friction surface) and the algorithms used to derive the cost surface and cost paths.

Least-cost analysis was conducted to examine the optimal routes between the source areas of lithic raw materials and four archaeological sites for which lithic provenance data are available. This was done to determine the proximity of the source areas to the sites (i.e., which source area is least costly?) and to determine the optimal route for moving lithic materials into the St. Johns River valley.

A friction surface was developed for peninsular Florida encompassing the St. Johns River valley and lithic source areas. Two variables were incorporated into the friction surface: slope and surface water. Primary digital data sets included a 15-m-resolution digital elevation model (DEM) and shapefiles containing surface water features digitized from USGS 7.5-minute topographic quadrangles.[1]

In this analysis it is assumed that travel by canoe was a more likely mode of transport than walking, given the density of vegetation across much of peninsular Florida and the potentially prohibitive weight of the lithic materials. Therefore, the friction surface was biased toward water travel. The surface water shapefile was processed to remove modern features (e.g., canals, retention ponds). Seasonal swamps and wetlands were then removed from the data set, as were smaller water bodies (ephemeral streams and lakes smaller than .25 km^2), since these were thought to be impediments to travel or not present during the middle Holocene. However, smaller water bodies named in the Geographic Names Information System were retained. The resulting hydrological shapefiles were then merged and converted to a raster with 15-m resolution. All cells containing surface water were assigned an arbitrary travel cost of 1.

The cost of terrestrial travel was based on the slope of the terrain. Slope was derived by geoprocessing the DEM and ranged from 0 to 79 degrees. I then used an equation proposed by Bell and Lock (2000) to model the relative cost of traversing terrains of different slopes. They demonstrate that the relative cost (C) can be calculated as the ratio of the tangent of the slope angle (s) to the tangent of 1 degree of slope:

$$C = \tan s \,/\, \tan 1$$

This results in a nonlinear relationship where steeper slopes become exponentially more difficult to travel. Applying this equation to the slope raster yielded values ranging 0–200.69. I scaled these values to set the cost of traveling across flat land at 5. This terrestrial friction surface was then combined with the hydrological friction surface to yield travel costs ranging 1–205.69 across the peninsula. Under this friction surface, the cost of traveling across one 15-m cell of water was 20 percent of the cost of traveling the same distance across flat land. The friction surface was then used to generate four cost surfaces, one originating at each of the four archaeological sites. Cost paths were then traced from each of the nine quarry clusters to the archaeological sites, resulting in 36 least-cost paths.

The least-cost analysis indicates that, in terms of cost-distance, the Ocala and Lake Panasoffkee quarry clusters are closest to Silver Springs (Figure 5.4). Least-cost paths for Silver Springs show that materials from quarry clusters to the north or south would likely be transported to Silver Springs by way of the Ocklawaha River. Southern quarry cluster materials (i.e., Lake Panasoffkee, Brooksville, Upper Withlacoochee, Caladesi, Hillsborough River, and Peace River) enter near the headwaters of the Ocklawaha River and travel downstream to the confluence with the Silver

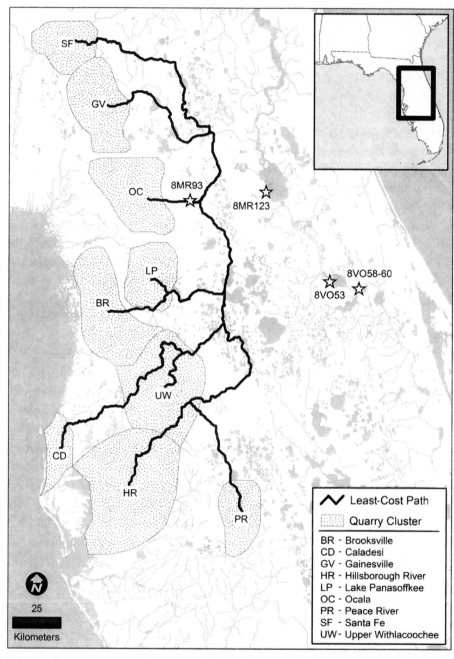

Figure 5.4. Least-cost pathways from lithic quarry clusters to Silver Springs (8MR93).

River. Northern quarry cluster materials (i.e., Santa Fe and Gainesville) enter the Ocklawaha River at Orange Springs before moving upstream to the Silver River. Only Ocala quarry cluster materials are likely to have been transported primarily over land, due to their proximity.

Likewise, least-cost paths to Silver Glen Springs primarily follow the Ocklawaha River, entering the St. Johns River north of Lake George and proceeding south from there (Figure 5.5). Again, Ocala and Lake Panasoffkee materials would be the least costly to transport. These least-cost paths also lend support to the hypothesis that Silver Springs was a gateway into the St. Johns River valley, as routes from six of nine quarry clusters pass through or near Silver Springs. Materials from the northernmost quarry clusters likely entered the Ocklawaha River downstream of Silver Springs, at Orange Springs, whereas Peace River materials would have taken an easterly route.

Least-cost paths to the Lake Monroe Outlet Midden and Thornhill Lake Complex are identical (Figure 5.6) and indicate that Lake Panasoffkee and Upper Withlacoochee quarry cluster materials would be least costly. Further, all materials except those originating in the Ocala quarry cluster would bypass Silver Springs on their optimal routes to these sites.

The least-cost analysis indicates which quarry clusters are the least costly source areas for the transport of lithic materials to the St. Johns River valley, and the likely transport paths those materials would have taken. This analysis suggests that if Silver Springs was a gateway, it was not so because of optimal travel routes. Only least-cost paths to Silver Glen Springs pass through Silver Springs for most quarry clusters. Least-cost paths to Lake Monroe Outlet Midden and Thornhill Lake largely bypass Silver Springs. Thus, if other lines of evidence support the hypothesis that Silver Springs was a gateway, this was not a result of optimizing transport costs.

The analysis also yields some predictions that, if confirmed by provenance data, would lend support to the least-cost model. Silver Springs and Silver Glen Springs should be dominated by Ocala and Lake Panasoffkee materials, whereas the Thornhill Lake Complex and Lake Monroe Outlet Midden should be dominated by Lake Panasoffkee and Upper Withlacoochee materials. Also, there should be a fall-off curve between Silver and Silver Glen springs for those materials originating from quarry clusters that would pass through Silver Springs on their way to Silver Glen

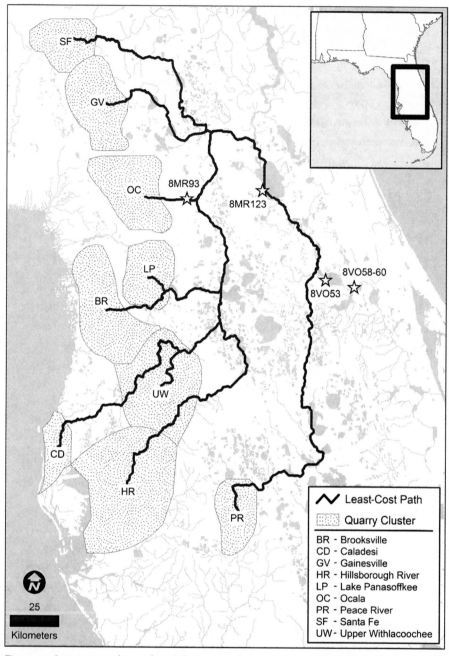

Figure 5.5. Least-cost pathways from lithic quarry clusters to Silver Glen Springs (8MR123).

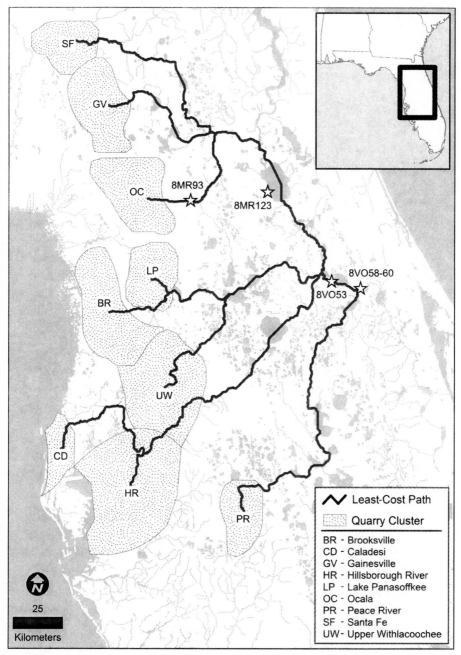

Figure 5.6. Least-cost pathways from lithic quarry clusters to the Lake Monroe Outlet Midden (8VO53) and the Thornhill Lake Complex (8VO58–60).

(Ocala, Lake Panasoffkee, Brooksville, Upper Withlacoochee, Caladesi, and Hillsborough River).

Lithic Provenance Determination

Lithic provenance determination was accomplished using techniques developed by Upchurch and colleagues (1982). The "quarry cluster" method uses a suite of visual characteristics, including rock fabric, fossil content, and secondary inclusions (crystal-lined voids, sand, porosity, etc.) to discriminate between materials from different chert-bearing geological formations (Upchurch et al. 1982). Provenance determination was conducted by Jon Endonino at Eastern Kentucky University using a stereoscopic microscope with magnification of .7–40×. Fossil content was the principal criterion for determining provenance, but rock fabric and secondary inclusions were also considered. For a detailed discussion of the microfossils, rock fabric, and secondary inclusions diagnostic of the various quarry clusters, see Upchurch and colleagues (1982), Austin (1997), Austin and Estabrook (2000), and Endonino (2007).

At Silver Springs, provenance was determined for 1,146 pieces of debitage. This represents approximately 10 percent of the total assemblage (n = 10,674) of debitage. Provenance was also determined for all tools recovered (n = 91). Similar sample sizes are available from Silver Glen Springs (n = 1,481 debitage, 107 tools), and Lake Monroe Outlet Midden (n = 1,270 debitage, 302 tools), whereas the Thornhill Complex sample is slightly smaller (n = 418 debitage, 29 tools).

The results of provenance analysis are presented in Tables 5.2 through 5.5, and Figure 5.7. Each site is dominated by one or two quarry clusters, with a range of others found in minor amounts. The assemblages at both Silver Springs and Silver Glen Springs are composed primarily of Ocala quarry cluster materials. Likewise, the Thornhill Lake assemblage is primarily composed of Upper Withlacoochee materials. The most abundant lithic material at the Lake Monroe Outlet Midden was not chert, but silicified coral. Silicified coral cannot be sourced using the quarry cluster method but is commonly found in the Upper Withlacoochee area (Endonino 2007). Amongst chert, Upper Withlacoochee and Lake Panasoffkee materials are most abundant. The provenance of lithic tools replicates the distribution of source areas in the debitage assemblages.

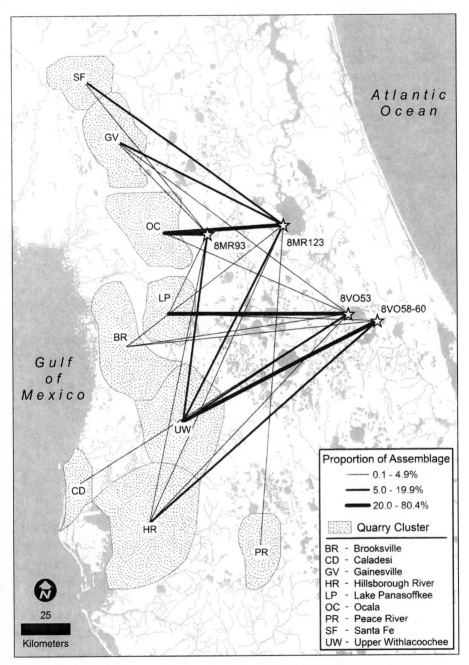

Figure 5.7. Comparison of lithic source areas in debitage assemblages from Silver Springs (8MR93), Silver Glen Springs (8MR123), Lake Monroe Outlet Midden (8VO53), and the Thornhill Lake Complex (8VO58–60). Line thickness varies according to quarry cluster abundance within each site assemblage.

By and large, these results bear out the implications of the least-cost analysis. The lithic materials at each site are primarily derived from one of the least-costly sources of procurement. There are, however, some discrepancies that are not explained by the least-cost model. First, there is a notable dearth of Lake Panasoffkee materials at all sites except the Lake Monroe Outlet Midden, despite its consistently low cost of acquisition. Ocala and Peace River materials are also underrepresented at the Thornhill Lake Complex and Lake Monroe Outlet Midden. Whether this represents a problem with the least-cost model, sampling bias, or preferences for stone from certain source areas over others is unclear.

If Silver Springs was a gateway into the St. Johns River valley, the distribution of source areas represented in the lithic assemblage there should be mirrored at the other sites. This is generally not the case. Both Silver Springs and Silver Glen are dominated by materials from the Ocala quarry cluster, whereas Lake Monroe and Thornhill are dominated by Lake Panasoffkee and Upper Withlacoochee materials, respectively. But there is some indication that Silver Springs did serve as a gateway, at least for materials moving into Silver Glen Springs and (perhaps) the northern portion of the St. Johns River valley. Although Ocala quarry cluster materials dominate at both sites, there is a drop-off in the relative frequency at Silver Glen. This is mirrored in the Upper Withlacoochee materials. However, Santa Fe and Gainesville materials are more frequent at Silver Glen, suggesting that these were procured directly rather than being funneled through Silver Springs.

Debitage Analysis

Lithic debitage was studied using individual flake analysis recording a series of attributes for each specimen. These attributes include: flake form (following Sullivan and Rozen 1985), technological categories (biface thinning flake, notching flake, shatter, etc.), striking platform type (prepared or unprepared), bulb of percussion morphology (salient vs. diffuse), presence of cortical material, presence of patination, raw material type, presence of thermal alteration, size (in square cm), and weight (g). Singly, many of these attributes are useful in discriminating between different lithic reduction activities. However, used in combination multiple lines of evidence provide a more robust interpretation of activities associated with the production and maintenance of stone tools. For purposes

Table 5.6. Summary results of debitage analysis from Silver Springs (8MR93) and Silver Glen Springs (8MR123)

| | Silver Springs (8MR93) | | | | Silver Glen Springs (8MR123) | | | |
Quarry cluster	n	Thinning Index	Mean Cortex	% Biface Thinning Flakes	n	Thinning Index	Mean Cortex	% Biface Thinning Flakes
Santa Fe	43	.66	0	44.2	325	.33	.2	65.2
Gainesville	1	.30		100.0	64	.48	.2	71.9
Ocala	868	.70	.3	50.6	818	.37	.2	67.8
Lake Panasoffkee	3	.48	.7	100.0	0	—	—	—
Brooksville	0	—	—	—	1	.10	0	0
Upper Withlacoochee	141	.63	.2	52.5	37	.69	.1	83.8
Caladesi	0	—	—	—	0	—	—	—
Hillsborough River	1	.07	0	100.0	4	.30	0	100.0
Peace River	0	—	—	—	1	.20	1.0	100.0
Silic. coral	25	.68	.3	44.0	171	.29	.1	67.8
Indet.	64	.28	.2	34.4	60	.28	.2	41.7
Total	1,146	.67	.3	49.7	1,481	.36	.2	66.8

of the present discussion, three metrics are highlighted in Table 5.6 and Table 5.7.

The thinning index is calculated as a ratio of weight to size grade. Although debitage weight and size grade themselves can be used to infer reduction activities, these data can be biased by, for example, a preponderance of broken flakes. One solution would be to weigh and measure only complete flakes, but this would significantly reduce the sample size. The thinning index is a useful alternative. This measure was originally proposed by Johnson (1981) as a proxy for stage of biface reduction (see also Beck et al. 2002). The logic behind it is that this ratio decreases from early- to late-stage manufacturing as the flint knapper attempts to minimize thickness while conserving surface area. This same logic can be applied to lithic debitage, as early-stage debitage is likely to be thicker for a given planar area than late-stage debitage. Further, since this is a ratio of the two values, it can be applied to both whole and broken specimens.

The second metric presented is mean cortex. The amount of cortex on the dorsal surface of a flake is instructive, as initial core reduction and early-stage tool production results in relatively more cortex, and

Table 5.7. Summary results of debitage analysis from the Lake Monroe Outlet Midden (8VO53) and Thornhill Lake Complex (8VO58–60)

| | Lake Monroe Outlet Midden (8VO53) | | | | Thornhill Lake Complex (8VO58–60) | | | |
Quarry cluster	n	Thinning Index	Mean Cortex	% Biface Thinning Flakes[a]	n	Thinning Index	Mean Cortex	% Biface Thinning Flakes
Santa Fe	0	—	—	—	0	—	—	—
Gainesville	11	.98	0	—	0	—	—	—
Ocala	38	.43	0	—	0	—	—	—
Lake Panasoffkee	258	.54	0	—	1	.13	0	100.0
Brooksville	38	.34	.1	—	19	.15	0	89.5
Upper Withlacoochee	162	.55	0	—	282	.32	.1	72.7
Caladesi	14	1.16	0	—	0	—	—	—
Hillsborough River	10	.44	0	—	33	.35	.2	84.8
Peace River	0	—	—	—	0	—	—	—
Silic. coral	664	.37	0	—	31	.25	.1	71.0
Indet.	75	.15	0	—	52	.25	.1	48.1
Total	1,270	.44	0	—	418	.30	.1	71.3

Note: [a] Data not available.

later-stage reduction less. Cortex was recorded as the proportion of the dorsal surface area on an interval scale from 0 to 5. This corresponds to 0 percent, 1–25 percent, 26–50 percent, 51–75 percent, 76–99 percent, and 100 percent.

The final variable presented is technological flake type (e.g., core reduction, biface thinning, notching). This value is likewise indicative of reduction activity. A higher proportion of biface-thinning flakes in the assemblage is reflective of later-stage tool production and maintenance.

Taking the aggregate assemblage data, it is clear that, relative to the other sites, reduction activities at Silver Springs involved larger packages at an earlier stage of reduction. Thinning index and cortex amount are highest in the Silver Springs assemblage, and the percentage of biface-thinning flakes is lowest. The other sites examined all have a lower thinning index, less cortex, and a greater proportion of biface-thinning flakes in their assemblages. This is again supportive of the gateway hypothesis but is also consistent with the proximity of Silver Springs to lithic source areas generally. As noted above, it may be the case that Silver Springs was a gateway for lithic materials moving only into the northern part of the study area, particularly to Silver Glen Springs. Relative to Silver Springs, there is a drop-off in frequency of both Ocala and Upper Withlacoochee materials at Silver Glen Springs. Specimens from these quarry clusters at Silver Glen Springs also tend to have less cortex and are more frequently biface-thinning flakes.

The Silver Springs Gateway?

The evidence from these analyses is somewhat conflicting. Overall, it suggests that proximity was the driving factor in lithic acquisition in the St. Johns River valley. There is little to support the idea that lithic raw materials were redistributed from Silver Springs to the Lake Monroe Outlet Midden and Thornhill Lake Complex. However, patterns do exist that indicate the movement of lithic materials from at least some source areas through Silver Springs to reach Silver Glen Springs. This is understandable when considered in the context of large-scale social gatherings taking place at Silver Glen, discussed in the previous chapter.

However, the least-cost paths indicate that some materials found in appreciable frequency at Silver Glen—from the Gainesville and Santa Fe quarry clusters—appear to have bypassed Silver Springs along their way. This is supported by the provenance determinations, inasmuch as materials from these quarry clusters are more abundant at Silver Glen than at Silver Springs. Nevertheless, the technological data indicate an earlier stage of reduction at Silver Springs, at least for the Santa Fe specimens. There is only one example of Gainesville quarry cluster material at Silver Springs, precluding inference from the technological attributes. If lithic materials did bypass Silver Springs on their way to Silver Glen, they would nevertheless enter into the St. Johns River basin, via the Ocklawaha River, at the juncture with Orange Spring, a smaller third-magnitude spring downstream from Silver.

The pattern that emerges is one of distinct spheres of circulation (Figure 5.8), whereby lithic materials entering the northern portion of the middle St. Johns River valley (i.e., the vicinity of Lake George) were obtained primarily from the northern quarry clusters and moved by way of Silver Springs, Orange Spring, and perhaps others. Lithic materials entering the southern portion of the middle St. Johns (i.e., the vicinity of lakes Monroe

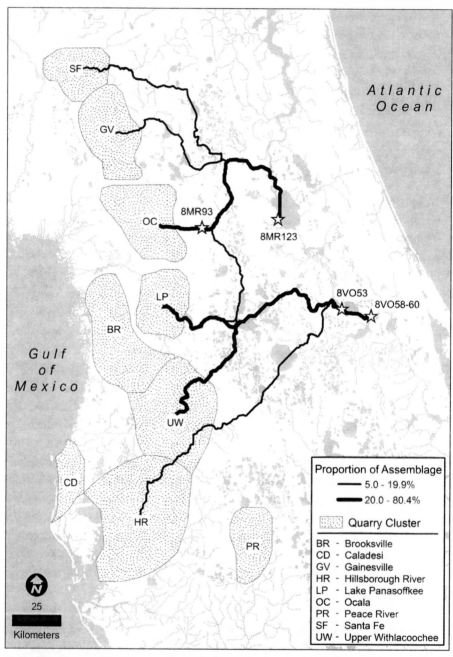

Figure 5.8. Aggregated least-cost paths, limited to those quarry clusters that compose greater than 5.0 percent of the lithic assemblage for a given site.

and Jesup) derived primarily from southern quarry clusters and entered via the numerous water bodies of the Central Lakes District. It is notable that these southern least-cost paths likewise enter the St. Johns River valley by way of springs—Hillsborough River chert via Wekiwa Spring and Lake Panasofﬄee, and Upper Withlacoochee chert via a concentration of a dozen springs in the Seminole National Forest. How these patterns of exchange and interaction manifested at intervening locales—for example at Alexander, Blue, or DeLeon springs—is unclear but could be elucidated with similar analyses in the future.

Rather than Silver Springs operating as the gateway into the St. Johns River valley, it appears that it may have been one of many springs that facilitated interaction and movement. If the patterns described above are murky, and the evidence contradictory, this is partially because of the lack of chronological control in the samples studied. The lithic assemblages from the Lake Monroe Outlet Midden and Thornhill Lake Complex were recovered during controlled excavations of relatively discrete Mount Taylor–aged deposits. The lithic assemblages from both Silver and Silver Glen, in contrast, were derived from reconnaissance survey. Although most of the lithic artifacts recovered at these sites are likely of Mount Taylor age, the assemblages nevertheless collapse millennia of activity proximate to the springs.

If other springs beyond Silver functioned as conduits or gateways for movement into the St. Johns, it remains to be determined whether they exhibit similar material records (i.e., a dense lithic assemblage and dearth of pottery, shell, and evidence of intensive habitation). Neither Orange, Wekiwa, nor the springs of the Seminole State Forest have been subject to intensive archaeological investigation that might address this. However, dense lithic assemblages adjacent to springs have been documented elsewhere, outside the St. Johns River valley. It is worth discussing these briefly to consider how they articulate with the springs examined above.

Beyond the St. Johns

In 2014 the LSA conducted an archaeological survey at Otter Springs Park, located in the Suwannee River valley of northwest peninsular Florida. This was done to aid the Suwannee River Water Management District in advance of infrastructural repair and maintenance dredging. Otter Springs Park is a 636-acre park and campground located in western

Gilchrist County, near the border with Dixie County. Otter is a second-magnitude spring consisting of two separate spring pools connected by a 75-m artificial channel that was excavated in the early 1960s. Otter Spring #1 is the main (original) spring and has a pool measuring approximately 40 m in diameter, with a concrete retaining wall on the southern margin. Otter Spring #2 is located approximately 45 m northeast of the main spring. It has a 21-m-diameter pool surrounded by a sand-cement retaining wall. It flows southwest into the pool of the main spring, through the artificial channel. Prior to the excavation of this channel, Otter Springs #2 did not flow onto the surface. It is visible on historic aerial photographs as a water-bearing sink or karst window. The spring run flows generally westward for approximately 1.3 km (0.8 mi), where it joins the Suwannee River.

The Otter Springs site (8GI12) had previously been recorded as encompassing both spring pools and the surrounding land, measuring approximately 4.8 acres in extent. This site was originally recorded in 1958 by John Goggin, based on his examination of material recovered from the spring by collectors. Little detail is given in Florida Master Site File records, but the collection consisted of potsherds and lithic tools. In 1974 two divers reported the recovery of potsherds and faunal remains from the cave system of Otter Springs, approximately 90 m back from the vent at a depth of 17 m.

In total 19 shovel test pits were excavated during the LSA survey. Subsurface disturbance was found to be extensive, with modern fill present over much of the project area. However, cultural materials were recovered from undisturbed contexts in all but one shovel test. As at Silver Springs, lithic artifacts were by far the most frequently recovered material, constituting 87.1 percent of the total (n = 474 out of 544 total). Pottery was the second-most frequent (6.6 percent; n = 36), followed in abundance by vertebrate fauna (6.3 percent; n = 34). These materials were spread across the project area, but artifact density was greatest proximate to and south of the spring. Artifact density was lower along the eastern and northern periphery of the project area.

The lithic assemblage is dominated by lithic debitage (n = 467). The bulk (73 percent) of this debitage consists of chert, although silicified coral is also well represented. The flakes are generally small (mean weight = .57 g) and lacking in dorsal cortex. Chert debitage is, on average, larger than silicified coral debitage, with a mean weight of .65 g for chert versus

.33 g for coral. We lack the contextual control to infer the full range of lithic reduction activities that occurred at Otter Springs, but the diminutive size of individual specimens in the assemblage is indicative of late-stage production and/or retouch.

Much as with Silver Springs, the bulk of the pottery assemblage consists of plain or eroded sand-tempered wares (72.2 percent). These have a wide spatial and temporal breadth, diminishing their utility as diagnostic artifacts. Diagnostic types recovered include Deptford Check Stamped, St. Johns plain or eroded, and Lochloosa Punctated. Both Deptford Check Stamped and St. Johns plain indicate a Woodland period occupation (ca. 2500–1800 BP), while the Lochloosa Punctated pottery indicates post-Woodland utilization of the site.

In sum, activities at Otter Springs are similar in many respects to those documented at Silver Springs and were largely centered on lithic reduction. The density of lithic artifacts at Otter Springs (99.8 artifacts/m³) is comparable to that at Silver Springs (91.9 artifacts/m³). Although pottery was considerably more dense (7.6 artifacts/m³ at Otter Springs vs. 1.1 artifacts/m³ at Silver Springs), it is still less than all but one of the large springs of the St. Johns River valley (cf. Table 5.1), indicating a lack of intensive habitation. This inference is supported by the lack of midden deposits and mounded features at Otter Springs. Likewise, the ratio of lithic to ceramic artifacts (13.17) is considerably higher at Otter than at St. Johns River valley springs. Where Otter Springs differs from Silver Spring is that the lithic assemblage is consistent with late-stage reduction and tool maintenance. This is somewhat confounding, given that Otter Springs is proximate to chert outcrops along the Suwannee River.

The survey at Otter Springs was not extensive, but limited to the area immediately surrounding the spring. So caution is warranted when drawing conclusions from these samples. Dense midden deposits may be present but slightly farther removed from the spring. However, an intensive survey at Fanning Springs, located just 7 km downstream from Otter Springs, documented similar results. Fanning is a first-magnitude spring consisting of a single main vent and numerous sand boils and seep springs. The pool measures some 60 m in diameter and 6 m deep, and is connected to the Suwannee River by a short (~140 m) spring run (Scott et al. 2004:212). Two intensive surveys (Bland and Chance 2000; Dickinson and Wayne 2003) resulted in the excavation of 507 shovel tests surrounding the spring and run. Although the overall density of artifacts was lower than at Otter Springs, lithic artifacts (n = 1,464) were similarly far more frequent than pottery (n = 88) and consistent with late-stage reduction. The ratio of lithic artifacts to pottery (16.63) was even higher than at Otter Springs. Likewise, the density of pottery (1.06 artifacts/m³) was lower and more consistent with that documented at Silver Springs.

It is tempting to infer from these surveys that springs in the Suwannee River valley frequently feature dense lithic assemblages absent midden deposits, pottery, or other indicators of intensive habitation. However, this is a small sample of the scores of springs along the Suwannee River. Indeed, at Manatee Springs, 12 km downstream from Fanning Springs, Bullen (1953) documented an intensively occupied village dating to the Early Weeden Island period. This underscores the observation that, as in the St. Johns River valley, a diversity of activities took place at springs in the western part of the peninsula. The inferences derived from a single spring do not necessarily apply to other springs, locally or regionally. Nevertheless, the lithic assemblages at Otter and Fanning springs are analogous to those at Silver Springs, if not as expansive or dense. This provides a clue to the importance of these deposits, which I discuss in the concluding section.

A Sense of Place

As discussed at the outset, the St. Johns River valley is bereft of outcrops of stone suitable for the manufacture of flaked-stone tools. Lithic raw materials were transported to the St. Johns River valley from source areas in northwest peninsular Florida. Recent archaeological survey at Silver Springs recovered a dense lithic assemblage absent pottery, fauna, shell deposits, or other evidence of intensive habitation. These results, combined with the proximity of Silver Springs to lithic source areas, led to the hypothesis that Silver Springs was a gateway or conduit for the movement of stone into the St. Johns River valley.

This hypothesis was evaluated with least-cost modeling, lithic provenance determinations, and technological analysis of lithic debitage from Silver Springs and three sites in the St. Johns River valley proper. These analyses indicate that if Silver Springs was a gateway, it was primarily for movement of lithic materials to Silver Glen Springs. The other sites under consideration—Lake Monroe Outlet Midden and Thornhill Lake Complex—lie at the southern end of the middle St. Johns and have lithic assemblages derived largely from different source areas than Silver or Silver Glen Springs.

If Silver Springs was a gateway for movement to Silver Glen and the pan-regional gatherings that took place there, the absence of shell at Silver Springs is nevertheless confounding. However, similarly dense lithic deposits have been documented at springs farther west in the Suwannee River valley. This, I argue, provides a key to understanding the deposits at Silver Springs.

Recall from above that the location of chert outcrops is coextensive with the densest concentrations of springs in Florida. As people, bearing stone, moved across the Florida peninsula from quarry areas toward the gatherings at Silver Glen, springs were a touchstone, a place at once unfamiliar but reminiscent of home. Through the process of flake removal, people left behind fragments of this stone along its journey. These fragments of stone indexed not only their place of origin—the locality and geologic formation from which they were acquired—but the events of fragmentation and stoppage at spring-side waypoints along their route. Perhaps the removal of a flake was an offering, perhaps simply lightening the load. Regardless, the fragmentation and deposition of stone effectively enchained places and people across the Florida peninsula, entangling them in social gatherings like those at Silver Glen Springs. Likewise, as this practice was repeated at springs along the journey—from the Gulf coastal lowlands, across interior highlands and scrub, and into the St. Johns River valley—people effectively re-created familiar places in an unfamiliar landscape through leaving behind fragments of stone from the homeland. Springs thus serve not only as nodes in social networks, but also as paths of connectivity. In this way springs themselves were "on-the-move" and contributed to the entanglement of communities across the Florida peninsula.

6

SPRINGS ETERNAL

Hope springs eternal in the human breast:
Man never is, but always to be blest:
The soul, uneasy and confined from home,
Rests and expatiates in a life to come.
    Lo, the poor Indian! whose untutor'd mind
Sees God in clouds, or hears him in the wind;
His soul, proud science never taught to stray
Far as the solar walk, or milky way;
Yet simple Nature to his hope has given,
Behind the cloud-topp'd hill, an humbler heaven;
Some safer world in depth of woods embrac'd,
Some happier island in the wat'ry waste,
Where slaves once more their native land behold,
No fiends torment, no Christians thirst for gold.

ALEXANDER POPE, *AN ESSAY ON MAN* (1848[1733])

Springs have been important places in Florida since humans first colonized the peninsula, and they continue to be today. Some were vital inland ports and conduits for travel prior to the widespread construction of railway lines and the advent of automobile travel (Figure 6.1; see also Berson 2011), and many were developed as health spas and tourist attractions in the nineteenth and twentieth centuries (Figure 6.2 and Figure 6.3). For modern Floridians, springs are popular recreation areas whose waters provide respite from oppressive summer heat. And today private campgrounds, and county, state, and federal parks, surround many springs, affording ample recreational opportunities. Springs are an important aspect of Florida's cultural heritage as well, the subject of paintings,

Figure 6.1. Steamboat approaching dock, view from the Morgan house, Silver Springs, Florida, in 1886. Photograph by George Barker, courtesy of the Library of Congress Prints and Photographs Division, Washington, D.C.

Figure 6.2. Interior of the health spa at White Springs, Hamilton County, Florida, in 1920. Courtesy of the State Archives of Florida.

Figure 6.3. View across Weeki Wachee Spring in 1952. Courtesy of the State Archives of Florida.

photographs, travelogues, poems, and literary works (e.g., Bartram 1996; Belleville 2000; Carr 1996; Douglas 1967; Earl 2009; Lanier 1876; Le Conte 1861; Moran 2004; Rawlings 1938; Tolbert 2010).

As noted at the outset of this book, Florida's springs face myriad threats. In addition to recreational impacts suffered at places like Silver Glen Springs, chemical pollutants from development and agricultural runoff are increasing, algal blooms proliferate, and spring flows decline as groundwater is pumped for human consumption (e.g., Florida Department of Community Affairs and Florida Department of Environmental Protection 2002; Florida Springs Initiative 2007; Florida Springs Task Force 2000; Knight 2015; Pittman 2012a). All of this has led to political wrangling over conservation measures and to tension between those who seek access to the water and those striving to protect fragile ecosystems and freshwater resources.

But, as relayed by Alexander Pope in the epigraph to this chapter, hope springs eternal. Advocates for springs conservation—spearheaded by organizations like the Springs Eternal Project and the Howard T. Odum Florida Springs Institute, and including scientists, artists, and members of the public—have been successful in increasing public awareness and garnering financial support for restoration and conservation projects. The 2015–2016 state budget included $40 million for 26 Florida Department of Environmental Protection (FDEP) springs restoration projects, the highest amount ever allocated (FDEP 2015; *Florida Trend* 2015). Matching funds from local governments and water management districts brought the total investment in springs restoration to $82 million. This amount was increased in the 2016–2017 budget to include $56.5 million from the state and a further $33.1 million in matching funds (FDEP 2016).

There is thus concerted effort to conserve springs, not only through public funding but outreach programs, media editorials, art installations, and museum exhibits (e.g., *Gainesville Sun* and *Ocala Star-Banner* 2013; Knight 2008, 2012, 2013, 2014, 2015; Moran 2013; Neeley 2015; Schofield 2013; *Tampa Bay Times* 2012). However, there are barriers and challenges as well, including the vast spatial and temporal scales of springs' hydrological processes and their entanglement with humans. Archaeology, with its long-term perspective, has ample data to provide policy makers, conservationists, and researchers interested in understanding the context of changes observed at springs and the consequences of human–spring interaction. However, the perceived disjuncture between modern experience of place and that of native Floridians centuries or millennia ago hamstrings attempts at dialogue (Sassaman 2012), as does the penchant of archaeologists to emphasize nuance and the complexity of individual cases. In this chapter I demonstrate the relevance of what has been presented thus far, of an archaeological sensibility, to issues facing springs today. I do so, first, by examining how the past is used, or constructed, in accounts of Florida springs as both a mythical Eden that modern humans have fallen from, and as target for springs restoration. Then, I return to Hodder's (2011a, 2011b, 2012) entanglement theory as a frame for exploring the interconnections between humans and things in the past and present. There is long-term continuity, or at least analogy, in the entanglement of humans and springs that bridges the chasm between ancient and modern experience. As a result, insights from the past are applicable to springs conservation today, despite appearances to the contrary.

THE PAST IN SPRINGS CONSERVATION NARRATIVES

The past is used in two ways, on two horizons, in narratives of springs conservation. The more recent past, the historical past of the last century or so, is generally used as baseline for the physical condition of springs in a pristine or untouched state. For example, consider the following quote from Bill Thompson of the *Ocala Star Banner*: "Though not as pristine as in the days when Hollywood icon Lloyd Bridges was filming his adventure series 'Sea Hunt' at the park, the water at Silver Springs is the main draw, and work is underway to reverse decades of inattention that have fed its decline" (Thompson 2013a:2). Similarly, in a special feature on Florida's vanishing springs, the *Tampa Bay Times* (2012) reported that "a century ago Florida's gin-clear springs drew presidents and millionaires and tourists galore who sought to cure their ailments by bathing in the healing cascades. Now the springs tell the story of a hidden sickness, one that lies deep within the earth." These appeals to the historic grandeur of springs imply that springs were untouched—in a natural state—prior to the mid-twentieth century. Jim Stevens, retired chair of the Florida Springs Task Force and the Florida Springs Initiative, wrote of his childhood visits to springs, "that was the 1950s, a time when our springs were still pristine with strong flow and clear water" (Knight 2015:xiii).

In addition to a baseline for measuring change, the recent past—and a pristine state—is used as a target for springs conservation: "True and meaningful restoration will require returning the springs back to their flows and nitrate levels of the 1950s and 1960s when significant changes were first apparent" (Knight 2015:101). And from a recent National Public Radio report: "Later this year, Florida's park service will take over Silver Springs and begin working to restore it to a more natural state" (Allen 2013). In this effort to restore springs to their "natural state," the material remains of modern humans are considered a blight; it is "too late to find [a spring] that is unaltered by the works of man" (Knight 2013). Where possible, these are removed and remediated, often at considerable cost. For example, "one condition of Palace's early departure [from Silver Springs] was that the vestiges of the attraction's past life as an amusement park and part-time zoo were to be removed—scuttled in favor of a return to a more natural setting" (Thompson 2013a).

The second horizon in which the past is used is a more distant one, and more rarely invoked. This is the "pre-historic" past of Native Americans.

Where it is mentioned at all, the roughly 13,000 years of pre-Columbian interaction with springs is largely glossed over. In his recent book *Silenced Springs*, Robert Knight, perhaps the most vocal and respected scientist advocating for springs conservation, summarizes 13 millennia in less than 300 words (Knight 2015:8–9). Likewise, the Florida DEP website states that "archaeological evidence indicates that people have been attracted to Florida's springs for thousands of years. The springs made the perfect home for Native Floridians who used them as a source of water and food. . . . As the last of the Ice Age came to a close in Florida, many environmental changes were occurring. . . . As these drastic changes were taking place, Florida's human inhabitants learned to adapt" (FDEP 2014). The next sentence continues: "Later arrivals to Florida, Ponce de Leon, John and William Bartram and other explorers, were drawn to the subterranean discharges of freshwater scattered across central and northern Florida." The narrative jumps from Paleoindian to Spanish explorer, glossing over some 10,000 years between. Similarly flattening time, a CNN report described the "cornucopia of history" recovered during dredge operations at Chassahowitzka Springs, with artifacts that "represent every period of human occupation in Florida" (Watkins 2013). And media coverage of the Laboratory of Southeastern Archeology (LSA) survey of Silver Springs reported a "treasure trove of artifacts" showing that "the renowned site's crystal clear waters were a draw for visitors long before the first modern tourists arrived" (Thompson 2013b).

I do not mean simply to criticize that nonspecialists are presenting superficial summaries of springs archaeology. Certainly, archaeologists are guilty of this as well, arguing (as I have done) that springs have been important as long as humans have been in Florida. This could perhaps be excused as the "distillation of extant complexity into tractable environmental [and archaeological] narratives, often a necessary step for political dialogue" (Heffernan et al. 2010:816). But this elision of the past creates a narrative of eternity, a history of springs existing largely unchanged: "Clear, temperate water flows through limestone channels beneath North Central Florida, rising to the surface to form scores of springs that sustained early natives, amazed European explorers and delight us today— but this may only be a memory in a generation or two" (*Gainesville Sun* and *Ocala Star-Banner* 2013).

The net effect of these two uses of the past is to recapitulate a perceived rupture, or revolution, at the onset of modernity that brought with it a "shift in temporality that jettisoned the ancient past to the scrapheap of irrelevance" (Sassaman 2012:251; see also Cobb 2005). The ancient past of springs has been compressed and discounted under the "springs eternal" trope as an interminable span of changelessness. Often, the ancient past is romanticized as an Edenic Florida, populated by noble natives living in harmony with nature—"the Indians named Silver Springs 'Sua-ille-aha,' sun-glinting water, and eventually came to regard the spring as sacred" (Martin 1966:49)—but this serves only to remind us of how far modern Floridians have fallen. Only the recent past—the past documented by written records and the memories of living people—is accepted as bearing relevance to the threats imperiling springs. So the best we can do is look back and, through some process of time reversal, restore springs to their remembered state, before the pace of change quickened. But the geological origin of springs, and the millennia of human–spring interaction described thus far, belie any notion of eternal sameness. In the following, I use entanglement theory as a framework for delineating these interactions and illuminating the various interdependencies of humans and springs. This framework summarizes the arguments presented earlier in the book, clarifies our understanding of spring dynamics, and opens an avenue for an archaeological sensibility that draws attention to springs' historical significance and the remnants of the past still visible in the present to assume its role in modern discourse.

Entanglement

Entanglement theory was developed by Hodder (2011a, 2011b, 2012), and the following summary is drawn from his work. This is an approach to describe the "complex networks, mixes, and engagements" that arise from human–thing interdependence (Hodder 2011a:162). Entanglement theory focuses on the *dependences* and *dependencies* between humans and things along multiple axes (Hodder 2011a, 2011b, 2012). Humans depend on things, for instance, as food, shelter, clothing, water, and the tools used to procure or manufacture these. But much recent literature in anthropology and social theory has revealed the ways that humans depend on things beyond subsistence and technology (e.g., DeMarrais et al. 2004; Gosden 2005; Ingold 2011, 2012, 2013; Meskell 2005; Miller 2005; Olsen 2010; Olsen et al. 2012; Skibo and Schiffer 2008; Webmoor and Witmore 2008). That is, things are increasingly recognized to facilitate social relations through exchange and interaction, personal and collective identities, negotiations of power and prestige, meanings, ideologies, and, embodiment.

Likewise, all things depend on other things through relations of interdependence. Human-crafted things rely, for example, on the tools used to make or repair them, and things that facilitate their use. So a wooden spoon depends on the tree from which the wood was harvested, the axe used to fell the tree, and the woodworking tools used to shape and smooth the wood into a spoon, but also the food that it stirs and scoops, the pot that contains that food, and the stove that provides heat. This thing–thing dependence may be obvious for human-manufactured things but is also true of natural things, which likewise depend on other things for their existence.

Things depend on humans as well, again most obviously for human-made goods, which depend on humans to manufacture and use them. This dependence of things on humans (and other things) creates relationships of *dependency*, that is, it imposes constraints on human activity. This is so because the things that humans depend on are not fixed and eternal but constantly "resist, decay, fall apart, run out, need replacing" (Hodder 2011b:180), and so humans must work to obtain, maintain, and replenish things. The net result is that humans become caught in a "double-bind," depending on things that, in turn, depend on people and other things (Hodder 2011a:164, 2012:88). This is the defining feature of entanglement. Human dependence on things creates obligations as people become drawn into relationships of care. The material properties of things thus create "specific practical entrapments" (Hodder 2011a:163) that, because of dependent relations, dictate and direct what people do.

This is entanglement: the dialectical relationship between dependence and dependency, between the enabling and constraining reliances of humans and things on each other (Hodder 2012:88–89). Entanglement is a directional process inasmuch as we humans are so dependent that our response to the breakdown of things is to fix them, tinkering and patching them up rather than scrapping the project and starting anew, to "find a solution that fits into what has been built" (Hodder 2011b:182). This is not to suggest that back-to-the-drawing-board innovations and course corrections never occur, but rather that there is a path-dependency and historical contingency to human–thing entanglement, that is, to social and technological change (Hodder 2012:167–171). Solutions and innovations—things—must fit into existing entanglements, phenomenal worlds, and conceptual ideologies.

The complexity of human–thing entanglement increases exponentially over the long term (Hodder 2012:174–177). The more people come to use and depend on things, the greater their entrapment in relations of dependency. The constant tinkering, maintaining, and repairing of things entails other people and things, expanding the web of entanglement. There is a temporal element to this as well, since humans and things operate on different time scales. As we depend on things, we become beholden to their own unique temporalities, and this introduces uncertainty to where and when intervention is needed (Hodder 2011a:164, 2011b:181, 2012:84–85). For example, the rate of decay differs for different things—a brick house, word-processing software, an automobile—as does the predictability of this decay, and thus the need for human intervention. So, over time, entanglement become more complex—entrapping more people and things in ever more complicated relationships.

Humans thus become caught up with things in various ways, through myriad relationships of reliance and care. And through these entanglements things and people are drawn together across multiple scales of space and time. Things can, of course, continue to exist absent human care, but "things cannot exist for humans, in the ways that humans want, without human intervention. Resources, wild or domesticated, animate or inanimate, need tending, conserving, protecting, if they are to exist in the ways that humans want them to" (Hodder 2011a:162). This is the crux of the issue and is true of springs as well. Our dependence on springs has entrapped us in relationships of care that necessitate certain actions. This is not a recent phenomenon but a process that has unfolded over millennia. The various dependences and dependencies of humans and springs are explored below to summarize the previous chapters of the book and illustrate the depth of human–spring entanglement. This analysis reveals not only the depth and complexity of problems currently plaguing springs but also the relevance of archaeological data to potential solutions and the crafting of alternative futures.

HUMANS DEPEND ON SPRINGS

Humans depend on springs in a variety of capacities. Minimally, springs are a source of clean, fresh water. This is particularly relevant in archaeological narratives of the Paleoindian period. As discussed in chapter 2, current reconstructions indicate that sea level was some 80 m lower than present when people first inhabited the peninsula. The climate was warmer and drier, with significantly lowered groundwater, reduced surface water availability, and xeric vegetative communities (Balsillie and Donoghue 2004; Otvos 2004; Watts et al. 1996; Watts and Hansen 1988). The fauna of the state was also quite different, with Pleistocene megafauna roaming what were likely arid plains and sandhills.

The *Oasis Model* of Paleoindian settlement, first proposed by Neill (1964) and later elaborated on by Dunbar (1991), posits that these early inhabitants of Florida were constrained by their need for reliable freshwater. Hydrological modeling of late Pleistocene Florida indicates that large springs were likely some of the few locales where freshwater could be obtained in the interior of the peninsula (Thulman 2009). Dunbar (2016:182) notes that "by any measure taken, the Floridan Aquifer, where it occurred near the surface [i.e., sinkholes and springs], represented the main source of potable water that attracted game animals and Paleoindian activity." Indeed, most well-documented inland sites of the Paleoindian period are associated with karst features like springs and sinkholes. For example, substantial late Pleistocene and early Holocene deposits have been recorded in northwest Florida at the Page-Ladson site, a submerged sinkhole in the Aucilla River system (Dunbar et al. 1988; Webb 2006), and the Wakulla Springs Lodge site (Rink, Dunbar, and Burdette 2012; Tesar and Jones 2004). Closer to the St. Johns River valley, Paleoindian artifacts and Pleistocene fauna have been recovered from Silver Springs (Neill 1958) and are frequently recovered from the Santa Fe and Ichetucknee rivers in north central Florida (Thulman 2009). The headwaters of the Ichetucknee River are formed by the Ichetucknee Springs group, while the Santa Fe River system incorporates numerous karst features, including sinkholes and dozens of springs.

This dependence on springs entailed dependence on other things as well. The presence of springs afforded the opportunity for humans to move into the otherwise arid interior of Florida. However, in many cases water from these springs did not flow onto the surface. For example, Paleoindian materials at Little Salt Spring were recovered from a ledge nearly 26 m below the current spring surface (Clausen et al. 1979). Similar materials were recovered 13 m beneath the surface of nearby Warm Mineral Spring (Clausen et al. 1975), including human remains dating to at least 12,000 cal BP. The recovery of objects from deep within cave systems at Silver, Silver Glen, and other springs suggests that these, too, were more akin to water-bearing caves or cenotes than to springs at the time. Thus, obtaining water from springs was no simple matter and in some cases involved considerable risk. This also implicates dependence on a suite of other things, for example, rope, cordage, or vines for descending into the spring, and waterskins or other containers to hold the water.

However, I have argued at length that the significance of springs was not merely their capacity to supply food and water. In chapter 3 I evaluated the hypothesis that the onset of spring flow was an ecological founding event underwriting riverine adaptation and the inception of shell mounding in the St. Johns River valley. Cores extracted adjacent to Salt and Silver Glen springs demonstrated that the onset of spring flow predated intensive shell mounding in the region by millennia. Meanwhile, stratigraphic testing at these and other springs indicated that sustained human activity at springs did not initially involve the deposition of shell. Thus, although people depended on springs, shell mounds apparently did not, or at least not initially.

Rather, the importance of springs increasingly turned on their role in facilitating movement and interaction across the Florida peninsula. Chapter 4 discussed the centrality of Silver Glen Springs as an extraregional gathering place that drew visitors from across the peninsula and enabled interaction and exchange. I argued that Silver Glen was made sacred by the confluence of dispersed people and things at a spring with an abundant material, historical record in the form of pits, shell ridges, and other deposits. People thus depended on springs as places of coalescence and community building.

Springs were similarly depended on to facilitate movement across the peninsula and, in this movement, became entangled with human dependence on stone. As discussed in chapter 5, stone suitable for tool production is absent in the St. Johns River valley. Silver Springs, among others, served as a conduit or way station along the path of stone from lithic source areas in northwest peninsular Florida to the St. Johns River valley. GIS-based least-cost analysis demonstrated that the optimal routes taken by stone from several distinct quarry clusters passed through Silver Springs on their way to Silver Glen. Provenance determinations and debitage analysis of lithic assemblages confirmed this hypothesis, particularly for Ocala quarry-cluster chert, which constituted 56 percent of the assemblage at Silver Glen. Based on these same analyses, sites farther to the south—Lake Monroe Outlet Midden and Thornhill Lake Complex—are dominated by different lithic source areas and do not appear to have been part of the same circulation network. However, the least-cost paths suggest that lithic resources at these sites may likewise have passed through springs along their routes.

Human dependence on springs continues today. We rely on springs in much the same way as ancient Floridians did, as sources of freshwater but also as sites for social gatherings. Here it is helpful to consider springs not just as points on the landscape but as windows into the hydrological web woven by the Floridan Aquifer. As noted in chapter 2, groundwater supplies potable water to 92 percent of Florida's population. The Floridan Aquifer provides the bulk of this potable water and is the primary source of freshwater for agricultural irrigation, industrial, mining, and commercial uses (Marella 2014). Although water is not typically extracted directly from springs, as it was in the past (the bottled water industry notwithstanding [Samek 2004]), over one million artificial wells in Florida act as proxy springs, discharging water from the Floridan Aquifer.

Likewise, modern Floridians continue to use springs as arenas for social gatherings, now in the context of recreation. Many canoe or kayak along spring runs in search of tranquility and communion with nature, and trips to the springs—for birthday parties, family outings, swimming, tubing, and fishing—are highly valued components of Floridian life. As Jim Stevenson wrote:

Springs are woven into the cultural fabric of rural North Florida. Springs were the gathering places for teens, much as malls are today. After a day of working in the fields, people would go to a spring to bathe and cool off. Springs were the social centers for family reunions, church baptisms, and school picnics. Health spas located at springs with hotels attracted invalids and tourists from the North expecting to be healed in the medicinal water of White, Wekiwa, and Hampton Springs. (Knight 2015:xiii)

These social gatherings may seem to be incommensurate with pan-regional gatherings that integrated far-flung people during the Archaic period, but springs today continue to draw a regional crowd (Bonn 2004). And activities like basking in the water, feasting on hot dogs, tossing a frisbee, imbibing, and singing by the campfire are not so different from those of the social gatherings millennia ago.

SPRINGS DEPEND ON OTHER THINGS

If humans depend on springs, springs, in turn, depend on other things. As detailed in chapter 2, springs depend on a number of materials, places, and processes, both immediate and far removed in space and time. I defined a spring broadly as a point on the landscape where groundwater flows onto the surface. As a point, or place, a spring thus draws together and is dependent on a number of other things. A spring, for example, is dependent on the water that flows and on the voids in the stone (i.e., pore, conduit, or cavern) that allow for the movement of water. Indeed, "in some usages 'spring' is restricted to the water that outflows, in other usages the word can refer to the water, the outlet, or the locality of the outflow" (U.S. Environmental Protection Agency 2002:157).

Spring water is ultimately derived from precipitation that percolates through overlying sediments to enter and recharge the Florida Aquifer. This recharge is facilitated or hindered by the thickness and hydraulic conductivity of sediments overlying the aquifer, which in turn are a product of ongoing geomorphological processes that have their roots in the establishment of Florida's siliciclastic mantle some 30 million years ago. These sediments (and atmospheric CO_2) also facilitate further karstification of the landscape, as they acidify percolating water and thus enhance dissolution of the limestone, creating and expanding pathways for water to flow from springs. This is also dependent on microbial activity and organic matter in soils, which further acidify the water. Local geomorphology and topography likewise influence the spatial position of springs, which are typically located at inflection points between high- and low-elevation terrain.

The water discharging from any given spring is primarily composed of relatively young (< 100 years residence time) water that fell on the local springshed—the surface and groundwater basins that contribute water to a spring. This springshed is not apparent from the surface terrain, but a product of largely invisible groundwater flow dynamics directing water to the spring. However, as outlets of the Floridan Aquifer, springs can also discharge water upwelling from deep in the system. This water recharged the aquifer as much as 30,000 years ago, and can include relict seawater trapped in the system after the Last Glacial Maximum (Moore et al. 2009; Morrissey et al. 2010; Plummer 1993; Toth and Katz 2006).

A spring is thus dependent on the motion of water through the cycle of recharge, flow, and discharge. Amongst artesian springs groundwater flow and discharge is driven by gradients of pressure (and temperature) in the confined aquifer. These pressure gradients are a result of elevation differentials between recharge and discharge zones, and fluctuate with changes in precipitation patterning and intensity, and the level of the seas surrounding the Florida peninsula. The motion of spring water is afforded by the carbonate limestone constituting the Florida aquifer, and the processes that have enhanced porosity and permeability of that stone.

The Irish poet-philosopher John O'Donohue described the karst landscape of western Ireland—the Burren region—as the product of "an ancient conversation between the ocean and the stone" (Tippett 2015), a description equally apt for the karst of Florida. Florida's carbonate limestone platform formed in a shallow marine environment and has been carved by the repeated transgressions and regressions of the sea. It was dependent on a confluence of conditions that favored the proliferation of specific organisms to produce and accumulate carbonate sediments.

Springs thus depend on, among other things, precipitation, stone, topography and terrain, springsheds, the sea, and the geologic processes and events that formed the Florida platform and Floridan Aquifer. Springs' entanglement with other things is open-ended. For example, over centennial and millennial scales, springs depend on fluctuations in sea level and precipitation resulting from hemispheric- and global-scale changes in atmospheric and oceanic circulation patterns, induced by postglacial warming and changes in the Earth's orbital dynamics and patterns of solar insolation. More recently, human activities have increasingly imposed dependencies on springs.

Springs Depend on Humans

Over the course of thirteen millennia of human–springs interaction, springs have come to increasingly depend on humans. On the one hand, springs' dependence on humans results from the long history of land alteration and terraforming adjacent to springs. As discussed in chapters 3 and 4, some of the earliest anthropogenic deposition at Salt and Silver Glen springs involved both the aggradation and progradation of the shoreline as midden accumulated in both terrestrial and subaqueous contexts during the Mount Taylor period. These elevated deposits facilitated access to the spring by covering over low-lying saturated areas on the margin of the spring pool and surrounding it with a high, dry platform. The emplacement of thick deposits of large, clastic particles (i.e., shells) likewise stabilized the shoreline of the spring pool. Indeed, as the water level in the spring fluctuated on seasonal, annual, and longer scales, shell deposits became concreted, and thus more durable, through these repeated cycles of wetting and drying.

The springs (as we know them today) continue to depend on anthropogenic shoreline stabilization and aggradation. Although the shell mounds surrounding Silver Glen Springs were removed by mining operations early in the twentieth century, intact deposits extend nearly 2 m beneath the current ground surface. The U.S. Forest Service recreation area—with its beach access, volleyball court, grassy fields, and picnic tables—is quite literally built on an Archaic-era foundation that continues to facilitate access to the spring by elevating the terrestrial surroundings and stabilizing the banks.

When compared to Silver Glen Springs, Salt Springs was home to relatively modest pre-Columbian anthropogenic deposits. Consequently, modern interventions toward shoreline stabilization and spring access have been more extensive. The pool of Salt Springs is now surrounded by a concrete retaining wall forming three sides of a rectangle. Salt Springs is not alone in this regard. Nearby Juniper Springs is surrounded by a circular wall, while Orange Spring "sits in a slightly ovoid depression entirely ringed with a rock retaining wall . . . the relatively short spring run exits the pool toward the northeast over a . . . man-made, limestone waterfall. Past the waterfall, the spring run is then channeled through a narrow concrete chute" (Scott et al. 2004:230). Likewise, DeLeon Spring features a circular concrete wall with access ladders and a sidewalk encircling the pool.

In addition to shoreline stabilization, shoreline aggradation and infilling is a common feature of springs. At Alexander Spring, access to the pool is provided by a beach contained behind a rock retaining wall. Longtime

Figure 6.4. Alexander Springs in 1947. Courtesy of the State Archives of Florida.

resident Robert Shepard reported that "the immediate area around the head spring was originally swamp. Approximately one acre . . . is now covered by artificial fill" (quoted in Willis 1995:5; see Figure 6.4). This was later confirmed by subsurface testing (Willis 1995). Archaeological reconnaissance conducted by the LSA has likewise documented large-scale anthropogenic infilling of spring-side wetlands in multiple locales. At Silver Springs, much of the main pool is surrounded a retaining wall and dock for the glass-bottom boats. During the LSA survey, modern fill was found to be discontinuous but widespread, particularly on the north side of the pool. The area adjacent to the retaining wall contains thick deposits of modern fill, in some cases exceeding 1 m deep, overlying the former wetland surface. Likewise at Otter Springs, fill sand and modern overburden of variable thickness overlie buried surface horizons and wetland deposits (O'Donoughue and Sassaman 2014).

Weeki Wachee Spring is perhaps the most heavily modified spring in Florida. Recreational facilities are extensive and include concessions, gift shops, water slides, a (constructed) beach at Buccaneer Bay Water Park, boat docks for the Wilderness River Cruise, nature trails, animal demonstrations, canoeing and kayaking down the Weeki Wachee River, and the famous Underwater Theater built into the west side of the spring pool. As at Otter and Silver springs, an LSA survey at Weeki Wachee springs documented widespread modern disturbance of variable depth (Figure 6.5; see O'Donoughue and Sassaman 2013), with fill sand and modern debris frequently overlying truncated soil profiles and buried surfaces. This was sometimes obvious, as in one shovel test that had to be terminated when it intercepted a concrete walkway *in situ* on a buried surface beneath 85 cm of fill. Proximate to the spring and river, fill typically overlies a dark-brown-to-black buried surface consisting of organically enriched, mucky sands and/or peat deposits. This indicates that sand was used to fill low-lying wetlands marginal to the spring.

In addition to the properties of springs' landscapes, spring flow is likewise dependent on human activity. As discussed in chapter 2, over 2,500 million gallons per day were pumped from the Floridan Aquifer in 2010 (Marella 2014). This groundwater extraction has caused significant reduction of water levels and pressure in the Floridan Aquifer over much of its extent. Historically, surface water was the primary source of freshwater use in Florida (Marella 2008) and, before the installation of artificial wells, springs were the primary outlet of groundwater from the Floridan Aquifer (Knight 2015:52). The first wells in Florida were drilled by the City of Jacksonville in 1884 (Bush and Johnston 1988; Knight 2015:277). The rate of groundwater extraction grew steadily over the course of the twentieth century, so that by 1980 groundwater had surpassed surface water as the primary freshwater source in Florida. In 1950 the amount of groundwater extracted for human consumption was 614 million gallons per day (Marella 2008). Sixty years later, in 2010, it had skyrocketed to 4,166 million gallons per day, an increase of nearly 600 percent.

As a result of this groundwater withdrawal, many springs across the peninsula have witnessed declining flows in recent decades. There is a spatial disjuncture to this, as the greatest reductions in spring flow do *not* occur in the same areas with the greatest groundwater consumption. The residents and businesses of Jacksonville currently withdraw daily some 90 million gallons of groundwater from the Floridan Aquifer, lowering the potentiometric surface of the aquifer in the immediate vicinity by 12 m. This groundwater reduction is not limited to pumping areas, however, as it creates a gradient of pressure, driving groundwater flow in the Floridan Aquifer from surrounding areas into the pressure sink beneath Jacksonville. The results radiate out into southern Georgia and

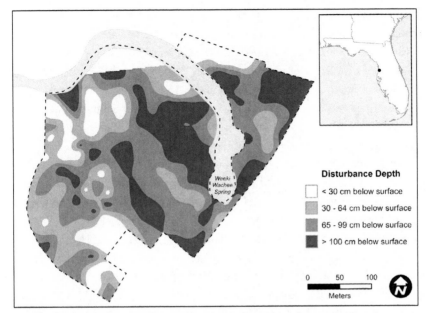

Figure 6.5. Interpolated depth of subsurface disturbance in the vicinity of Weeki Wachee Spring. Modified from O'Donoughue and Sassaman (2013).

north-central Florida, affecting areas more than 100 km distant and reducing flow in springs of the Ichetucknee, Santa Fe, and Suwannee rivers (Florida Springs Institute Members 2015; Knight 2015).

Groundwater extraction is not the only anthropogenic impact reducing aquifer pressure and spring flow. As noted above, spring flow is dependent on precipitation recharging the Floridan Aquifer. Over the course of the twentieth century, there has been a broad trend toward decreased precipitation and increased daily maximum temperature in Florida. This has been attributed to the drainage and conversion of millions of acres of wetlands to agricultural, residential, and industrial uses. The conversion of these wetlands has reduced the landscape's capacity for surface-water storage and decreased the temperature and humidity gradients that drive sea breezes and convective summer rainfall (Marshall et al. 2004; Pielke et al. 1999). Thus, development and landscape alterations over the past century have altered local climate in Florida and reduced recharge to the Floridan Aquifer.

Water quality is also dependent on human activity. As noted at the outset of this book, increased nitrate in springs and the Floridan Aquifer is a threat to both human health and local ecologies. Nitrate has been the prime culprit in attempts to explain the proliferation of filamentous algal mats covering spring bottoms and floating on the surface. Nitrate, a form of nitrogen, is an essential nutrient for plant and animal life. The primary source of nitrate entering the aquifer is fertilizer, but other sources include human wastewater treatment and disposal (whether from municipal facilities or septic tanks), animal waste, and industrial byproducts. The aquifer is particularly susceptible to pollution from surface applications in recharge areas where it is unconfined or near the surface.

It is generally thought that at lower concentrations nutrients, like nitrate, are beneficial to native vegetation in springs, which includes a variety of submerged, floating, and emergent vascular plants. Unfortunately, at higher concentrations nutrients favor fast-growing algae, which then outcompete native plants (Brown et al. 2008; Knight 2015). However, several factors suggest that increased nitrate may not be the primary factor driving algal proliferation in springs (Heffernan et al. 2010). Experimental and observational studies indicate that there is not a strong correlation between elevated nitrate and algal growth in springs, and that increases in the two are often spatially and temporally disconnected. Silver Glen Springs, for example, has seen a rapid increase in algal biomass, but without a corresponding increase in nitrate levels (Knight 2015:79; Pandion Systems 2013; Pittman 2012b). This implicates other forcing mechanisms and has led to alternative hypotheses.

Researchers from the University of Florida have argued that invertebrate grazers, such as aquatic gastropods, exert a strong predatory control on filamentous algae (Heffernan et al. 2010; Liebowitz et al. 2014). Grazer populations have been reduced in recent decades as a result of declining dissolved oxygen levels in spring water. This decrease in dissolved oxygen is attributed to groundwater pumping and the concomitant incorporation of deeper, older, more oxygen-depleted water in spring discharge. The depression of grazer populations has allowed algae to proliferate and reach a tipping point beyond which grazers can no longer effectively control algal populations.

While acknowledging the role of grazers in algal control, Knight (2015:77–78) suggests that a complex interaction of physical, chemical, and biological forces controls the balance of vascular plants and algae. Rather than focusing on factors that favor algal growth, Knight emphasizes changes that have negatively impacted native plants. These include increased nitrate and reduced dissolved oxygen and grazer populations, but also reduced flow velocity because of groundwater extraction, trampling from recreational activities, and the application of herbicides to control invasive plant species. In this view, those springs most vulnerable to algal proliferation are those in which native plants are heavily stressed by these activities.

Although the precise mechanisms for increased algal dominance are debated, human activity is universally implicated (Heffernan et al. 2010; Knight 2015; Liebowitz et al. 2014). Whether from nutrient enrichment, grazer population depression, or some combination of factors, it is clear that pollution, pumping, and physical damage are responsible for reduced flows and degradation of water quality in springs. Absent future interventions, springs will continue to decline. Thus, they depend on humans for their continued existence.

SPRINGS ENTANGLED

Entanglement involves not only dependent relations, like those outlined above, but also dependencies as humans are entrapped in the downstream reliances of things. Humans depend on springs that themselves depend on humans and other things, and so humans are entwined in relationships of care. Springs are not eternal. Springs fall apart. They require maintenance and repair, imposing constraints on and directing human activity. At Silver Glen Springs, aging recreational facilities are in need of replacement, and eroding midden deposits along the mining escarpment and pool entrance require periodic stabilization with clean fill (Randall et al. 2011). At Salt Springs, a portion of a relict timber retaining wall was removed and replaced with concrete in 2009. As described in chapter 3, the coffer dam installed to facilitate this repair exposed subaqueous midden that was subsequently tested by the LSA (see also O'Donoughue et al. 2011). And at Alexander Spring, "erosion and sedimentation have been a constant maintenance problem . . . sedimentation occurs in two ways: 1) Runoff from the parking lot and roads courses through the recreation area during downpours that wash into the spring . . . 2) Erosion from the beach due to intense foot traffic and the constant movement of 76,000,000 gallons of water per day downstream from the boil" (Willis 1995:11). This has required repeated dredging to remove introduced sand from the spring and constant replenishment of the beach with fresh fill sand. This is a consequence of several factors, including the removal of vegetation that would otherwise stabilize slopes, the infilling of the wet-land that acted as a sediment trap, and the introduction of unconsolidated sediment through beach construction in the 1950s. The beach at Weeki Wachee Spring necessitates similar dredging and rejuvenation (Spicuzza 2005), and facilities like the Underwater Theater require maintenance and upkeep for both safety and aesthetics.

Silver Springs' transition to a state park in 2013 brought with it several million dollars of repairs and renovations, paid for by the former lessee, Palace Entertainment. This included rehabilitating walkways and boardwalks, replacing rotted wood, painting structures, removing invasive plants, and demolishing zoological exhibits. However, the Florida Department of Environmental Protection "halted much of the work, with less than half of Palace's money spent, because some problems were bigger than first imagined" (Thompson 2013a:3). Indeed, the state's acquisition of both Silver and Weeki Wachee springs from private entertainment companies, and their conversion to state parks, was motivated by the failure (or inability) to maintain aging facilities and ensure protection of the springs from degradation. Rehabilitating and redeveloping these facilities necessitated the archaeological surveys conducted by the LSA.

State agencies have resorted to mechanical and suction dredging to remove benthic algae from several springs (e.g., Chassahowitzka, Otter, and Weeki Wachee). And tens of millions of dollars have been spent constructing wastewater facilities and purchasing land around springs to protect them from pollution. The City of Tallahassee, for instance, spent over a quarter of a billion dollars on wastewater treatment facilities to reduce nitrate pollution in Wakulla Springs (Shockman 2015). Similarly, the proximity of Weeki Wachee Springs to U.S. Highway 19 and a massive parking lot required the installation of facilities to capture and treat stormwater runoff (Southwest Florida Water Management District 2009).

Springs are thus entangled with anthropogenic and planetary processes and events at multiple temporal and spatial scales. Springs are unique and complex hydrological and ecological entities, and so their extensive entanglement is perhaps not surprising. But out of this web I want to draw two salient features of springs entanglement as they pertain to springs archaeology and conservation. The first is that springs entanglement itself is in many ways a barrier to conservation. Predicting the impacts of interventions on springs ecology and hydrology is fraught with uncertainty, because of their dynamic complexities—that is, their entanglement with forces operating at divergent spatial and temporal scales. Changes taking place at springs (i.e., flow and pollution) have been ongoing for decades, with a temporality scarcely perceptible on the scale of the human lifetime.

Likewise, the spatial scale of springs' hydrological ties is largely obscured from human perception. Springsheds—the basins contributing water to a spring—are not visible on the surface and vary in size and extent over time. It is not at all apparent where, for example, nitrates from fertilizers on an agricultural field will end up after percolating through the soil and recharging the aquifer. Protecting springs' water quality is largely a matter of managing land-use practices within springsheds. However, because these are moving targets, the process is not straightforward. It is therefore difficult to determine what actions need to be taken on what portions of the land surrounding a spring to best protect it from further pollution. It is likewise not obvious to the casual observer that—because of the entanglement of springs—actions in a given locality can have impacts in distant parts of the Floridan Aquifer (e.g., groundwater pumping in Jacksonville impacting springs 100 km distant).

The spatial scale and invisibility of springs' entanglement has economic implications as well. As noted in chapter 2, springs are found primarily in the karst regions of northern Florida. This area has a relatively low population density, in comparison to largely springs-free southern Florida. Much of Florida's financial abundance is also located away from springs. Figure 6.6 shows the distribution of springs in Florida, per Florida DEP data (2012), and median per capita income (PCI) by county in 2013. Count PCI ranged from $20,294 to $64,872, and counties can be divided into low, medium, and high income tiers in roughly $15,000 increments. These data reveal that 82.7 percent of springs are located in low-income counties, 16.8 percent in medium-income counties, and .5 percent in high-income counties. Financial, and thus political, capital is largely concentrated in areas of the state devoid of springs.

Recent research has demonstrated that those living close to a spring are more vested in springs conservation (Alenicheva 2012). This is problematic, since actions taking place in distant locales can negatively impact springs. Protecting springs requires people to change their behavior with regard to water use and the application of polluting substances (e.g., fertilizers) over a wide swath that may be far removed from springs. As Jim Stevenson, retired chair of the Florida Springs Task Force quoted above, said in a recent interview: "we have spent substantial time and funding

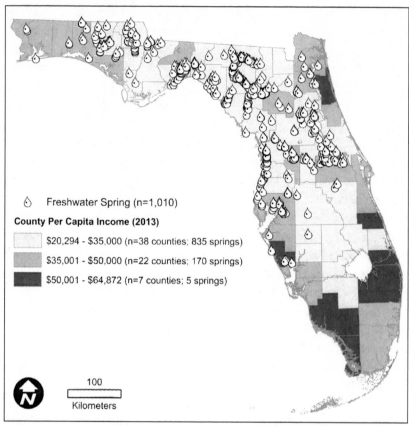

Figure 6.6. County median per capita income and the distribution of springs in Florida. Springs data from the Florida Department of Environmental Protection (2012). Economic data from the U.S. Department of Commerce, Bureau of Economic Analysis (www.bea.gov).

to educate Floridians about the plight of our springs and what citizens can do to overcome the degradation. . . . Optimism may be in order if we can convince the public that they must be outraged by the loss of their springs. . . . Our springs will survive or die by the level of public sentiment" (quoted in Swihart 2013). Education has not been enough, partially because of the entrapment of our entanglements. Floridians are so reliant on groundwater, so entangled with it, that actions proposed to reduce withdrawals are difficult to implement. And the prospect of divesting ourselves of pumped groundwater completely and turning to other sources of freshwater is not considered possible, or not considered at all.

The second salient feature of springs entanglement is the long-term continuity in human activity at springs. The myriad ways that springs and humans are now codependent are historically contingent and a result of the path dependencies instigated by human–springs engagement in the past. Our entanglement has increased through time, but ancient human activities at springs (e.g., extracting water, infilling marginal wetlands, aggrading shorelines, gathering for social events) are the same as those taking place today, scalar differences notwithstanding.

The continuity of human–springs entanglement over millennia undercuts narratives of changelessness invoked by the springs eternal trope. Likewise, the path dependency and historical trajectories of springs entanglement points to the futility of backward-looking conservation goals seeking a pristine or more natural state for springs. Referring to water usage in Marion County and flow reduction in Silver Springs, Ed Lowe, chief scientist of the St. Johns River Water Management District, said recently, "I think the district is realizing we are beyond the point of sustainable use" (quoted in *Ocala Star-Banner* 2015). Likewise, Knight (2015:102) acknowledges that "pragmatically, we may have to accept that springs will never be returned to their former natural majesty." Nevertheless, this continues to be the target of springs conservation. Knight continues that "ethically, this should not be an option seriously considered by the concerned public or by those public officials who are in leadership or regulatory positions and who can potentially contribute to a reversal in the trajectory of depletion and pollution that has engulfed Florida's springs." Conservation efforts that seek either to reverse time to a pristine state or to maintain the status quo (i.e., "sustainable use") are unlikely to succeed. Indeed, the long-term record of human landscape alteration at springs like Silver Glen discounts the very existence of a pristine or natural state to return to. We cannot escape our entanglement with springs by looking back. We cannot "fix" springs by fixing them in time, locking them in the past of an imagined pristine state. Conservation efforts must be *future*-oriented, targeting activities and goals consonant with ongoing human–spring interaction.

My argument is not that springs will cease to exist without human intervention—although their water quality and flow may be impaired—but rather that they cannot continue to exist in *the ways that people want them to* without care. A key question for springs conservation, then, is, What are springs for? Today, springs are for many things: swimming, tubing, and camping with family and friends; contemplating, painting, photographing; studying, excavating, legislating. They are recreation areas, research subjects, and places of employment. The activities that people engage in to maintain springs (e.g., repairing aging facilities, remediating algal proliferation) serve to maintain the aesthetic and ecological integrity of springs that underwrites all the ways that people seek to use them. There are, however, competing interests. Take, for example, the case of Silver Springs. After becoming a state park in October 2013, renovations and facility repairs continued under the management of the Florida DEP. As of late 2014, over 20 buildings had been demolished, and all zoological exhibits removed as part of returning the park to a more pristine state:

> [Park Manager Sally] Lieb walked the east side of the park on a recent day and stood by the remains of a 1-foot-thick, 10-foot-high wall. She pointed to an empty field that was once home to the park's cougars. The few feet of wall is all that remains. Lieb hopes to let the field return to its natural state. Then she pointed to a canal dividing where she stood and the five-acre Ross Allen Island, where captive alligators once were housed behind glass. The two bridges onto the island are gone now. They didn't meet state standards. All remnants of the boardwalk on the island are also gone. The old boardwalk overwhelmed and took away from the island experience, Lieb said, adding, "Now it's a community with cypress trees and beautiful wildlife." (Hiers 2014:2)

However, the DEP also has to accommodate park visitors, some of whom are less enthusiastic about the changes. Hiers (2014:4) quoted one, among many disappointed visitors, as saying: "We thought there were still animals here. . . . It's great that they're bringing it back to its natural state, but all you have is boat rides for the kids now." And so future interventions at springs and the direction of their entanglement hinges on the question, What are springs for?

As noted above, research has demonstrated that proximity is an important factor motivating public will toward springs conservation, as those living less than five miles from a spring "value the springs to a greater extent, more often engage in local volunteer actions, and have a greater willingness to increase personal knowledge and share their knowledge with others" (Alenicheva 2012:14). As a corollary to this, direct experience with springs is also an important factor determining public sentiment for springs conservation. In other words, if people are to value springs, and thus be motivated to take actions to protect them, springs must be experienced. People must develop relationships with these places. However, it is not enough for people to visit or admire springs. As Keith Basso (1996b:56–57) wrote, "it is simply not the case, as some phenomenologists and growing numbers of nature writers would have us believe, that relationships to places are lived exclusively or predominantly in contemplative moments of social isolation. On the contrary, relationships to places are lived most often in the company of other people." Indeed, if places like Silver Glen Springs are any guide, the value attached to springs is amplified and manifested in moments of social gathering. And these gatherings do not (and did not) take place in a historical vacuum but are most affecting in the context of social memories of past gatherings, once materialized in the form of various pits, mounds, interments, and offerings.

Continued recreation, then, is a key to mobilizing public sentiment for springs protection and conservation. Through recreational gathering at springs, people can continue to develop the relationships with these places that are necessary for their ongoing cultural valuation. Likewise, the long-term historical import of springs should be brought to the fore in conservation narratives and highlighted at recreational facilities. The goal here is not to provide a baseline for comparison or to construct simplistic narratives of people living in harmony with springs, but to emphasize the generations of people who have come before, the "continuum from the time of the ancestors to the current-day people, all of whom *shared parts of this one place*" (Fowler and Fowler 2008:2, emphasis added). Springs can be made meaningful by accentuating the continuity of place, enlivening it with history, despite the gulf of experience that seemingly separates the ancient and the modern.

If I may return once more to *The Yearling*, and Rawlings' (1938:4) description of Silver Glen Springs as it "bubbled up . . . cut itself a channel" to join Lake George and, flowing northward with the St. Johns River, the sea: "It excited Jody to watch the beginning of the ocean. There were other beginnings, true, but this one was his own." This book too is a beginning, and there is much yet to be learned about the history and significance of Florida's springs. But I am hopeful that it will contribute in some small way to springs conservation, and that generations to come will continue to be enamored and enchanted by these magical waters.

NOTES

Chapter 1. Smoke on the Water

1. Public Law 88–577 (16 U.S. C. 1131–1136), 88th Congress, Second Session, September 3, 1964.

Chapter 2. Springs Geology

1. Confining and semi-confining units are sometimes referred to as *aquicludes* or *aquitards*. Confining units can also occur within or above the surficial aquifer, where they create a perched aquifer. These typically have a relatively small areal extent but can form lakes or ponds whose water level is independent of the surrounding water table.

2. For the sake of simplicity, I forgo discussion of local aquifers, such as the Biscayne and sand and gravel aquifers, which, while important to regional water supply, are less relevant to the distribution and mechanics of artesian springs.

3. We can further differentiate between primary and secondary porosity. Primary porosity is inherent in the material as a result of deposition. Secondary porosity is formed by weathering and diagenesis, for example, as a result of tectonic fracturing or chemical dissolution.

4. Geomorphologically, the lower St. Johns more properly begins where the western offset ends, near present-day Palatka and approximately 15 km north of the confluence with the Ocklawaha River.

Chapter 3. Spring Origins

1. Florida accounts for some 30 percent of global phosphate production. The Port of Tampa exports more phosphate fertilizer than any other port in the world (Hine 2013:159–163).

2. In the following I use "shell site" or "shell deposit" to refer to anthropogenic deposits dominated by shells. When referring specifically to elevated deposits, I use "shell mound" generically, and "shell ridge" to refer specifically to elongated (linear, crescentic, or lenticular) forms.

3. However, many of these large springs originate from deep caverns that likely contained fresh groundwater, even if that water did not flow onto the surface.

Chapter 4. Sacred Spring

1. Dunbar and Waller (1983:19–20) include sites adjacent to Salt and Silver Glen springs as St. Johns River Paleoindian sites. The Silver Glen Springs site is presumably

D.B.'s Cave (8MR162), but I can find no documented Paleoindian site adjacent to Salt Springs. The Guest Mammoth Site (8MR130 [Rayl 1974]) in Silver River is another purported Paleoindian site, but the association of the fauna and artifacts is dubious.

2. Thermal alteration of lithic artifacts is thought to have been most prevalent during the preceramic Archaic in Florida (Ste. Claire 1987).

Chapter 5. Springs On the Move

1. These data sets were obtained from the Florida Geographic Data Library (FGDL).

REFERENCES CITED

Abshire, A. E., Alden L. Potter, Allen R. Taylor, Clyde H. Neil, Walter H. Anderson, John
  I. Rutledge, and Stevenson B. Johnson (editors)
1935   *Some Further Papers on Aboriginal Man in the Neighborhood of the Ocala
         National Forest.* Civilian Conservation Corps, Company 1420, Ocala Camp,
         Florida.

Alenicheva, Diana
2012   Assessing Springshed Residents' Perceptions of North Central Florida
         Springs. Unpublished master's thesis, Interdisciplinary Ecology Program,
         School of Natural Resources and Environment, University of Florida,
         Gainesville.

Allen, Greg
2013   Now Endangered, Florida's Silver Springs Once Lured Tourists. Electronic
         document, http://www.npr.org/2013/04/13/177105692/before-disney-flori-
         das-silver-springs-lured-tourists, accessed October 9, 2015.

Alley, Richard B., Paul A. Mayewski, Todd Sowers, Minze Stuiver, Kendrick C. Taylor,
  and Peter U. Clark
1997   Holocene Climatic Instability: A Prominent, Widespread Event 8200 yr Ago.
         Geology 25:483–486.

Alt, David, and H. K. Brooks
1965   Age of the Florida Marine Terraces. *Journal of Geology* 73:406–411.

Anderson, David G.
1994   *The Savannah River Chiefdoms: Political Change in the Late Prehistoric South-
         east.* University of Alabama Press, Tuscaloosa.

Anderson, David G., and Thaddeus G. Bissett
2015   The Initial Colonization of North America: Sea-Level Change, Shoreline
         Movement, and Great Migrations. In *Mobility and Ancient Society in Asia
         and the Americas: Proceedings of the Second International Conference on
         "Great Migrations,"* edited by Michael Frachetti and Robert Spengler, pp.
         59–88. Springer, New York.

Anderson, David G., Lisa S. O'Steen, and Kenneth E. Sassaman
1996   Environmental and Chronological Considerations. In *The Paleoindian and
         Early Archaic Southeast,* edited by David G. Anderson and Kenneth E. Sassa-
         man, pp. 3–15. University of Alabama Press, Tuscaloosa.

Anderson, David G., Michael Russo, and Kenneth E. Sassaman
2007   Mid-Holocene Cultural Dynamics in Southeastern North America. In *Climate Change and Cultural Dynamics: A Global Perspective on Mid-Holocene Transitions*, edited by David G. Anderson, Kirk A. Maasch, and Daniel H. Sandweiss, pp. 457–489. Academic Press, London.

Anderson, David G., and Kenneth E. Sassaman
2012   *Recent Developments in Southeastern Archaeology: From Colonization to Complexity.* Society for American Archaeology, Washington, D.C.

Anderson, Elyse
2015   Draft Report: Silver Glen Run, Locus C & D (8LA1-W). Manuscript on file, Laboratory of Southeastern Archaeology, University of Florida, Gainesville.

Andrews, Travis DeWitt
2012   Testate Amoebae as Hydrological Proxies in the Florida Everglades. Unpublished master's thesis, Earth and Environmental Sciences, Lehigh University, Bethlehem, Pennsylvania.

Archaeological Consultants Inc., and Janus Research
2001   *Phase III Mitigative Excavations at Lake Monroe Outlet Midden (8VO53), Volusia County, Florida.* Report submitted to U.S. Department of Transportation Federal Highway Administration and Florida Department of Transportation District Five, Sarasota. Copies available from the Florida Master Site Files, Tallahassee.

Arthur, Jonathan D., P. G. 1149, Alan E. Baker, James R. Cichon, Alex R. Wood, and Andrew Rudin
2005   *Florida Aquifer Vulnerability Assessment (FAVA): Contamination Potential of Florida's Principal Aquifer Systems.* Division of Resource Assessment and Management, Florida Geological Survey, Tallahassee.

Arz, Helge W., Frank Lamy, and Jürgen Pätzold
2006   A Pronounced Dry Event Recorded around 4.2 ka in Brine Sediments from the Northern Red Sea. *Quaternary Research* 66:432–441.

Ashley, Keith H., and Nancy Marie White (editors)
2012   *Late Prehistoric Florida: Archaeology at the Edge of the Mississippian World.* University Press of Florida, Gainesville.

Aten, Lawrence E.
1999   Middle Archaic Ceremonialism at Tick Island, Florida: Ripley Bullen's 1961 Excavation at the Harris Creek Site. *TheFlorida Anthropologist* 52:131–200.

Aucott, Walter R.
1988   *Areal Variation in Recharge to and Discharge from the Floridan Aquifer System in Florida.* Water-Resources Investigations Report 88–4057. U.S. Geological Survey, Reston, Virginia.

Austin, Robert J.
1997   The Economics of Lithic-Resource Use in South Central Florida. Unpublished Ph.D. dissertation, Department of Anthropology, University of Florida, Gainesville.

Austin, Robert J., and Richard W. Estabrook

2000 Chert Distribution and Exploitation in Peninsular Florida. *The Florida Anthropologist* 53:116–130.

Bair, Cinnamon

2011 Polk Chronicles: Kissengen Spring Was Spot for Fun. Electronic document, http://www.theledger.com/article/20110823/COLUMNISTS/108235000, accessed August 14, 2015.

Balsillie, James H., and Joseph F. Donoghue

2004 *High Resolution Sea-Level History for the Gulf of Mexico since the Last Glacial Maximum.* Report of Investigations 103. Florida Geological Survey, Tallahassee.

2011 Northern Gulf of Mexico Sea-Level History for the Past 20,000 Years. In *Gulf of Mexico: Origin, Waters, and Biota*, Vol. 3: *Geology*, edited by Noreen A. Buster and Charles W. Holmes, pp. 53–69. Texas A&M University Press, College Station.

Barber, D. C., A. Dyke, C. Hillaire-Marcel, A. E. Jennings, J. T. Andrews, M. W. Kerwin, G. Bilodeau, R. McNeely, J. Southon, M. D. Morehead, and J.-M. Gagnon

1999 Forcing of the Cold Event of 8,200 Years Ago by Catastrophic Drainage of Laurentide Lakes. *Nature* 400:344–348.

Barrett, John C.

1999 The Mythical Landscapes of the British Iron Age. In *Archaeologies of Landscape: Contemporary Perspectives*, edited by Wendy Ashmore and A. Bernard Knapp, pp. 253–265. Blackwell, Malden.

2001 Agency, the Duality of Structure, and the Problem of the Archaeological Record. In *Archaeological Theory Today*, edited by Ian Hodder, pp. 141–164. Blackwell, Malden.

Bartram, John

1769 *A Description of East-Florida, with a Journal, kept by John Bartram of Philadelphia, Botanist to His Majesty for the Floridas.* William Stork, London.

Bartram, William

1996 *Travels and Other Writings.* Library of America, New York.

Basso, Keith H.

1996a *Wisdom Sits in Places: Landscape and Language among the Western Apache.* University of New Mexico Press, Albuquerque.

1996b Wisdom Sits in Places: Notes on a Western Apache Landscape. In *Senses of Place*, edited by Steven Feld and Keith H. Basso, pp. 53–90. School for Advanced Research Press, Santa Fe.

Beasley, Virgil R. III

2009 Monumentality during the Mid-Holocene in the Upper and Middle St. Johns River Basins, Florida. Unpublished Ph.D. dissertation, Department of Anthropology, Northwestern University, Evanston, Illinois.

Beck, Charlotte, Amanda K. Taylor, George T. Jones, Cynthia M. Fadem, Caitlyn R. Cook, and Sara A. Millward

2002 Rocks Are Heavy: Transport Costs and Paleoarchaic Quarry Behavior in the Great Basin. *Journal of Anthropological Archaeology* 21:481–507.

Beck, Robin A., Douglas J. Bolender, James A. Brown, and Timothy K. Earle
2007   Eventful Archaeology: The Place of Space in Structural Transformation. *Current Anthropology* 48:833–860.

Belaineh, Getachew, Joseph Stewart, Peter Sucsy, Louis H. Motz, Kijin Park, Shahrokh Rouhani, and Michael Cullum
2012   Groundwater Hydrology. In *St. Johns River Water Supply Impact Study*, edited by Edgar F. Lowe, Lawrence E. Battoe, Hal Wilkening, Michael Cullum, and Tom Bartol, pp. 4-i–4-100. Technical Publication SJ2012-1. St. Johns River Water Management District, Palatka, Florida.

Belcourt, Andrew N., Martin F. Dickinson, and Lucy B. Wayne
2009   *Cultural Resources Survey and Assessment, Silver Springs Retention Pond, Marion County, Florida*. SouthArc Inc. Copies available from the Florida Master Site Files, Tallahassee.

Bell, Catherine
1992   *Ritual Theory, Ritual Practice*. Oxford University Press, New York.

Bell, Tyler, and Gary Lock
2000   Topographic and Cultural Influences on Walking the Ridgeway in Later Prehistoric Times. In *Beyond the Map: Archaeology and Spatial Technologies*, edited by Gary Lock, pp. 85–100. IOS Press, Amsterdam.

Belleville, Bill
2000   *River of Lakes: A Journey on Florida's St. Johns River*. University of Georgia Press, Athens.

2011   *Salvaging the Real Florida: Lost and Found in the State of Dreams*. University Press of Florida, Gainesville.

Bender, Barbara
2001   Landscapes On-the-Move. *Journal of Social Archaeology* 1:75–89.

Bennett Michael W.
2004   *Hydrogeologic Investigation of the Floridan Aquifer System: Big Cypress Preserve Collier County, Florida*. Technical Publication WS–18. South Florida Water Management District, West Palm Beach, Florida.

Berson, Thomas R.
2011   Silver Springs: The Florida Interior in the American Imagination. Unpublished Ph.D. dissertation, Department of History, University of Florida, Gainesville.

Blakeslee, Donald J.
2010   *Holy Ground, Healing Water: Cultural Landscapes at Waconda Lake, Kansas*. Texas A&M University Press, College Station.

Bland, Myles C. P., and Marsha A. Chance
2000   *An Intensive Cultural Resource Assessment Survey of the Fanning Springs State Recreation Area, Levy County, Florida*. Report of Investigations 191. Environmental Services, Inc., Jacksonville, Florida.

Bleicher, Niels, and Carsten Schubert
2015   Why Are They Still There? A Model of Accumulation and Decay of Organic Prehistoric Cultural Deposits. *Journal of Archaeological Science* 61:277–286.

Blessing, Meggan E.
2011   Zooarchaeological Assemblage. In *Archaeological Investigations at Salt Springs (8MR2322), Marion County, Florida*, edited by Jason M. O'Donoughue, Kenneth E. Sassaman, Meggan E. Blessing, Johanna B. Talcott, and Julie C. Byrd, pp. 65–85. Technical Report 11. Laboratory of Southeastern Archaeology, Department of Anthropology, University of Florida.

Blum, Michael D., and Torbjörn E. Törnqvist
2000   Fluvial Responses to Climate and Sea-Level Change: A Review and Look Forward. *Sedimentology* 47(s1):2–48.

Bonn, Mark A.
2004   *Visitor Profiles, Economic Impacts and Recreational Aesthetic Values Associated with Eight Priority Florida Springs Located in the St. Johns River Water Management District*. Special Publication SJ2004-SP35. St. Johns River Water Management District, Palatka, Florida.

Bonn, Mark A., and Frederick W. Bell
2003   *Economic Impact of Selected Florida Springs on Surrounding Local Areas*. Report prepared for the Florida Department of Environmental Protection, Division of State Lands, Florida Springs Task Force, Tallahassee.

Booth, Robert K., Stephen T. Jackson, Steven L. Forman, John E. Kutzbach, E. A. Bettis, Joseph Kreigs, and David K. Wright
2005   A Severe Centennial-Scale Drought in Midcontinental North America 4200 Years Ago and Apparent Global Linkages. *The Holocene* 15:321–328.

Booth, R. K., M. Lamentowicz, and D. J. Charman
2010   Preparation and Analysis of Testate Amoebae in Peatland Paleoenvironmental Studies. *Mires and Peat* 7(2):1–7.

Bradley, Richard
2000   *An Archaeology of Natural Places*. Routledge, London.
2005   *Ritual and Domestic Life in Prehistoric Europe*. Routledge, London.

Brady, James E., and Wendy Ashmore
1999   Mountains, Caves, Water: Ideational Landscapes of the Ancient Maya. In *Archaeologies of Landscape: Contemporary Perspectives*, edited by Wendy Ashmore and A. Bernard Knapp, pp. 124–145. Blackwell, Malden.

Brenneman, Walter L., and Mary G. Brenneman
1995   *Crossing the Circle at the Holy Wells of Ireland*. University Press of Virginia, Charlottesville.

Brenner, Mark, Lawrence W. Keenan, Steven J. Miller, and Claire L. Schelske
1999   Spatial and Temporal Patterns of Sediment and Nutrient Accumulation in Shallow Lakes of the Upper St. Johns River Basin, Florida. *Wetlands Ecology and Management* 6:221–240.

Brenner, Mark, Claire L. Schelske, and Lawrence W. Keenan
2001   Historical Rates of Sediment and Nutrient Accumulation in Marshes of the Upper St. Johns River Basin, Florida, USA. *Journal of Paleolimnology* 26:241–257.

Brinton, Daniel G.
1859   *Notes on the Florida Peninsula, Its Literary History, Indian Tribes and Antiqui-*
        ties. Joseph Sabin, Philadelphia.
Broecker, Wallace S.
2006   Was the Younger Dryas Triggered by a Flood? *Science* 312:1146–1148.
Broecker, Wallace S., George H. Denton, R. Lawrence Edwards, Hai Cheng, Richard B.
        Alley, and Aaron E. Putnam
2010   Putting the Younger Dryas Cold Event into Context. *Quaternary Science Re-*
        views 29:1078–1081.
Brooks, H. K.
1981   *Guide to the Physiographic Divisions of Florida.* Institute of Food and Agri-
        cultural Sciences, University of Florida, Gainesville.
Brown, Bill
2001   Thing Theory. *Critical Inquiry* 28:1–22.
Brown, Canter Jr.
1991   *Florida's Peace River Frontier.* University of Central Florida Press, Orlando.
Brown, D. P.
1984   *Impact of Development on Availability and Quality of Ground Water in East-*
        ern Nassau County, Florida, and Southeastern Camden County, Georgia. Wa-
        ter-Resources Investigations Report 83-4190. U.S. Geological Survey, Reston,
        Virginia.
Brown, James A., and Robert K. Vierra
1983   What Happened in the Middle Archaic? Introduction to an Ecological Ap-
        proach to Koster Site Archaeology. In *Archaic Hunters and Gatherers in the*
        American Midwest, edited by James L. Phillips and James A. Brown, pp. 165–
        195. Academic, New York.
Brown, Kenneth M., Dennis Varza, and Terry D. Richardson
1989   Life Histories and Population Dynamics of Two Subtropical Snails (Proso-
        branchia: Viviparidae). *Journal of the North American Benthological Society*
        8:222–228.
Brown, Mark T., Kelly Chinners Reiss, Matthew J. Cohen, Jason M. Evans, Patrick W.
        Inglett, Kanika Sharma Inglett, K. Ramesh Reddy, Thomas K. Frazer, Charles
        A. Jacoby, Edward J. Phlips, Robert L. Knight, Sky K. Notestein, Richard G.
        Hamann, and Kathleen A. McKee
2008   *Summary and Synthesis of Available Literature on the Effects of Nutrients on*
        Springs Organisms and Systems. University of Florida Water Institute. Report
        submitted to the Florida Department of Environmental Protection, Tallahas-
        see.
Brück, Joanna
1999   Ritual and Rationality: Some Problems of Interpretation in European Ar-
        chaeology. *European Journal of Archaeology* 2(3):313–344.
Bullen, Ripley P.
1953   Excavations at Manatee Springs, Florida. *The Florida Anthropologist* 6:53–67.

Burt, Al

2003   Healing Waters: Springs Represent a Disappearing Part of Florida. *Tallahassee Democrat* 27 April:E1, E5. Tallahassee, Florida.

1975   *A Guide to the Identification of Florida Projectile Points.* Rev. ed. Kendall Books, Gainesville.

Bush, P. W., and R. H. Johnston

1988   *Ground-Water Hydraulics, Regional Flow, and Ground-Water Development of the Floridan Aquifer System in Florida and in Parts of Georgia, South Carolina, and Alabama.* Professional Paper 1403-C. U.S. Geological Survey, Washington, D.C.

Butt, Peter, Alaa Aly, and David Toth

2006   *Silver Springs Spring Vent Documentation and Geochemical Characterization.* Special Publication SJ2008-SP6. St. Johns River Water Management District, Palatka, Florida.

Byrd, Julia C.

2011   Archaic Bone Tools in the St. Johns River Basin, Florida: Microwear and Manufacture Traces. Unpublished master's thesis, Department of Anthropology, Florida State University, Tallahassee.

Carmichael, David, Jane Hubert, and Brian Reeves

1994   Introduction. In *Sacred Sites, Sacred Places,* edited by David L. Carmichael, Jane Hubert, Brian Reeves, and Audchild Schanche, pp. 1–8. Routledge, New York.

Carr, Archie

1996   *A Naturalist in Florida: A Celebration of Eden.* Yale University Press, New Haven.

Carr, Susan Latham

2009   Soiling Glen Springs. Electronic document, http://www.ocala.com/article/20090803/ARTICLES/908031008, accessed October 2, 2015.

Casey, Edward S.

1996   How to Get from Space to Place in a Fairly Short Stretch of Time: Phenomenological Prolegomena. In *Senses of Place,* edited by Steven Feld and Keith H. Basso, pp. 13–52. School for Advanced Research Press, Santa Fe.

Chambers, Frank M., Robert K. Booth, Francois De Vleeschouwer, Mariusz Lamentowicz, Gael Le Roux, Dmitri Mauquoy, Jonathan E. Nichols, and Bas van Geel

2012   Development and Refinement of Proxy-Climate Indicators from Peats. *Quaternary International* 268:21–33.

Chapman, John

2000   *Fragmentation in Archaeology: People, Places and Broken Objects in the Prehistory of South-Eastern Europe.* Routledge, New York.

Chapman, John, and Bisserka Gaydarska

2007   *Parts and Wholes: Fragmentation in Prehistoric Context.* Oxbow Books, Oxford.

Charlton, Ro

2008   *Fundamentals of Fluvial Geomorphology.* Routledge, New York.

Claassen, Cheryl

2010   *Feasting with Shellfish in the Southern Ohio Valley: Archaic Sacred Sites and Rituals.* University of Tennessee Press, Knoxville.

Clausen, Carl J., H. K. Brooks, and Al B. Wesolowsky

1975   The Early Man Site at Warm Mineral Springs, Florida. *Journal of Field Archaeology* 2(3):191–213

Clausen, Carl J., A. D. Cohen, Cesare Emiliani, J. A. Holman, and J. J. Stipp

1979   Little Salt Spring, Florida: A Unique Underwater Site. *Science* 203(4381):609–614.

Cobb, Charles C.

2005   Archaeology and the "Savage Slot": Displacement and Emplacement in the Premodern World. *American Anthropologist* 107:563–574.

Connoly, James, and Mark Lake

2006   *Geographical Information Systems in Archaeology.* Cambridge University Press, New York.

Connor, Jody N., and Thomas V. Belanger

1981   Ground Water Seepage in Lake Washington and the Upper St. Johns River Basin, Florida. *Journal of the American Water Resources Association* 17:799–805.

Cooke, C. Wythe

1939   *Scenery of Florida, Interpreted by a Geologist.* Bulletin 17. Florida Geological Survey, Tallahassee.

1945   *The Geology of Florida.* Bulletin 29. Florida Geological Survey, Tallahassee.

Copeland, Rick (compiler)

2003   *Florida Springs Classification System and Spring Glossary.* Special Publication 52. Florida Geological Survey, Tallahassee.

Cordell, Ann S.

2004   Paste Variability and Possible Manufacturing Origins of Late Archaic Fiber-Tempered Pottery from Selected Sites in Peninsular Florida. In *Early Pottery: Technology, Function, Style, and Interaction in the Lower Southeast*, edited by Rebecca Saunders and Christopher T. Hays, pp. 63–104. University of Alabama Press, Tuscaloosa.

Delcourt, Paul A., and Hazel R. Delcourt

2004   *Prehistoric Native Americans and Ecological Change: Human Ecosystems in Eastern North America since the Pleistocene.* Cambridge University Press, New York.

DeMarrais, Elizabeth, Chris Gosden, and Colin Renfrew (editors)

2004   *Rethinking Materiality: The Engagement of Mind with the Material World.* McDonald Institute for Archaeological Research, Cambridge.

DeMort, Carole L.

1991   The St. Johns River System. In *The Rivers of Florida*, edited by Robert J. Livingston, pp. 97–120. Springer-Verlag, New York.

Denevan, William M.

1992   The Pristine Myth: The Landscape of the Americas in 1492. *Annals of the Association of American Geographers* 82:369–385.

Denson, Robin L., Gary D. Ellis, and Russell Dorsey

1995 *Archaeological Survey of De Leon Springs State Recreation Area.* Ellis Archaeology. Submitted to Florida Department of Environmental Protection. Copies available from the Florida Master Site Files, Tallahassee.

Dickinson, Martin F., and Lucy B. Wayne

1994 *Cultural Resources Survey and Assessment, Salt Springs Recreation Area, Marion County, Florida.* SouthArc, Inc. Copies available from the Florida Master Site Files, Tallahassee.

2002 *Cultural Resources Survey and Assessment, Silver Springs Boat Landing & Train Depot, Marion County, Florida.* SouthArc, Inc. Submitted to Smart Parks of Florida, Inc. Copies available from the Florida Master Site Files, Tallahassee.

2003 *Cultural Resources Survey and Assessment: Fanning Springs State Recreation Area Proposed Cabin Sites, Levy County, Florida.* SouthArc, Inc. Copies available from the Florida Master Site Files, Tallahassee.

Donar, Christopher, Eugene F. Stoermer, and Mark Brenner

2009 The Holocene Paleolimnology of Lake Apopka, Florida. *Nova Hedwigia* 135:57–70.

Donders, Timme H.

2014 Middle Holocene Humidity Increase in Florida: Climate or Sea-Level? *Quaternary Science Reviews* 103:170–174.

Donders, Timme H., Hugo Jan de Boer, Walter Finsinger, Eric C. Grimm, Stefan C. Dekker, Gert Jan Reichart, and Friederike Wagner-Cremer

2011 Impact of the Atlantic Warm Pool on Precipitation and Temperature in Florida during North Atlantic Cold Spells. *Climate Dynamics* 36:109–118.

Donders, Timme H., Friederike Wagner, David L. Dilcher, and Henk Visscher

2005 Mid-to Late-Holocene El Niño-Southern Oscillation Dynamics Reflected in the Subtropical Terrestrial Realm. *Proceedings of the National Academy of Sciences of the United States of America* 102:10904–10908.

Donoghue, Joseph F.

2011 Sea Level History of the Northern Gulf of Mexico Coast and Sea Level Rise Scenarios for the Near Future. *Climatic Change* 107:17–33.

Doran, Glen H. (editor)

2002 *Windover: Multidisciplinary Investigations of an Early Archaic Florida Cemetery.* University Press of Florida, Gainesville.

Douglas, Marjory Stoneman

1967 *Florida: The Long Frontier.* Harper and Row, New York.

Dunbar, James S.

1990 8MR162: D.B.'s Cave Site. Field Survey Form. Copies available from the Florida Master Site Files, Tallahassee.

1991 Resource Orientation of Clovis and Suwannee Age Paleoindian Sites in Florida. In *Clovis: Origins and Adaptations*, edited by Robson Bonnichsen and Karen L. Turnmire, pp. 185–213. Center for the Study of the First Americans, Oregon State University, Corvallis.

2002   Chronostratigraphy and Paleoclimate of Late Pleistocene Florida and the Implications of Changing Paleoindian Land Use. Unpublished master's thesis, Department of Anthropology, Florida State University, Tallahassee.

2003   *Alexander Springs Inspection of August 4, 2003*. Bureau of Archaeological Research, CARL Archaeological Survey. Submitted to Florida Division of Historical Resources. Copies available from the Florida Master Site Files, Tallahassee.

2006   Paleoindian Archaeology. In *First Floridians and Last Mastodons: The Page-Ladson Site in the Aucilla River*, edited by S. David Webb, pp. 403–435. Springer, New York.

2016   *Paleoindian Societies of the Coastal Southeast*. University of Florida Press, Gainesville.

Dunbar, James S., and Glen Doran

2010   *Paleoindian Sites Revisited—Known Sites and New Perspectives*. Florida State University. Copies available from the Florida Master Site Files, Tallahassee.

Dunbar, James S., Michael K. Faught, and S. David Webb

1988   Page/Ladson (8JE591): An Underwater Paleo-Indian Site in Northwestern Florida. *The Florida Anthropologist* 41:442–452.

Dunbar, James S., and Ben I. Waller

1983   A Distribution Analysis of the Clovis/Suwannee Paleo-Indian Sites of Florida—A Geographic Approach. *The Florida Anthropologist* 36:18–30.

Dwyer, Peter D.

1996   The Invention of Nature. In *Redefining Nature: Ecology, Culture and Domestication*, edited by Roy Ellen and Katsuyoshi Fukui, pp. 157–186. Berg, Oxford.

Dye, David H.

1996   Riverine Adaptation in the Midsouth. In *Of Caves and Shell Mounds*, edited by Kenneth C. Carstens and Patty Jo Watson, pp. 140–158. University of Alabama Press, Tuscaloosa.

Earl, Steven

2009   *Ichetucknee: Sacred Waters*. University Press of Florida, Gainesville.

Edwards, W. E.

1954   The Helen Blazes Site of Central Eastern Florida: A Study in Method utilizing the Disciplines of Archaeology, Geology, and Pedology. Unpublished Ph.D. dissertation, Department of Geology, Columbia University, New York.

Eliade, Mircea

1958   *Patterns in Comparative Religion*. Translated by Rosemary Sheen. Sheed and Ward, New York.

Emerson, Thomas E., Dale L. McElrath, and Andrew C. Fortier (editors)

2009   Archaic Societies: Diversity and Complexity across the Midcontinent. State University of New York Press, Albany.

Endonino, Jon C.

2007   A Reevaluation of the Gainesville, Ocala, and Lake Panasoffkee Quarry Clusters. *The Florida Anthropologist* 60:19–38.

2009   The Thornhill Lake Archaeological Research Project: 2005–2008. *The Florida Anthropologist* 61:149–165.

2010   Thornhill Lake: Hunter-Gatherers, Monuments, and Memory. Unpublished Ph.D. dissertation, Department of Anthropology, University of Florida, Gainesville.

Enfield, David B., Alberto M. Mestas-Nuñez, and Paul J. Trimble

2001   The Atlantic Multidecadal Oscillation and Its Relation to Rainfall and River Flows in the Continental U.S. *Geophysical Research Letters* 28:2077–2080.

Escobar, Jaime, Mark Brenner, Thomas J. Whitmore, William F. Kenney, and Jason H. Curtis

2008   Ecology of Testate Amoebae (Thecamoebians) in Subtropical Florida Lakes. *Journal of Paleolimnology* 40:715–731.

Estabrook, Richard W., and Laura M. Weant

1993   *Cultural Resource Assessment Survey of the Gemini Springs Project Site, Volusia County, Florida.* Janus Research. Submitted to Pinnacle Companies, Orlando. Copies available from the Florida Master Site Files, Tallahassee.

Faught, Michael K.

2009   *Silver Spring Paleoindian Research Project, Report of Field Operations, 15–17 December 2003.* Archaeological Research Cooperative, Inc. Copies available from the Florida Master Site Files, Tallahassee.

Faught, Michael K., and Joseph F. Donoghue

1997   Marine Inundated Archaeological Sites and Paleofluvial Systems: Examples from a Karst-Controlled Continental Shelf Setting in Apalachee Bay, Northeastern Gulf of Mexico. *Geoarchaeology* 12:417–458.

Faught, Michael K., and James C. Waggoner Jr.

2012   The Early Archaic to Middle Archaic transition in Florida: An Argument for Discontinuity. *The Florida Anthropologist* 65:153–175.

Faure, Hugues, Robert C. Walter, and Douglas R. Grant

2002   The Coastal Oasis: Ice Age Springs on Emerged Continental Shelves. *Global and Planetary Change* 33:47–56.

Ferguson, G. E., C. W. Lingham, S. K. Love, and R. O. Vernon

1947   *Springs of Florida.* Bulletin 31. Florida Geological Survey, Tallahassee.

Ferring, C. Reid

1986   Rates of Fluvial Sedimentation: Implications for Archaeological Variability. *Geoarchaeology* 1:259–274.

Filley, T. R., K. H. Freeman, T. S. Bianchi, M. Baskaran, L. A. Colarusso, and P. G. Hatcher

2001   An Isotopic Biogeochemical Assessment of Shifts in Organic Matter Input to Holocene Sediments from Mud Lake, Florida. *Organic Geochemistry* 32:1153–1167.

Fleury, Perrine, Michel Bakalowicz, and Ghislain de Marsily

2007   Submarine Springs and Coastal Karst Aquifers: A Review. *Journal of Hydrogeology* 339:79–92.

Florea, Lee J., and H. L. Vacher

2006   Springflow Hydrographs: Eogenetic vs. Telogenetic Karst. *Ground Water* 44:352–361.

2007   Eogenetic Karst Hydrology: Insights from the 2004 Hurricanes, Peninsular Florida. *Ground Water* 45: 439–446.

Florida Department of Community Affairs and Florida Department of Environmental Protection

2002   *Protecting Florida's Springs: Land Use Planning Strategies and Best Management Practices.* Florida Department of Community Affairs and Florida Department of Environmental Protection, Tallahassee.

Florida Department of Environmental Protection (FDEP)

2012   FDEP GeoData Directory. Electronic document, http://www.dep.state.fl.us/gis/datadir.htm/, accessed July 1, 2015.

2014   About Florida Springs. Electronic document, http://www.dep.state.fl.us/springs/about.htm, accessed October 8, 2015.

2015   DEP Springs Funding Projects. Electronic document, http://fdep.maps.arcgis.com/apps/MapJournal/index.html?appid=002cea9e3e454943aa67ae0934c2b3f1, accessed October 8, 2015.

2016   Springs Restoration Projects Identified to Receive More than $56 Million in Funding. Electronic document, https://content.govdelivery.com/accounts/FLDEP/bulletins/1555b80, accessed July 15, 2016.

Florida Springs Initiative

2007   *Program Summary and Recommendations.* Florida Department of Environmental Protection, Tallahassee.

Florida Springs Institute Members

2015   Guest Column: Jacksonville Has Serious Groundwater Issues. Electronic document, http://jacksonville.com/business/columnists/2015-09-04/story/guest-column-jacksonville-has-serious-groundwater-issues, accessed October 7, 2015.

Florida Springs Task Force

2000   *Florida's Springs: Strategies for Protection & Restoration.* Submitted to the Florida Department of Environmental Protection. Copies available from the Florida Department of Environmental Protection, Tallahassee.

Florida Trend

2015   Florida Springs to Receive $82 Million toward Restoration Projects. Electronic document, http://www.floridatrend.com/article/19068/gov-scott-distributes-82-million-for-florida-springs-restoration-projects, accessed October 8, 2015.

Fogelson, Raymond D.

1989   The Ethnohistory of Events and Nonevents. *Ethnohistory* 36(2):133–147.

Fowler, Catherine S., and Don D. Fowler (editors)

2008   *The Great Basin: People and Place in Ancient Times.* School for Advanced Research Press, Santa Fe.

Frazier, Charles

2006   *Thirteen Moons.* Random House, New York.

Gainesville Sun and *Ocala Star-Banner*

2013   Fragile Springs. Electronic document, http://fragilesprings.com/, accessed October 9, 2015.

Gaiser, E. E., B. E. Taylor, and M. J. Brooks
2001   Establishment of Wetlands on the Southeastern Atlantic Coastal Plain: Pa-
        leolimnological Evidence of a Mid-Holocene Hydrologic Threshold from a
        South Carolina Pond. *Journal of Paleolimnology* 26:373–391.
Gibson, Jon L.
2001   *The Ancient Mounds of Poverty Point: Place of Rings.* University Press of Flor-
        ida, Gainesville.
Gillespie, Susan D.
2007   Comment on "Eventful Archaeology: The Place of Space in Structural Trans-
        formation" by R. Beck, D. Bolender, J. Brown, and T. Earle. *Current Anthro-
        pology* 48:846–847.
Gilmore, Zackary I.
2011   Silver Glen Run, Locus B (8LA1-West). In *St. Johns Archaeological Field
        School 2007–10: Silver Glen Run (8LA1),* by Kenneth E. Sassaman, Zackary I.
        Gilmore, and Asa R. Randall, pp. 171–314. Technical Report 12. Laboratory
        of Southeastern Archaeology, Department of Anthropology, University of
        Florida, Gainesville.
2014   Gathering Places: Histories of Material and Social Interaction at Late Ar-
        chaic Shell Mounds in Florida. Unpublished Ph.D. dissertation, Department
        of Anthropology, University of Florida, Gainesville.
2015   Subterranean Histories: Pit Events and Place-Making in Late Archaic Flori-
        da. In *The Archaeology of Events: Cultural Change and Continuity in the An-
        cient Southeast,* edited by Zackary I. Gilmore and Jason M. O'Donoughue,
        pp. 119–140. University of Alabama Press, Tuscaloosa.
2016   *Gathering at Silver Glen: Community and History in Late Archaic Florida.*
        University of Florida Press, Gainesville.
Gilmore, Zackary I., and Jason M. O'Donoughue
2015   Introduction: The Enigma of the Event. In *The Archaeology of Events: Cul-
        tural Change and Continuity in the Pre-Columbian Southeast,* edited by Zack-
        ary I. Gilmore and Jason M. O'Donoughue, pp. 1–22. University of Alabama
        Press, Tuscaloosa.
Gleason, Patrick J., and Peter Stone
1994   Age, Origin, and Landscape Evolution of the Everglades Peatland. In *Ever-
        glades: The Ecosystem and Its Restoration,* edited by Steven Davis and John
        Ogden, pp. 149–197. St. Lucie Press, Boca Raton.
Goggin, John M.
1947   A Preliminary Definition of Archaeological Areas and Periods in Florida.
        American Antiquity 13:114–127.
1952   *Space and Time Perspective in Northern St. Johns Archeology, Florida.* Univer-
        sity Press of Florida, Gainesville.
Gosden, Chris
2005   What Do Objects Want? *Journal of Archaeological Method and Theory* 12:193–
        211.

Gribben, Arthur
1992   *Holy Wells and Sacred Water Sources in Britain and Ireland: An Annotated Bibliography*. Garland, New York.
Grimm, E.C., G.L. Jacobson Jr, W.A. Watts, B.C.S. Hansen, and K.A. Maasch
1993   A 50,000-Year Record of Climate Oscillations from Florida and Its Temporal Correlation. *Science* 61:9.
Grimm E. C., S. Lozano-Garcia, H. Behling, and V. Markgraf
2001   Holocene Vegetation and Climate Variability in the Americas. In *Interhemispheric Climate Linkages*, edited by V Markgraf, pp. 352–370. Academic, San Diego.
Grimm, E. C., W. A. Watts, G. L. Jacobson, B. Hansen, H.R. Almquist, and A.C. Diefenbacher-Krall
2006   Evidence for Warm Wet Heinrich Events in Florida. *Quaternary Science Reviews* 25:2197–2211.
Hays, Christopher T., and Richard A. Weinstein
2004   Early Pottery at Poverty Point: Origins and Functions. In *Early Pottery: Technology, Function, Style, and Interaction in the Lower Southeast*, edited by Rebecca Saunders and Christopher T. Hays, pp. 150–168. University of Alabama Press, Tuscaloosa.
Heffernan, James B., Dina M. Liebowitz, Thomas K. Frazer, Jason M. Evans, and Matthew J. Cohen
2010   Algal Blooms and the Nitrogen-Enrichment Hypothesis in Florida Springs: Evidence, Alternatives, and Adaptive Management. *Ecological Applications* 20:816–829.
Heidegger, Martin
1971   *Poetry, Language, Thought*. Harper, London.
Hemmings, E. Thomas
1975   The Silver Springs Site, Prehistory in the Silver Springs Valley, Florida. *The Florida Anthropologist* 28:141–158.
Hiers, Fred
2014   Silver Springs' Anniversary: State Operation a Work in Progress. Electronic document, http://www.ocala.com/article/20141002/ARTICLES/141009969, accessed October 7, 2015.
Hine, Albert C.
2013   *Geologic History of Florida*. University Press of Florida, Gainesville.
Hodder, Ian
2011a   Human-Thing Entanglement: Towards an Integrated Archaeological Perspective. *Journal of the Royal Anthropological Institute* 17:154–177.
2011b   Wheels of Time: Some Aspects of Entanglement Theory and the Secondary Products Revolution. *Journal of World Prehistory* 24:175–187.
2012   *Entangled: An Archaeology of the Relationships between Humans and Things*. Wiley-Blackwell, Malden.

Horton, B. P., W. R. Peltier, S. J. Culver, R. Drummond, S. E. Engelhart, A. C. Kemp, and
K. H. Thomson
2009   Holocene Sea-Level Changes along the North Carolina Coastline and Their
        Implications for Glacial Isostatic Adjustment Models. *Quaternary Science
        Reviews* 28:1725–1736.
Howey, Meghan C. L.
2007   Using Multi-Criteria Cost Surface Analysis to Explore Past Regional Land-
        scapes: A Case Study of Ritual Activity and Social Interaction in Michigan,
        AD 1200–1600. *Journal of Archaeological Science* 34:1830–1846.
Huang, Yongsong, Bryan Shuman, Yi Wang, Thompson Webb III, Eric C. Grimm, and
George L. Jacobson Jr.
2006   Climatic and Environmental Controls on the Variation of C_3 and C_4 Plant
        Abundances in Central Florida for the Past 62,000 Years. *Palaeogeography,
        Palaeoclimatology, Palaeoecology* 237:428–435.
Huber, Red
2012   Looking Back at Winter Park's Famous Sinkhole. Electronic document,
        http://www.orlandosentinel.com/os-fla360-looking-back-at-winter-parks-
        famous-sinkhole-20121113-story.html, accessed July 31, 2015.
Hubert, Jane
1994   Sacred Beliefs and Beliefs of Sacredness. In *Sacred Sites, Sacred Places*, edited
        by David L. Carmichael, Jane Hubert, Brian Reeves, and Audchild Schanche,
        pp. 9–19. Routledge, New York.
Hudson, Charles M.
1976   *The Southeastern Indians*. University of Tennessee Press, Knoxville.
Hughes, J. D., H. L. Vacher, and Ward E. Sanford
2009   Temporal Response of Hydraulic Head, Temperature, and Chloride Concen-
        trations to Sea-Level Changes, Floridan Aquifer System, USA. *Hydrogeology
        Journal* 17:793–815.
Huntsinger, Lynn, and María Fernández-Giménez
2000   Spiritual Pilgrims at Mount Shasta, California. *Geographical Review* 90:536–
        558.
Ingold, Tim
2011   *Being Alive: Essays on Movement, Knowledge and Description*. Routledge,
        New York.
2012   Toward an Ecology of Materials. *Annual Review of Anthropology* 41:427–442.
2013   *Making: Anthropology, Archaeology, Art and Architecture*. Routledge, New
        York.
Jahn, Otto L., and Ripley P. Bullen
1978   *The Tick Island Site, St. Johns River, Florida*. Publication 10. Florida Anthro-
        pological Society, Gainesville.
Johnson, Jay K.
1981   *Yellow Creek Archaeological Project, Volume 2*. Publications in Anthropology
        2. Tennessee Valley Authority, Chattanooga.

Jones, Gregg W., Sam B. Upchurch, and Kyle M. Chapman
1996   *Origin of Nitrate in Ground Water Discharging from Rainbow Springs, Marion County, Florida*. Southwest Florida Water Management District, Brooksville, Florida.

Joyce, Rosemary A., and Susan D. Gillespie (editors)
2015   *Things in Motion: Object Itineraries in Anthropological Practice*. School for Advanced Research Press, Santa Fe.

Karst Environmental Services, Inc.
2008   *Submerged Springs Site Documentation: August and September 2007*. Special Publication SJ2008-SP7. St. Johns River Water Management District, Palatka, Florida.

Katz, B. G.
2004   Sources of Nitrate Contamination and Age of Water in Large Karstic Springs of Florida. *Environmental Geology* 46:689–706.

Kelly, Martin H., and James A. Gore
2008   Florida River Flow Patterns and the Atlantic Multidecadal Oscillation. *River Research Applications* 24:598–616.

Kidder, Tristram R.
2002   Mapping Poverty Point. American Antiquity (67):89–101.
2010   Hunter-Gatherer Ritual and Complexity: New Evidence from Poverty Point, Louisiana. In *Ancient Complexities: New Perspectives in Precolumbian North America*, edited by Susan M. Alt, pp. 32–51. University of Utah Press, Salt Lake City.

Kindinger, Jack L., Jeffrey B. Davis, and James G. Flocks.
1994   *High-Resolution Single-Channel Seismic Reflection Surveys of Orange Lake and Other Selected Sites of North Central Florida*. Open-File Report 94–616. U.S. Geological Survey, St. Petersburg, Florida.
1999   Geology and Evolution of Lakes in North-Central Florida. *Environmental Geology* 38:301–321.
2000   *Subsurface Characterization of Selected Water Bodies in the St. Johns River Water Management District, Northeast Florida*. Open File Report 2000–180. U.S. Geological Survey, St. Petersburg, Florida.

Knight, Robert L.
2008   Saving Silver Springs Can't Wait Forever. Electronic document, http://www.gainesville.com/article/20080928/OPINION03/809280253, accessed October 9, 2015.
2012   The River of Denial. Electronic document, http://www.gainesville.com/article/20121216/OPINION03/121219918, accessed October 20, 2015.
2013   Restoring Florida's Springs. Electronic document, http://www.gainesville.com/article/20131020/opinion03/131019617, accessed October 20, 2015.
2014   Paying the Springs Bill. Electronic document, http://www.gainesville.com/article/20140824/OPINION03/140829810, accessed October 20, 2015.
2015   *Silenced Springs: Moving from Tragedy to Hope*. Howard T. Odum Florida Springs Institute, Gainesville.

Knight, Vernon James

1989   Symbolism of Mississippian Mounds. In *Powhatan's Mantle: Indians in the Colonial Southeast*, edited by P. H. Wood, Gregory A. Waselkov, and W. T. Hatley, pp. 279–291. University of Nebraska Press, Lincoln.

Knowles, Leel Jr., Andrew M. O'Reilly, and James C. Adamski

2002   *Hydrogeology and Simulated Effects of Ground-Water Withdrawals from the Floridan Aquifer System in Lake County and in the Ocala National Forest and Vicinity, North-Central Florida.* Water-Resources Investigations Report 02–4207. U.S. Geological Survey, Tallahassee, Florida.

Knox, J. C.

1995   Fluvial Systems since 20,000 Years BP. In *Global Continental Palaeohydrology*, edited by K. J. Gregory, L. Starkel, and V. R. Baker, pp. 87–108. Wiley, Chichester.

Kroening, Sharon E.

2004   *Streamflow and Water-Quality Characteristics at Selected Sites of the St. Johns River in Central Florida, 1933 to 2002.* Scientific Investigations Report 2004–5177. U.S. Geological Survey, Altamonte Springs, Florida.

Kurek, Joshua, Les C. Cwynar, and Ray W. Spear

2004   The 8200 cal yr BP Cooling Event in Eastern North America and the Utility of Midge Analysis for Holocene Temperature Reconstructions. *Quaternary Science Reviews* 23:627–639.

Land, L. A., and C. K. Paull

2000   Submarine Karst Belt Rimming the Continental Slope in the Straits of Florida. *Geo-Marine Letters* 20:123–132.

Lane, Ed

1986   *Karst in Florida.* Special Publication 29. Florida Geological Survey, Tallahassee.

2001   *The Spring Creek Submarine Springs Group, Wakulla County, Florida.* Special Publication 47. Florida Geological Survey, Tallahassee.

Lanier, Sidney

1876   *Florida: Its Scenery, Climate, and History: With an Account of Charleston, Savannah, Augusta, and Aiken, a Chapter for Consumptives, Various Papers on Fruit-Culture, and a Complete Hand-Book and Guide.* J B. Lippincott, Philadelphia.

Le Conte, John

1861   On the Optical Phenomena Presented by the "Silver Spring," in Marion County, Florida. *American Journal of Science and Arts* 31:1–11.

Liebowitz, Dina M., Matthew J. Cohen, James B. Heffernan, Lawrence V. Korhnak, and Thomas K. Frazer

2014   Environmentally-Mediated Consumer Control of Algal Proliferation in Florida Springs. *Freshwater Biology* 59: 2009–2023.

Livingston, Robert J.

1991   The Oklawaha River System. In *The Rivers of Florida*, edited by Robert J. Livingston, pp. 85–95. Springer-Verlag, New York.

Logan, Patrick
1980   *The Holy Wells of Ireland*. Colin Smythe Limited, Gerrards Cross, Buckinghamshire.

Lucas, Gavin
2008   Time and the Archaeological Event. *Cambridge Archaeological Journal* 18:59–65.

Lucero, Lisa J., and Andrew Kinkella
2015   Pilgrimage to the Edge of the Watery Underworld: An Ancient Maya Water Temple at Cara Blanca, Belize. *Cambridge Archaeological Journal* 25:163–185.

McCall, George A.
1974[1868]   *Letters from the Frontiers*. University Press of Florida, Gainesville.

McCarthy, Helen
2004   Assaulting California's Sacred Mountains: Shamans vs. New Age Merchants of Nirvana. In *Beyond Primitivism: Indigenous Religious Traditions and Modernity*, edited by Jacob K. Olupona, pp. 172–178. Routledge, New York.

McGee, Ray M., and Ryan J. Wheeler
1994   Stratigraphic Excavations at Groves' Orange Midden, Lake Monroe, Volusia County, Florida: Methodology and Results. *The Florida Anthropologist* 47:333–349.

McLeod, Michael
1986   That Sinking Feeling in Florida, You Never Know When Your Lawn—or Your Neighborhood—Will Be Swallowed Up by Nature's Vacuum. Electronic document, http://articles.orlandosentinel.com/1986-01-19/news/0190220042_1_mae-rose-sinkhole-rose-owens, accessed July 31, 2015.

Magny, Michel, Boris Vannière, Gianni Zanchetta, Eric Fouache, Gilles Touchais, Lera Petrika, Céline Coussot, Anne-Véronique Walter-Simonnet, and Fabien Arnaud
2009   Possible Complexity of the Climatic Event around 4300–3800 cal. BP in the Central and Western Mediterranean. *The Holocene* 19:823–833.

Mann, Charles C.
2006   *1491: New Revelations of the Americas before Columbus*. Vintage Books, New York.

Marella, Richard L.
2008   *Water Use in Florida, 2005 and Trends 1950–2005*. Fact Sheet 2008–3080. U.S. Geological Survey, Reston, Virginia.
2014   *Water Withdrawals, Use, and Trends in Florida, 2010*. Scientific Investigations Report 2014–5088. U.S. Geological Survey, Reston, Virginia.

Marquardt, William H., and Patty Jo Watson (editors)
2005   *Archaeology of the Middle Green River Region, Kentucky*. University Press of Florida, Gainesville.

Marrinan, Rochelle A., H. Stephen Hale, and William M. Stanton
1990   *Test Excavations at Silver Glen Springs, Florida (8MR123)*. Miscellaneous Report Series 2. Department of Anthropology, Florida State University, Tallahassee.

Marshall, Curtis H., Roger A. Pielke Sr., Louis T. Steyaert, and Debra A. Willard
2004   The Impact of Anthropogenic Land-Cover Change on the Florida Peninsula Sea Breezes and Warm Season Sensible Weather. *Monthly Weather Review* 132:28–52.

Martin, Jonathan B., and Randolph W. Dean
2001   Exchange of Water between Conduits and Matrix in the Floridan Aquifer. *Chemical Geology* 179: 145–165.

Martin, Richard A.
1966   *Eternal Spring: Man's 10,000 Years of History at Florida's Silver Springs*. Great Outdoors, St. Petersburg, Florida.

Mauss, Marcel
1990 [1925] *The Gift: The Form and Reason for Exchange in Archaic Societies*. W. W. Norton, New York.

Mayewski, Paul A., Eelco E. Rohling, J. Curt Stager, Wibjörn Karlén, Kirk A. Maasch, L. David Meeker, Eric A. Meyerson, Francoise Gasse, Shirley van Kreveld, Karin Holmgren, Julia Lee-Thorp, Gunhild Rosqvist, Frank Rack, Michael Staubwasser, Ralph R. Schneider, and Eric J. Steig
2004   Holocene Climate Variability. *Quaternary Research* 62:243–255.

Meskell, Lynn (editor)
2005   *Archaeologies of Materiality*. Blackwell, Malden.

Milanich, Jerald T.
1994   *Archaeology of Precolumbian Florida*. University Press of Florida, Gainesville.

Miller, Daniel
2005   *Materiality*. Duke University Press, Durham, North Carolina.

Miller, James A.
1986   Hydrogeologic Framework of the Floridan Aquifer System in Florida and in Parts of Georgia, Alabama, and South Carolina. Professional Paper 1403-B. U.S. Geological Survey, Washington, D.C.
1997   Hydrogeology of Florida. In *The Geology of Florida*, edited by Anthony F. Randazzo and Douglas S. Jones, pp. 69–88. University Press of Florida, Gainesville.

Miller, James J.
1992   Effects of Environmental Change on Late Archaic People of Northeast Florida. *The Florida Anthropologist* 45:100–106.
1998   *An Environmental History of Northeast Florida*. University Press of Florida, Gainesville.

Mitchell, Edward A. D., Daniel J. Charman, and Barry G. Warner
2008   Testate Amoebae Analysis in Ecological and Paleoecological Studies of Wetlands: Past, Present and Future. *Biodiversity and Conservation* 17(9):2115–2137.

Moore, Clarence B.
1894a   Certain Sand Mounds of the St. Johns River, Florida. Part I. *Journal of the Academy of Natural Sciences of Philadelphia* 10:4–128.
1894b   Certain Sand Mounds of the St. Johns River, Florida. Part II. *Journal of the Academy of Natural Sciences of Philadelphia* 10:129–246.

1895   Certain Sand Mounds of the Ocklawaha River, Florida. *Journal of the Academy of Natural Sciences of Philadelphia* 10:518–543.

Moore, Paul J., Jon B. Martin, and Elizabeth J. Screaton

2009   Geochemical and Statistical Evidence of Recharge, Mixing, and Controls on Spring Discharge in an Eogenetic Karst Aquifer. *Journal of Hydrology* 376:443–455.

Moran, John

2004   *Journal of Light: The Visual Diary of a Florida Nature Photographer.* University Press of Florida, Gainesville.

2013   Reclaiming Our Springs. Electronic document, http://www.gainesville.com/article/20131229/OPINION03/131229706/-1/opinion03?Title=John-Moran-Reclaiming-our-springs, accessed October 9, 2015.

Morphy, Howard

1995   Landscape and the Reproduction of the Ancestral Past. In *Anthropology of Landscape: Perspectives on Place and Space*, edited by Eric Hirsch and Michael O'Hanlon, pp. 184–209. Clarendon Press, Oxford.

Morrissey, Sheila K., Jordan F. Clark, Michael Bennett, Emily Richardson, and Martin Stute

2010   Groundwater Reorganization in the Floridan Aquifer Following Holocene Sea-Level Rise. *Nature Geoscience* 3:683–687.

Motz, Louis H., and Ahmet Dogan

2004   *North-Central Florida Active Water-Table Regional Groundwater Flow Model.* Special Publication SJ2005-SP16. St. Johns River Water Management District, Palatka, Florida.

Munch, Douglas A., David J. Toth, Ching-tzu Huang, Jeffery B. Davis, Carlos M. Fortich, William L. Osburn, Edward J. Phlips, Erin L. Quinlan, Michael S. Allen, Melissa J. Woods, Patrick Cooney, Robert L. Knight, Ronald A. Clarke, and Scott L. Knight

2006   *Fifty-Year Retrospective Study of the Ecology of Silver Springs, Florida.* Special Publication SJ2007-SP4. St. Johns River Water Management District, Palatka, Florida.

Nash, Ronald J.

1997   Archetypal Landscapes and the Interpretation of Meaning. *Cambridge Archaeological Journal* 7:57–69.

Neeley, Michelle

2015   Art Exhibit Featuring Florida's Springs Opens at Thomas Center. Electronic document, http://www.wuft.org/news/2015/10/01/art-exhibit-featuring-floridas-springs-opens-at-thomas-center/, accessed October 9, 2015.

Neill, Wilfred T.

1958   A Stratified Early Site at Silver Springs, Florida. *The Florida Anthropologist* 11:33–52.

1964   Association of Suwannee Points and Extinct Animals. *The Florida Anthropologist.* 17:17–32.

Norman, Robert
2010   *Images of America: Ocala National Forest.* Arcadia, Charleston.
Ocala Star Banner
2015   Editorial: Science Enough? Electronic document, http://www.ocala.com/article/20150913/OPINION01/150919948, accessed October 2, 2015.
O'Donoughue, Jason M.
2010   Shell Springs Eternal. Paper presented at the 67th Annual Meeting of the Southeastern Archaeological Conference, Lexington, Kentucky.
2013   Conspicuous in Their Absence: Shell Sites and Freshwater Springs in the St. Johns River Valley. Paper presented at the 70th Annual Meeting of the Southeastern Archaeological Conference, Tampa, Florida.
2015   Beyond the Event Horizon: Moments of Consequence (?) in the St. Johns River Valley. In *The Archaeology of Events: Cultural Change and Continuity in the Pre-Columbian Southeast*, edited by Zackary I. Gilmore and Jason M. O'Donoughue, pp. 46–61. University of Alabama Press, Tuscaloosa.
O'Donoughue, Jason M., and Kenneth E. Sassaman
2013   *Phase I Archaeological Survey of Weeki Wachee Springs State Park, Hernando County, Florida.* Technical Report 18. Laboratory of Southeastern Archaeology, Department of Anthropology, University of Florida, Gainesville.
2014   *Cultural Resources Assessment Survey within Otter Spring Park, Gilchrist County, Florida.* Technical Report 19. Laboratory of Southeastern Archaeology, Department of Anthropology, University of Florida, Gainesville.
O'Donoughue, Jason M., Kenneth E. Sassaman, Meggan E. Blessing, Johanna B. Talcott, and Julie C. Byrd
2011   *Archaeological Investigations at Salt Springs (8MR2322), Marion County, Florida.* Technical Report 11. Laboratory of Southeastern Archaeology, Department of Anthropology, University of Florida, Gainesville.
Odum, Howard T.
1957a   Primary Production Measurements in Eleven Florida Springs and a Marine Turtle-Grass Community. *Limnology and Oceanography* 2:85–97.
1957b   Trophic Structure and Productivity of Silver Springs, Florida. *Ecological Monographs* 27:55–112.
Olsen, Bjørnar
2003   Material Culture after Text: Re-membering Things. *Norwegian Archaeological Review* 36:87–104.
2010   *In Defense of Things.* Alta Mira, Walnut Creek.
Olsen, Bjørnar, Michael Shanks, Timothy Webmoor, and Christopher Witmore
2012   *Archaeology: The Discipline of Things.* University of California Press, Berkeley.
Olwig, Kenneth
1993   Sexual Cosmology: Nation and Landscape at the Conceptual Interstices of Nature and Culture; or What Does Landscape Really Mean? In *Landscape: Politics and Perspective*, edited by Barbara Bender, pp. 307–343. Berg, Oxford.

Ortmann, Anthony L., and Tristram R. Kidder
2013   Building Mound A at Poverty Point, Louisiana: Monumental Public Archi-
          tecture, Ritual Practice, and Implications for Hunter-Gatherer Complexity.
          Geoarchaeology 28:66–86.

Otvos, Ervin G.
2004   Holocene Gulf Levels: Recognition Issues and an Updated Sea-Level Curve.
          Journal of Coastal Research 20:680–699.

Pandion Systems, Inc.
2003   *Carrying Capacity Study of Silver Glen Spring and Run.* DEP Contract Num-
          ber SL 982. Submitted to the Florida Department of Environmental Protec-
          tion. Copies available from Florida Department of Environmental Protec-
          tion, Tallahassee.

Patrick, G. E.
1879   The Great Spirit Spring. *Transactions of the Kansas Academy of Science (1872–
          1880)* 7(1879–1880):22–26.

Peek, Harry M.
1951   *Cessation of Flow of Kissengen Spring in Polk County, Florida.* Report of In-
          vestigations 7. Florida Geological Survey, Tallahassee.

Phelps, G. G.
2004   *Chemistry of Ground Water in the Silver Springs Basin, Florida, with an Em-
          phasis on Nitrate.* Scientific Investigations. Report 2004-5144. U.S. Geologi-
          cal Survey, Reston, Virginia.

Phelps, G.G., and K. P. Rohrer
1987   *Hydrogeology in the Area of a Freshwater Lens in the Floridan Aquifer System,
          Northeast Seminole County, Florida.* Water Resources Investigation Report
          86-4097. U.S. Geological Survey, Washington, D.C.

Piatek, Bruce J.
1994   The Tomoka Mound Complex in Northeast Florida. *Southeastern Archaeol-
          ogy* 13:109–118.

Pielke, Roger A. Sr., Curtis Marshall, Robert L. Walko, Louis T. Steyaert, Pier-Luigi Vi-
          dale, Glen E. Liston, Walter A. Lyons, and Thomas N. Chase
1999   The Influence of Anthropogenic Landscape Changes on Weather in South
          Florida. *Monthly Weather Review* 127:1663–1673.

Pirkle, William A.
1971   The Offset Course of the St. Johns River, Florida. *Southeastern Geology* 13:39–
          59.

Pittman, Craig
2012a   Florida's Vanishing Springs. Electronic document, http://www.tampabay.
          com/news/environment/water/floridas-vanishing-springs/1262988, accessed
          August 20, 2013.
2012b   Scientists Puzzled by Silver Glen's Mystery Algae. Electronic document,
          http://www.tampabay.com/news/environment/water/scientists-puzzled-by-
          silver-glens-mystery-algae/1262974, accessed April 23, 2013.

Plummer, L. Niel

1993   Stable Isotope Enrichment in Paleowaters of the Southeast Atlantic Coastal Plain, United States. *Science* 262:2016–2020.

Pope, Alexander

1848[1733]   *An Essay on Man in Four Epistles.* Merriam, Moore, Troy, New York.

Porter, Kevin M.

2009   Possible Dugout Canoe (8MR3554) at Silver Glen Springs Recreational Area, Marion County, Florida. Florida Bureau of Archaeological Research. Copies available from the Florida Master Site Files, Tallahassee.

Potter, Alden L.

1935   The Remains at Silver Glen Springs. In *Some Further Papers on Aboriginal Man in the Neighborhood of the Ocala National Forest,* edited by A. E. Abshire, Alden L. Potter, Allen R. Taylor, Clyde H. Neil, Walter H. Anderson, John I. Rutledge, and Stevenson B. Johnson, pp. 13–14. Civilian Conservation Corps, Company 1420, Ocala Camp, Florida.

Prufer, Keith M., and James E. Brady (editors)

2005   *Stone Houses and Earth Lords: Maya Religion in Cave Context.* University Press of Colorado, Boulder.

Purdy, Barbara A.

1991   *The Art and Archaeology of Florida's Wetlands.* CRC Press, Boca Raton.

Quillen, Amanda K., Evelyn E. Gaiser, and Eric C. Grimm

2013   Diatom-Based Paleolimnological Reconstruction of Regional Climate and Local Land-Use Change from a Protected Sinkhole Lake in Southern Florida, USA. *Journal of Paleolimnology* 49:15–30.

Quinn, Rhonda L., Bryan D. Tucker, and John Krigbaum

2008   Diet and Mobility in Middle Archaic Florida: Stable Isotopic and Faunal Evidence from the Harris Creek Archaeological Site (8VO24), Tick Island. *Journal of Archaeological Science* 35:2346–2356.

Randall, Asa R.

2007   *St. Johns Archaeological Field School 2005: Hontoon Island State Park. Technical Report 7.* Laboratory of Southeastern Archaeology, Department of Anthropology, University of Florida, Gainesville.

2010   Remapping Histories: Preceramic Archaic Community Construction along the Middle St. Johns River, Florida. Unpublished Ph.D. dissertation, Department of Anthropology, University of Florida, Gainesville.

2011   Remapping Archaic Social Histories along the St. Johns River, Florida. In *Hunter-Gatherer Archaeology as Historical Process,* edited by Kenneth E. Sassaman and Donald H. Holly Jr., pp. 120–142. University of Arizona Press, Tucson.

2013   The Chronology and History of Mount Taylor Period (ca. 7400–4600 cal B.P.) Shell Sites on the Middle St. Johns River, Florida. *Southeastern Archaeology* 32:193–217.

2014a   Freshwater Shellfishing 9,000 Years Ago in Northeast Florida. Paper presented at the 71st Annual Meeting of the Southeastern Archaeological Conference, Columbia, South Carolina.

2014b   LiDAR-Aided Reconnaissance and Reconstruction of Lost Landscapes: An Example of Freshwater Shell Mounds (ca. 7500–500 Cal B.P.) in Northeast Florida. *Journal of Field Archaeology* 39(2):162–179.

2015   *Constructing Histories: Archaic Freshwater Shell Mounds and Social Landscapes of the St. Johns River, Florida.* University Press of Florida, Gainesville.

Randall, Asa R., Meggan E. Blessing, and Jon C. Endonino

2011   *Cultural Resource Assessment Survey of Silver Glen Springs Recreational Area in the Ocala National Forest, Florida.* Technical Report 13. Laboratory of Southeastern Archaeology, Department of Anthropology, University of Florida, Gainesville.

Randall, Asa R., and Kenneth E. Sassaman

2005   *St. Johns Archaeological Field School 2003–2004: Hontoon Island State Park.* Technical Report 6. Laboratory of Southeastern Archaeology, Department of Anthropology, University of Florida, Gainesville.

2010   (E)mergent Complexities during the Archaic in Northeast Florida. In *Ancient Complexities: New Perspectives in Precolumbian North America,* edited by Susan M. Alt, pp. 8–31. University of Utah Press, Salt Lake City.

2012   2012 Field School Summaries: St. Johns Archaeological Field School: Silver Glen Springs Run. *The Florida Anthropologist* 65:248–250.

Randall, Asa R., Kenneth E. Sassaman, Zackary I. Gilmore, Meggan E. Blessing, and Jason M. O'Donoughue.

2014   Archaic Histories beyond the Shell "Heap" on the St. Johns River. In *New Histories of Pre-Columbian Florida,* edited by Neill J. Wallis and Asa R. Randall, pp. 18–37. University Press of Florida, Gainesville.

Randall, Asa R., and Bryan Tucker

2012   A Mount Taylor Period Radiocarbon Assay from the Bluffton Burial Mound (8VO23). *The Florida Anthropologist* 65:219–225.

Randazzo, Anthony F.

1997   The Sedimentary Platform of Florida: Mesozoic to Cenozoic. In *The Geology of Florida,* edited by Anthony F. Randazzo and Douglas S. Jones, pp. 39–58. University Press of Florida, Gainesville.

Rattue, James

1995   *The Living Stream: Holy Wells in Historical Context.* Boydell Press, Woodbridge, Suffolk.

Rawlings, Marjorie Kinnan

1938   *The Yearling.* Collier Macmillan, New York.

Ray, Celeste

2011   The Sacred and the Body Politic at Ireland's Holy Wells. *International Social Science Journal* 62(205–206):271–285.

2014   *The Origin of Ireland's Holy Wells.* Archaeopress, Oxford.

Reese, Ronald S., and Emily Richardson

2008   *Synthesis of the Hydrogeologic Framework of the Floridan Aquifer System and*

Delineation of a Major Avon Park Permeable Zone in Central and Southern Florida. Scientific Investigations Report 2007–5207. U.S. Geological Survey, Washington, D.C.

Rink, W. Jack, James S. Dunbar, and Kevin E. Burdette

2012   The Wakulla Springs Lodge Site (8WA329): 2008 Excavations and New OSL Dating Evidence. *The Florida Anthropologist* 65:5–22.

Rink, W. Jack, James S. Dunbar, Glen H. Doran, Charles Frederick, and Brittney Gregory

2012   Geoarchaeological Investigations and OSL Dating Evidence in an Archaic and Paleoindian Context at the Helen Blazes Site (8BR27), Brevard County, Florida. *The Florida Anthropologist* 65:85–105.

Robison, Jim

1987   A Sinkhole Chronology. Electronic document, http://articles.orlandosentinel.com/1987-12-27/news/0170120189_1_sinkhole-winter-park-mae-rose, accessed July 21, 2015.

Rosenau, Jack C., Glen L. Faulkner, Charles W. Hendry Jr., and Robert W. Hull

1977   *Springs of Florida.* Bulletin 31 (revised). Bureau of Geology, Tallahassee.

Rosenswig, Robert M.

2015   A Mosaic of Adaptation: The Archaeological Record for Mesoamerica's Archaic Period. *Journal of Archaeological Research* 23:115–162.

Rupert, Frank R.

1988   *The Geology of Wakulla Springs.* Open File Report 22. Florida Geological Survey, Tallahassee.

Russo, Michael

1994   Why We Don't Believe in Archaic Mounds and Why We Should: The Case from Florida. *Southeastern Archaeology* 13:93–109.

2004   Measuring Shell Rings for Social Inequality. In *Signs of Power: The Rise of Cultural Complexity in the Southeast,* edited by Jon L. Gibson and Philip J. Carr, pp. 26–70. University of Alabama Press, Tuscaloosa.

Sahlins, Marshall

1985   *Islands of History.* University of Chicago Press, Chicago.

1991   The Return of the Event, Again: With Reflections on the Beginnings of the Great Fijian War of 1843 to 1855 between the Kingdoms of Bau and Rewa. In *Clio in Oceania: Toward a Historical Anthropology,* edited by Aletta Biersack, pp. 37–99. Smithsonian Institution Press, Washington, D.C.

St. Johns River Water Management District (SJRWMD)

2015a   GIS Download Library. Electronic document, http://floridaswater.com/gis-development/docs/themes.html, accessed July 1, 2015.

2015b   Springs of the District. Electronic document, http://floridaswater.com/springs/springslist.html, accessed September 17, 2015.

Ste. Claire, Dana

1987   The Development of Thermal Alteration Technologies in Florida: Implications for the Study of Prehistoric Adaptation. *The Florida Anthropologist* 40:203–208.

Samek, Kelly
2004   Unknown Quantity: The Bottled Water Industry and Florida's Springs. *Journal of Land Use & Environmental Law* 19:569–595.
Santos-Granero, Fernando
1998   Writing History into the Landscape: Space, Myth, and Ritual in Contemporary Amazonia. *American Ethnologist* 25(2):128–148.
Sassaman, Kenneth E.
1993   *Early Pottery in the Southeast: Tradition and Innovation in Cooking Technology.* University of Alabama Press, Tuscaloosa.
2003a   *St. Johns Archaeological Field School 2000–2001: Blue Spring and Hontoon Island State Parks.* Technical Report 4. Laboratory of Southeastern Archaeology, Department of Anthropology, University of Florida, Gainesville.
2003b   *Crescent Lake Archaeological Survey, 2002: Putnam and Flagler Counties, Florida.* Technical Report 5. Laboratory of Southeastern Archaeology, Department of Anthropology, University of Florida, Gainesville.
2003c   New AMS Dates on Orange Fiber-Tempered Pottery from the Middle St. Johns Valley and Their Implications for Culture History in Northeast Florida. *The Florida Anthropologist* 56:5–13.
2004   Common Origins and Divergent Histories in the Early Pottery Traditions of the American Southeast. In *Early Pottery: Technology, Function, Style, and Interaction in the Lower Southeast,* edited by Rebecca Saunders and Christopher T. Hays, pp. 23–39. University of Alabama Press, Tuscaloosa.
2010   *The Eastern Archaic, Historicized.* AltaMira, Lanham.
2012   Futurologists Look Back. *Archaeologies* 8:250–268.
2013   Drowning Out the Past: How Humans Historicize Water as Water Historicizes Them. In *Big Histories, Human Lives: Tackling Problems of Scale in Archaeology,* edited by John Robb and Timothy R. Pauketat, pp. 171–192. School for Advanced Research Press, Santa Fe.
Sassaman, Kenneth E., Zackary I. Gilmore, and Asa R. Randall
2011   *St. Johns Archaeological Field School 2007–10: Silver Glen Run (8LA1).* Technical Report 12. Laboratory of Southeastern Archaeology, Department of Anthropology, University of Florida, Gainesville.
Sassaman, Kenneth E., and Asa R. Randall
2012   Shell Mounds of the Middle St. Johns Basin, Northeast Florida. In *The Origins of New World Monumentality,* edited by Richard L. Burger and Robert M. Rosenswig, pp. 53–77. University Press of Florida, Gainesville.
Saunders, Joe W., Rolfe D. Mandel, C. Garth Sampson, Charles M. Allen, E. Thurman Allen, Daniel A. Bush, James K. Feathers, Kristen J. Gremillion, C. T. Hallmark, H. Edwin Jackson, Jay K. Johnson, Reca Jones, Roger T. Saucier, Gary L. Stringer, and Malcolm F. Vidrine
2005   Watson Brake, a Middle Archaic Mound Complex in Northeast Louisiana. *American Antiquity* 70:631–668.
Saunders, Rebecca, and Michael Russo
2011   Coastal Shell Middens in Florida: A View from the Archaic Period. *Quaternary International* 239:38–50.

Scherer, Reed P.
1988   Freshwater Diatom Assemblages and Ecology/Paleoecology of the Okefe-
        nokee Swamp/Marsh Complex, Southern Georgia, U.S.A. *Diatom Research*
        3:129–157.
Schiffer, Donna M.
1998   *Hydrology of Central Florida Lakes—A Primer.* Circular 1137. U.S. Geological
        Survey, Reston, Virginia.
Schmidt, Walter
1997   Geomorphology and Physiography of Florida. In *The Geology of Florida*, ed-
        ited by Anthony F. Randazzo and Douglas S. Jones, pp. 1–12. University Press
        of Florida, Gainesville.
Schofield, Kate
2013   Fla. Museum Opens New Exhibits Saturday Highlighting State's Springs,
        Cultural History. Electronic document, https://www.flmnh.ufl.edu/press-
        room/2013/03/19/fla-museum-opens-new-exhibits-saturday-highlighting-
        states-springs-cultural-history/, accessed October 9, 2015.
Scott, Thomas M.
1983   *The Hawthorn Formation of Northeast Florida, Part I: The Geology of the
        Hawthorn Formation of Northeast Florida.* Report of Investigations 94. Flor-
        ida Geological Survey, Tallahassee.
1988   *The Lithostratigraphy of the Hawthorn Group (Miocene) of Florida.* Bulletin
        59. Florida Geological Survey, Tallahassee.
1997   Miocene to Holocene History of Florida. In *The Geology of Florida*, edited
        by Anthony F. Randazzo and Douglas S. Jones, pp. 57–69. University Press of
        Florida, Gainesville.
2011   Geology of the Florida Platform—Pre-Mesozoic to Recent. In *Gulf of Mexico:
        Origin, Waters, and Biota*, Vol. 3: Geology, edited by Noreen A. Buster and
        Charles W. Holmes, pp. 17–31. Texas A&M University Press, College Station.
Scott, Thomas M., Guy H. Means, Ryan C. Means, and Rebecca P. Morgan
2002   *First Magnitude Springs of Florida.* Open File Report 85. Florida Geological
        Survey, Tallahassee.
Scott, Thomas M., Guy H. Means, Rebecca P. Meegan, Ryan C. Means, Sam B. Upchurch,
        R. E. Copeland, J. Jones, Tina Roberts, and Alan Willet
2004   *Springs of Florida.* Bulletin 66. Florida Geological Survey, Tallahassee.
Screaton, Elizabeth, Jonathan B. Martin, Brian Ginn, and Laren Smith
2004   Conduit Properties and Karstification in the Unconfined Floridan Aquifer.
        Ground Water 42:338–346.
Sears, William H.
1960   The Bluffton Burial Mound. *The Florida Anthropologist* 13:55–60.
Seinfeld, Daniel M.
2013   *An Assessment of Submerged Archaeological Deposits and Evidence for Looting
        at the Silver Glen Springs Run Site (8MR3605/8LA1).* Report on File, Florida
        Bureau of Archaeological Research, Tallahassee.

Sewell, William H. Jr.

2005   *Logics of History: Social Theory and Social Transformation.* University of Chicago Press, Chicago.

Shelton, Douglas N.

2005   *The Rare and Endemic Snails of Selected Springs within the St. Johns River Water Management District.* Special Publication SJ2006-SP17. St. Johns River Water Management District, Palatka, Florida.

Shockman, Elizabeth

2015   Florida's Natural Springs Are Changing—And Disappearing. Electronic document, http://www.pri.org/stories/2015-09-05/floridas-natural-springs-are-changing-and-disappearing, accessed October 7, 2015.

Shoemaker, W. Barclay, Andrew M. O'Reilly, Nicasio Sepúlveda, Stanley A. Williams, Louis H. Motz, and Qing Sun

2004   *Comparison of Estimated Areas Contributing Recharge to Selected Springs in North-Central Florida by Using Multiple Ground-Water Flow Models.* Open-File Report 03-448. U.S. Geological Survey, Tallahassee, Florida.

Siddall, Mark, Eelco J. Rohling, Ahuva Almogi-Labin, C. Hemleben, D. Meischner, I. Schmelzer, and David A. Smeed

2003   Sea-Level Fluctuations during the Last Glacial Cycle. *Nature* 423:853–858.

Simms, Alexander R., Kurt Lambeck, Anthony Purcell, John B. Anderson, and Antonio B. Rodriguez

2007   Sea-Level History of the Gulf of Mexico since the Last Glacial Maximum with Implications for the Melting History of the Laurentide Ice Sheet. *Quaternary Science Reviews* 26:920–940.

Skibo, James M., and Michael Brian Schiffer

2008   *People and Things: A Behavioral Approach to Material Culture.* Springer, New York.

Smith, Bruce D.

1986   Archaeology of the Southeastern United States: From Dalton to DeSoto 10,500–500 BP. In *Advances in World Archaeology,* edited by Fred Wendorf and Angela E. Close, pp. 5:1–92. Academic, New York.

Smith, D. E., S. Harrison, C. R. Firth, and J. T. Jordan

2011   The Early Holocene Sea Level Rise. *Quaternary Science Reviews* 30:1846–1860.

Smith, Douglas L., and Kenneth M. Lord

1997   Tectonic Evolution and Geophysics of the Florida Basement. In *The Geology of Florida,* edited by Anthony F. Randazzo and Douglas S. Jones, pp. 13–26. University Press of Florida, Gainesville.

Smock, Leonard A., Anne B. Wright, and Arthur C. Benke

2005   Atlantic Coastal Rivers of the Southeastern United States. In *Rivers of North America,* edited by Arthur C. Benke and Colbert F. Cushing, pp. 73–124. Elsevier Academic Press, Burlington.

Sommer, Eleanor K.

2012   Fountains of Life: A Look at Florida Springs from Sacred Waters to Green

Slime. University of Florida College of Journalism and Communications. Electronic document, http://stateofwater.org/ecosystems/springs/, accessed October 7, 2015.

Southeastern Archaeological Research, Inc.

2008   *Cultural Resource Assessment Survey of State Road 40 from One Mile West of State Road 326 to State Road 15 (US 17) PD&E Study, Marion, Lake, and Volusia Counties, Florida.* Submitted to Inwood Consulting Engineers, Project No. 2018–05177. Copies Available from SEARCH, Inc., Jonesville, Florida.

Southwest Florida Water Management District (SWFWMD)

2009   Weeki Wachee Springs Restoration Project. Electronic document, http://www.swfwmd.state.fl.us/springs/weeki-wachee/restoration-project.php, accessed October 6, 2015.

Spechler, Rick M.

1994   *Saltwater Intrusion Quality of Water in Floridan Aquifer System, Northeastern Florida.* Water Resources Investigation Report 92–4174. U.S. Geological Survey, Tallahassee.

Spicuzza, Mary

2005   Restoration of Sea Wall Under Way. Electronic document, http://www.sptimes.com/2005/09/24/news_pf/Hernando/Restoration_of_sea_wa.shtml, accessed October 6, 2015.

Spivey, S. Margaret, Tristram R. Kidder, Anthony L. Ortmann, and Lee J. Arco

2015   Pilgrimage to Poverty Point? In *The Archaeology of Events: Cultural Change and Continuity in the Pre-Columbian* Southeast, edited by Zackary I. Gilmore and Jason M. O'Donoughue, pp. 141–159. University of Alabama Press, Tuscaloosa.

Springs Eternal Project

2013   Why We Love This Spring—Silver Glen Springs. Electronic document, http://springseternalproject.org/springs/silver-glen/why-we-love-this-spring-silver-glen/, accessed September 15, 2015.

Stanton, William M.

1995   Archaic Subsistence in the Middle St. Johns River Valley: Silver Glen Springs and the Mt. Taylor Period. Unpublished master's thesis, Department of Anthropology, Florida State University, Tallahassee.

Steponaitis, Vincas P.

1986   Prehistoric Archaeology in the Southeastern United States, 1970–1985. *Annual Review of Anthropology* 15:363–404.

Sterling, Maurice, and C. A. Padera

1998   *The Upper St. Johns River Project—The Environmental Transformation of a Public Flood Control Project.* Professional Paper SJ98-PP1. St. Johns River Water Management District, Palatka, Florida.

Stevenson, R. Jan, Agnieszka Pinowska, Andrea Albertin, James O. Sickman

2007   *Ecological Condition of Algae and Nutrients in Florida Springs.* DEP Grant Number S0291. Report submitted to the Florida Department of Environmental Protection, Tallahassee.

Stewart, Joseph, Peter Sucsy, and John Hendrickson

2006   Meteorological and Subsurface Factors Affecting Estuarine Conditions with-
        in Lake George in the St. Johns River, Florida. Proceedings of the Seventh
        International Conference on Hydroscience and Engineering, Philadelphia.

Strang, Veronica

2005   Common Senses: Water, Sensory Experience and the Generation of Mean-
        ing. *Journal of Material Culture* 10:92–120.

2008   The Social Construction of Water. In *Handbook of Landscape Archaeology*,
        edited by Bruno David and Julian Thomas, pp. 123–130. Left Coast Press,
        Walnut Creek.

Strathern, Marilyn

1988   *The Gender of the Gift: Problems with Women and Problems with Society in
        Melanesia.* University of California Press, Berkeley.

Stringfield, V. T., and H. H. Cooper Jr.

1951   *Geologic and Hydrologic Features of an Artesian Submarine Spring East of
        Florida.* Report of Investigations 7. Florida Geological Survey, Tallahassee.

Strong, William A.

2004   Temporal Water Chemistry Trends within Individual Springs and within
        a Population of Florida Springs. Unpublished master's thesis, University of
        Florida, Gainesville.

Sullivan, Alan P. III, and Kenneth C. Rozen

1985   Debitage Analysis and Archaeological Interpretation. *American Antiquity*
        50:755–779.

Swarzenski, P. W., C. D Reich, R. M. Spechler, J. L Kindinger, and W. S. Moore

2001   Using Multiple Geochemical Tracers to Characterize the Hydrogeology of
        the Submarine Spring off Crescent Beach, Florida. *Chemical Geology* 179:187–
        202.

Swihart, Tom

2013   Four Questions for Jim Stevenson. Electronic document, http://www.watery-
        foundation.com/?p=8887, accessed October 2, 2015.

Swineford, Ada, and John C. Frye

1955   Notes on Waconda or Great Spirit Spring, Mitchell County, Kansas. *Transac-
        tions of the Kansas Academy of Science (1903–)* 58(2):265–270.

Taçon, Paul S.

1999   Identifying Ancient Sacred Landscapes in Australia: From Physical to Social.
        In *Archaeologies of Landscape: Contemporary Perspectives*, edited by Wendy
        Ashmore and A. Bernard Knapp, pp. 33–57. Blackwell, Malden.

Talcott, Johanna B.

2011   Paleoethnobotanical Assemblage. In *Archaeological Investigations at Salt
        Springs (8MR2322), Marion County, Florida*, edited by Jason M. O'Donoughue,
        Kenneth E. Sassaman, Meggan E. Blessing, Johanna B. Talcott, and Julie C.
        Byrd, pp. 85–104. Technical Report 12, Laboratory of Southeastern Archaeol-
        ogy, Department of Anthropology, University of Florida.

Tampa Bay Times
2012   Florida's Vanishing Springs. Electronic document, http://www.tampabay. com/specials/2012/reports/florida-springs/, accessed October 9, 2015.

Tarasov, Lev, and W. R. Peltier
2005   Arctic Freshwater Forcing of the Younger Dryas Cold Reversal. *Nature* 435:662–665.

Tesar, Louis D., and Calvin B. Jones
2004   *Wakulla Springs Lodge Site (8WA329) in Edward Ball Wakulla Springs State Park, Wakulla County, Florida.* Florida Bureau of Archaeological Research, Tallahassee.

Theodoratus, Dorothea J., and Frank LaPena
1994   Wintu Sacred Geography of Northern California. In *Sacred Sites, Sacred Places*, edited by David L. Carmichael, Jane Hubert, Brian Reeves, and Audchild Schanche, pp. 20–31. Routledge, New York.

Thomas, Julian
1999   An Economy of Substances in Earlier Neolithic Britain. In *Material Symbols: Culture and Economy in Prehistory*, edited by John E. Robb, pp. 70–89. Center for Archaeological Investigations, Occasional Paper 26. Southern Illinois University, Carbondale.

Thompson
1964   Archaeological Site Form, 8MR83. Copies available from the Florida Master Site Files, Tallahassee.

Thompson, Bill
2013a   Silver Springs' Unveiling as State Park Set Tuesday. Electronic document, http://www.ocala.com/article/20130930/ARTICLES/130939978, accessed October 6, 2015.
2013b   Treasure Trove of Artifacts Found at Silver Springs. Electronic document, http://www.ocala.com/article/20130812/ARTICLES/130819934, accessed October 9, 2015.

Thulman, David K.
2009   Freshwater Availability as the Constraining Factor in the Middle Paleoindian Occupation of North-Central Florida. *Geoarchaeology* 24:243–276.
2012   Paleoindian Occupations along the St. Johns River, Florida. *The Florida Anthropologist* 65:79–83.

Tippett, Krista
2015   Transcript for John O'Donohue—The Inner Landscape of Beauty. Electronic document, http://www.onbeing.org/program/john-odonohue-the-inner-landscape-of-beauty/transcript/7801, accessed September 7, 2015.

Tolbert, Margaret Ross
2010   *AQUIFERious*. Fidelity Press, Addison.

Törnqvist, Torbjörn E., Juan L. González, Lee A. Newsom, Klaas van der Borg, Arie F. M. de Jong, and Charles W. Kurnik
2004   Deciphering Holocene Sea-Level History on the US Gulf Coast: A High-

Resolution Record from the Mississippi Delta. *Geological Society of America Bulletin* 116:1026–1039.

Toscano, Marguerite A., and Joyce Lundberg

1999   Submerged Late Pleistocene Reefs on the Tectonically-Stable SE Florida Margin: High-Precision Geochronology, Stratigraphy, Resolution of Substage 5a Sea-Level Elevation, and Orbital Forcing. *Quaternary Science Reviews* 18:753–767.

Toscano, Marguerite A., and Ian G. Macintyre

2003   Corrected Western Atlantic Sea-Level Curve for the Last 11,000 Years Based on Calibrated ^{14}C dates from *Acropora palmata* Framework and Intertidal Mangrove Peat. *Coral Reefs* 22:257–270.

Toth, David J., and Brian G. Katz

2006   Mixing of Shallow and Deep Groundwater as Indicated by the Chemistry and Age of Karstic Springs. *Hydrogeology Journal* 14:827–847.

Tucker, Bryan D.

2009   Isotopic Investigations of Archaic Period Subsistence and Settlement in the St. Johns River Drainage, Florida. Unpublished Ph.D. dissertation, Department of Anthropology, University of Florida, Gainesville.

Turner, Ernest

1989   The Souls of My Dead Brothers. In *Conflict in the Archaeology of Living Traditions*, edited by Robert Layton, pp. 189–194. Unwin Hyman, Boston.

Upchurch, Sam B., Richard N. Strom, and Mark G. Nuckels

1982   Methods of Provenance Determination of Florida Cherts. Department of Geology, University of South Florida, Tampa. Submitted to the Florida Division of Archives, History, and Records Management, Bureau of Historic Sites and Properties, Tallahassee.

U.S. Environmental Protection Agency

2002   *A Lexicon of Cave and Karst Terminology with Special Reference to Environmental Karst Hydrology*. U.S. Environmental Protection Agency, Washington, D.C.

Van Soelen, E. E., G. R. Brooks, R. A. Larson, J. S. Sinninghe Damsté, and G. J. Reichart

2012   Mid- to Late-Holocene Coastal Environmental Changes in Southwest Florida, USA. *The Holocene* 22:929–938.

Vernon, Robert O.

1951   *Geology of Citrus and Levy Counties, Florida*. Geological Bulletin 33. Florida Geological Survey, Tallahassee.

Walsh, Stephen J.

2001   Freshwater Macrofauna of Florida Karst Habitats. In *U.S. Geological Survey Karst Interest Group Proceedings, St. Petersburg, Florida, February 13–16, 2001*, edited by Eve L. Kuniansky, pp. 78–88. Water-Resources Investigations Report 01–4011. U.S. Geological Survey, Denver, Colorado.

Waters, Michael R., and Thomas W. Stafford

2007   Redefining the Age of Clovis: Implications for the Peopling of the Americas. *Science* 315:1122–1126.

Watkins, Tom
2013   In Florida, a Spring Cleanup Yields Cornucopia of History. Electronic document, http://www.cnn.com/2013/11/16/us/florida-spring-artifacts/index. html, accessed October 9, 2015.

Watts, William A.
1969   A Pollen Diagram from Mud Lake, Marion County, North-Central Florida. *Geological Society of America Bulletin* 80:631–642.
1971   Postglacial and Interglacial Vegetation History of Southern Georgia and Central Florida. *Ecology* 52:676–690.
1975   A Late Quaternary Record of Vegetation from Lake Annie, South-Central Florida. *Geology* 3:344–346.
1980   The Late Quaternary Vegetation History of the Southeastern United States. *Annual Review of Ecology and Systematics* 11:387–409.

Watts, William A., Eric C. Grimm, and T. C. Hussey
1996   Mid-Holocene Forest History of Florida and the Coastal Plain of Georgia and South Carolina. In *Archaeology of the Mid-Holocene Southeast*, edited by Kenneth E. Sassaman and David G. Anderson, pp. 28–40. University Press of Florida, Gainesville.

Watts, William A., and Barbara C. S. Hansen
1988   Environments of Florida in the Late Wisconsin and Holocene. In *Wet Site Archaeology*, edited by Barbara A. Purdy, pp. 307–323. Telford, Caldwell.
1994   Pre-Holocene and Holocene Pollen Records of Vegetation History from the Florida Peninsula and Their Climatic Implications. *Palaeogeography, Palaeoclimatology, Palaeoecology* 109:163–176.

Watts, William A., Barbara C. S. Hansen, and Eric C. Grimm
1992   Camel Lake: A 40 000-r Record of Vegetational and Forest History from Northwest Florida. *Ecology* 73:1056–1066.

Watts, William A., and M. Stuiver
1980   Late Wisconsin Climate of Northern Florida and the Origin of Species-Rich Deciduous Forest. *Science* 210:325–327.

Webb, S. David (editor)
2006   First Floridians and Last Mastodons: The Page-Ladson Site in the Aucilla River. Springer, New York.

Weber, Kenneth A., and Robert G. Perry
2006   Groundwater Abstraction Impacts on Spring Flow and Base Flow in the Hillsborough River Basin, Florida, USA. *Hydrogeology Journal* 14:1252–1264.

Webmoor, Timothy, and Christopher Witmore
2008   Things Are Us! A Commentary on Human/Things Relations under the Banner of a "Social" Archaeology. *Norwegian Archaeological Review* 41:53–70.

Weiner, Annette B.
1992   *Inalienable Possessions: The Paradox of Keeping-While-Giving*. University of California Press, Berkeley.

Wharton, Barry, George Ballo, and Mitchell Hope
1981   The Republic Groves Site, Hardee County, Florida. *The Florida Anthropologist* 34:59–80.

Wheeler, Ryan J.

2001   8MR3173: FBAR Canoe and Log Boat Recording Form. Copies available from the Florida Master Site Files, Tallahassee.

Wheeler, Ryan, and Ray M. McGee

1994   Technology of Mount Taylor Period Occupation, Groves' Orange Midden (8VO2601). *The Florida Anthropologist* 47:350–379.

Wheeler, Ryan J., James J. Miller, Ray M. McGee, Donna Ruhl, Brenda Swann, and Melissa Memory

2003   Archaic Period Canoes from Newnans Lake, Florida. *American Antiquity* (68):533–551.

Wheeler, Ryan J., Christine L. Newman, and Ray M. McGee

2000   A New Look at the Mount Taylor and Bluffton Sites, Volusia County, with an Outline of the Mount Taylor Culture. *The Florida Anthropologist* 53:133–157.

White, Devin A., and Sarah L. Surface-Evans (editors)

2012   *Least Cost Analysis of Social Landscapes: Archaeological Case Studies.* University of Utah Press, Salt Lake City.

White, William A.

1970   *The Geomorphology of the Florida Peninsula.* Geological Bulletin 51. Florida Bureau of Geology, Tallahassee.

White, William B.

2002   Karst Hydrology: Recent Developments and Open Questions. *Engineering Geology* 65(2):85–105.

Willard, Debra A., and Christopher E. Bernhardt

2011   Impacts of Past Climate and Sea Level Change on Everglades Wetlands: Placing a Century of Anthropogenic Change into a Late-Holocene Context. *Climatic Change* 107:59–80.

Willard, Debra A., Christopher E. Bernhardt, Gregg R. Brooks, Thomas M. Cronin, Terence Edgar, and Rebekka Larson

2007   Deglacial Climate Variability in Central Florida, USA. *Palaeogeography, Palaeoclimatology, Palaeoecology* 251:366–382.

Williams, Lester J., and Joann F. Dixon

2015   *Digital Surfaces and Thicknesses of Selected Hydrogeologic Units of the Floridan Aquifer System in Florida and Parts of Georgia, Alabama, and South Carolina.* Data Series 926. U.S. Geological Survey, Reston, Virginia.

Williams, Lester J., and Eve L. Kuniansky

2015   *Revised Hydrogeologic Framework of the Floridan Aquifer System in Florida and Parts of Georgia, Alabama, and South Carolina.* Professional Paper 1807. U.S. Geological Survey, Reston, Virginia.

Williams, Stanley A.

2006   *Simulation of the Effects of Groundwater Withdrawals from the Floridan Aquifer System in Volusia County and Vicinity.* Technical Publication SJ2006-4. St. Johns River Water Management District, Palatka, Florida.

Willis, Raymond F.
1972   8MR123: Silver Glen Springs. Archaeological Site Form. Copies available from the Florida Master Site Files, Tallahassee.
1995   *Alexander Springs Beach Reconstruction, Seminole Ranger District, Ocala National Forest, Lake County.* FY-1995 Heritage Resources Status Report 10. U.S. Forest Service, Tallahassee.

Winnemem Wintu Tribe
2015   Mt. Shasta: Desecration of Panther Spring, Our Genesis Place. Electronic document, http://www.winnememwintu.us/mount-shasta/, accessed September 7, 2015.

Woodfill, Brent K. S., Jon Spenard, and Megan Parker
2015   Caves, Hills, and Caches: The Importance of Karst Landscapes for the Prehispanic and Contemporary Maya. *Geological Society of America Special Papers* 516, in press, doi:10.1130/2015.2516(16).

Wright, Eric E., Albert C. Hine, Steven L. Goodbred Jr., and Stanley D. Locker
2005   The Effect of Sea-Level and Climate Change on the Development of a Mixed Siliciclastic–Carbonate, Deltaic Coastline: Suwannee River, Florida, U.S.A. *Journal of Sedimentary Research* 75:621–635.Wyman, Jeffries
1875   *Fresh-Water Shell Mounds of the St. Johns River, Florida.* Memoir 4. Peabody Academy of Science, Salem.

Zarikian, Carlos A. Alvarez, Peter K. Swart, John A. Gifford, and Patricia L. Blackwelder
2005   Holocene Paleohydrology of Little Salt Spring, Florida, Based on Ostracod Assemblages and Stable Isotopes. *Palaeogeography, Palaeoclimatology, Palaeoecology* 225:134–156.

INDEX

Alachua (biface type). *See* Florida Archaic Stemmed

Alexander Spring: artifact density, 149–51; land alteration, 188–89; maintenance, 193–94

algae, in springs, 6, 176, 191–93, 194. *See also* springs, pollution of

Altithermal. *See* Hypsithermal

Appalachian Mountains, 27, 29

apple snail (*Pomacea paludosa*), 63, 84, 114, 116

aquifer: artesian, 21; Biscayne, 201; confined, 20–21; confining units, 21, 75, 201; defined, 20; in Florida, 21–23; Intermediate, 23; sand and gravel, 201; surficial, 20, 23; unconfined, 20–21; water table, 20. *See also* Floridan Aquifer; karst aquifer

Arcadia Formation, 153. *See also* Hawthorn Group

Archaic period, 9, 61–64; Early Archaic, 11, 61–62, 111; Late Archaic, 61, 63; Middle Archaic, 10, 11, 61–63, 111. *See also* Mount Taylor period; Orange period

assemblage, residuality and reversibility of, 74. *See also* event

Atlantic Ocean: and the Floridan Aquifer, 37, 38, 39; geologic history, 25, 28

banded mystery snail (*Viviparus georgianus*): in shell mounds, 63, 65, 84, 123; springs as habitat for, 136–37, 141; unusual specimens from Silver Glen Springs, 126, 133

bannerstone, 68–69, 119

Bartram, John, 108

Bartram, William, 3, 140

Basso, Keith, 199

beads, 119; shell, 64, 68; stone, 64, 68–69

Bender, Barbara, 141–42

bivalve. *See* freshwater bivalve (*Unionidae* sp.)

Blue Cypress Marsh, 47

Blue Spring Midden B (8VO43), 98–99; artifact density, 149–51

Bluffton site (8VO22), 68, 69

Bolen: biface type, 62, 147; drought, 62

Bølling-Allerød interstadial, 40

Bullen, Ripley, 66, 172

burial mounds: Mount Taylor period, 66, 68–70, 116–17, 130–31; non-local individuals in, 66, 99; Orange period, 119, 121–22, 123, 131–32; at Silver Springs, 143, 149; St. Johns period, 125, 128, 133. *See also* Bluffton site (8VO22); Harris Creek site (8VO24); Silver Glen Complex; Thornhill Lake Complex

Burren region (Ireland), 187

California, springs in, 100–102

carbonate aquifer. *See* aquifer; karst aquifer

carbonate rock: and Floridan Aquifer, 21–23, 26–27, 187; formation of chert, 153; weathering of, 28–30, 31. *See also* Florida Platform; Floridan Aquifer; karst

carbonate sediments, 25–27. *See also* carbonate rock

Carr, Archie, 4

Casey, Edward, 141

cenote, 30, 184; sacred to the Maya, 105. *See also* sinkhole

Central Florida Phosphate District, 55–56

Central Lakes District, 51–52, 169

C_4 plant, 41–42

chert: geology, 153; movement/circulation in Florida, 142, 167–69, 172, 185; source areas, 141, 153–54; in the St. Johns River valley, 15, 138–39, 141, 172, 184. *See also* lithic artifacts; quarry cluster

Chief Seattle (Duwamish tribe), 138

Jason O'Donoughue is an archaeologist with the Florida Bureau of Archaeological Research. He is coeditor of *The Archaeology of Events: Cultural Change and Continuity in the Pre-Columbian Southeast.*

Ancient Earthen Enclosures of the Eastern Woodlands, edited by Robert C. Mainfort Jr. and Lynne P. Sullivan (1998)

An Environmental History of Northeast Florida, by James J. Miller (1998)

Precolumbian Architecture in Eastern North America, by William N. Morgan (1999)

Archaeology of Colonial Pensacola, edited by Judith A. Bense (1999)

Grit-Tempered: Early Women Archaeologists in the Southeastern United States, edited by Nancy Marie White, Lynne P. Sullivan, and Rochelle A. Marrinan (1999)

Coosa: The Rise and Fall of a Southeastern Mississippian Chiefdom, by Marvin T. Smith (2000)

Religion, Power, and Politics in Colonial St. Augustine, by Robert L. Kapitzke (2001)

Bioarchaeology of Spanish Florida: The Impact of Colonialism, edited by Clark Spencer Larsen (2001)

Archaeological Studies of Gender in the Southeastern United States, edited by Jane M. Eastman and Christopher B. Rodning (2001)

The Archaeology of Traditions: Agency and History Before and After Columbus, edited by Timothy R. Pauketat (2001)

Foraging, Farming, and Coastal Biocultural Adaptation in Late Prehistoric North Carolina, by Dale L. Hutchinson (2002)

Windover: Multidisciplinary Investigations of an Early Archaic Florida Cemetery, edited by Glen H. Doran (2002)

Archaeology of the Everglades, by John W. Griffin (2002)

Pioneer in Space and Time: John Mann Goggin and the Development of Florida Archaeology, by Brent Richards Weisman (2002)

Indians of Central and South Florida, 1513–1763, by John H. Hann (2003)

Presidio Santa Maria de Galve: A Struggle for Survival in Colonial Spanish Pensacola, edited by Judith A. Bense (2003)

Bioarchaeology of the Florida Gulf Coast: Adaptation, Conflict, and Change, by Dale L. Hutchinson (2004)

The Myth of Syphilis: The Natural History of Treponematosis in North America, edited by Mary Lucas Powell and Della Collins Cook (2005)

The Florida Journals of Frank Hamilton Cushing, edited by Phyllis E. Kolianos and Brent R. Weisman (2005)

The Lost Florida Manuscript of Frank Hamilton Cushing, edited by Phyllis E. Kolianos and Brent R. Weisman (2005)

The Native American World Beyond Apalachee: West Florida and the Chattahoochee Valley, by John H. Hann (2006)

Tatham Mound and the Bioarchaeology of European Contact: Disease and Depopulation in Central Gulf Coast Florida, by Dale L. Hutchinson (2006)

Taino Indian Myth and Practice: The Arrival of the Stranger King, by William F. Keegan (2007)

An Archaeology of Black Markets: Local Ceramics and Economies in Eighteenth-Century Jamaica, by Mark W. Hauser (2008; first paperback edition, 2013)

Mississippian Mortuary Practices: Beyond Hierarchy and the Representationist Perspective, edited by Lynne P. Sullivan and Robert C. Mainfort Jr. (2010; first paperback edition, 2012)

Bioarchaeology of Ethnogenesis in the Colonial Southeast, by Christopher M. Stojanowski (2010; first paperback edition, 2013)

French Colonial Archaeology in the Southeast and Caribbean, edited by Kenneth G. Kelly and Meredith D. Hardy (2011; first paperback edition, 2015)

Late Prehistoric Florida: Archaeology at the Edge of the Mississippian World, edited by Keith Ashley and Nancy Marie White (2012; first paperback edition, 2015)

Early and Middle Woodland Landscapes of the Southeast, edited by Alice P. Wright and Edward R. Henry (2013)

Trends and Traditions in Southeastern Zooarchaeology, edited by Tanya M. Peres (2014)

New Histories of Pre-Columbian Florida, edited by Neill J. Wallis and Asa R. Randall (2014; first paperback edition, 2016)

Discovering Florida: First-Contact Narratives from Spanish Expeditions along the Lower Gulf Coast, edited and translated by John E. Worth (2014; first paperback edition, 2015)

Constructing Histories: Archaic Freshwater Shell Mounds and Social Landscapes of the St. Johns River, Florida, by Asa R. Randall (2015)

Archaeology of Early Colonial Interaction at El Chorro de Maíta, Cuba, by Roberto Valcárcel Rojas (2016)

Fort San Juan and the Limits of Empire: Colonialism and Household Practice at the Berry Site, edited by Robin A. Beck, Christopher B. Rodning, and David G. Moore (2016)

Rethinking Moundville and Its Hinterland, edited by Vincas P. Steponaitis and C. Margaret Scarry (2016)

Handbook of Ceramic Animal Symbols in the Ancient Lesser Antilles, by Lawrence Waldron (2016)

Paleoindian Societies of the Coastal Southeast, by James S. Dunbar (2016)

Gathering at Silver Glen: Community and History in Late Archaic Florida, by Zackary I. Gilmore (2016)

Cuban Archaeology in the Caribbean, edited by Ivan Roksandic (2016)

Archaeologies of Slavery and Freedom in the Caribbean: Exploring the Spaces in Between, edited by Lynsey A. Bates, John M. Chenoweth, and James A. Delle (2016)

Setting the Table: Ceramics, Dining, and Cultural Exchange in Andalusia and La Florida, by Kathryn L. Ness (2017)

Simplicity, Equality, and Slavery: An Archaeology of Quakerism in the British Virgin Islands, 1740–1780, by John M. Chenoweth (2017)

Fit For War: Sustenance and Order in the Mid-Eighteenth-Century Catawba Nation, by Mary Elizabeth Fitts (2017)

Water from Stone: Archaeology and Conservation at Florida's Springs, by Jason O'Donoughue (2017)

CPSIA information can be obtained
at www.ICGtesting.com
Printed in the USA
LVOW07*1918190817

545630LV00008B/135/P